Programming

IBM PC BASIC

Programming IBM PC BASIC

Chao C. Chien
Pasadena City College

Macmillan Publishing Company
New York

Collier Macmillan Publishers
London

Phoebe, Les and little Robbie

Printed in the United States of America

Library of Congress Cataloging-in-Publication Data

Chien, Chao.
Programming IBM PC BASIC.

Includes index.
1. IBM Personal Computer—Programming. 2. BASIC (Computer program language) I. Title.
QA76.8.I2594C448 1987 005.265 86-21540

Macmillan Publishing Company
866 Third Avenue, New York, New York 10022

Collier Macmillan Canada, Inc.

Printing: 1 2 3 4 5 6 7 8 Year: 7 8 9 0 1 2 3 4

ISBN 0-02-322392-8

CONTENTS

PREFACE

BASIC (Beginners' All-purpose Symbolic Instruction Code) was originally created for educational purposes to be implemented on the minicomputer in a time-sharing environment. But in recent years, due to the rapid development of microcomputers and the fact that BASIC is usually their resident high-level language, BASIC not only has grown dramatically in popularity but also has become at least as sophisticated as some of the older high-level languages, such as FORTRAN or COBOL. The power of the new breed of microcomputer BASIC dialects, of which the IBM PC BASIC is one, is indeed impressive.

The fundamental structure of BASIC is unique in that most of its statements can be executed individually. Most other high-level languages require that programs be executed in their entirety. This unique feature of BASIC is a great advantage for programmers, allowing them to test program statement syntax line by line, and thus perform detailed program diagnosis. However, this versatility also permits the BASIC programmer to skip much of the initial organizational work before committing the program logic to code. This possibility has led to the criticism that BASIC is an unstructured language.

Actually, program structure—that is, the organization of the program logic—is the programmer's, not the language's, responsibility. Well-conceived program logic will be translated into well-structured program code regardless of the language used. Similarly, poorly organized program logic will lead to inefficient code. Thus, the program structure must be developed during the design phase, and it is, by and large, language independent. Because of this, and because this book has been designed primarily with the beginning programmer in mind, we will pay as much attention here to the training of the thought process and its eventual conversion to code as to the BASIC language itself.

ORGANIZATION

This book is organized into three major sections. Chapters 1 through 4 introduce the preliminary concept of the data cycle along with the necessary language supports. Chapters 5 through 11 deal with logic structuring and the fundamental techniques for thought development and coding preparation. Finally Chapter 12 introduces the student to the very powerful and popular IBM PC BASIC graphics.

All of this material is presented in a coherent manner; the knowledge, techniques, and philosophies explained in the earlier chapters are continually applied to the material in later chapters. The programming process is therefore always illustrated in its entirety.

This book is also organized so that it can be used as an easy reference. The chapters are formed around distinct language features. For example, chapters 5 and 6 deal with looping, chapters 7 and 8 are strictly concerned with branching, while chapter 11 covers modular programming. Within the chapters, important major topics comprise separate sections that can be referenced easily from the table of contents.

SPECIAL FEATURES

To develop programming discipline, this book emphasizes the technique of flowcharting. Flowcharting as a tool for the organization and expression of thought is illustrated throughout the book, and the fundamental flowcharting philosophy and methods are collected in appendix A.

Small example programs are used throughout the book to illustrate specific language features. Large application program examples are then presented to demonstrate how these features are used in coordination to achieve more complex objectives. These large programs also illustrate the structured programming philosophy. Program documentation is included with each example, and the program listings and output are printed in a second color.

After each language feature is introduced and explained, the syntax is summarized in a box separate from the rest of the text for easy reference.

LEARNING AIDS

To ensure student mastery of the language features and programming concepts, the book provides abundant section exercises following each major topic. These exercises are divided into groups designed to develop various specific skills. For example, to enhance the fundamental understanding of the language syntax, we list prewritten programs containing possible language errors for the student to correct or modify. The student is also asked to design small programs in order to practice using the specific language features. Following these preliminary exercises, the student is asked to design complete programs beginning with flowcharting.

At the end of each chapter more exercises are provided that check the student's acquisition of the skills taught to that point. Selected exercise answers are provided in appendix B.

INSTRUCTIONAL AIDS

An instructor's manual and an example diskette accompany the book. The manual provides the following aids:

- Discussion of approaches to teaching BASIC
- Suggested course outlines
- Discussion chapter objectives
- Language features that are nonportable, and common portable versions
- Suggested topics and example programs to be highlighted in the classroom.

The example diskette contains all the examples used in the book as well as a processing program that allows the instructor to select specific examples for laboratory use.

ACKNOWLEDGMENTS

Much appreciation must be extended to the reviewers Joseph Waters of Santa Rosa Junior College and Hyatt Barnes of Napa Valley College. I also wish to thank Philip Cecchettini, Larry Lazopoulos, and the editors at Burgess, for their guidance and their unrelenting faith in this book.

1 / FUNDAMENTALS OF PROGRAMMING

INTRODUCTION

The computer, despite its inherent versatility as a computational machine, is basically incapable of functioning on its own without instructions issued by humans. These instructions are known as *computer instructions.* A set of computer instructions put together specifically for the purpose of solving a problem is called a *program.* Certain groups of computer instructions, called *languages,* cause the computer to do different things well. For example, one language may be most appropriate for reading and printing out masses of business data, while another language may be best suited for performing very complicated arithmetic on a small amount of engineering data.

The computer's "native" language, constructed from binary code, is called the *machine language.* Because machine language is difficult for people to use, high-level languages have been developed to express our directions and make working with the computer easier. High-level languages are similar to human languages in that they use recognizable code words such as **PRINT** and **IF**. BASIC is a high-level computer language, and this book will teach you how to use BASIC to express your directions—in other words, how to program.

BASIC has fairly simple grammar (called language *syntax*) and rules, and it is capable of expressing many useful problem-solving operations. Like human languages, computer languages have verbs and sentences. The language verbs are often called *keywords* or *reserved words*: Keywords are the words the language relies on to understand your directions; reserved words are those that the programmer can only use to express the meaning stipulated by the language. The BASIC used by the IBM PC was developed by Microsoft Corporation; the BASIC dialect introduced in this book is the IBM PC Advanced BASIC called BASICA, Version 1.10. Throughout this book, when we use the term BASIC, we are actually referring to BASICA.

A program written in a high-level language such as BASIC is called an *applications* program, and its purpose is to solve a real-life problem. Because the computer only understands machine language, an applications program must be decoded, in a process known as *interpretation* or *compilation*, by an interpreter or compiler before it can work. An interpreter decodes one applications program instruction and executes it immediately before moving on to the next. A compiler decodes the entire applications program first, turns it into machine language instructions, and then executes the program as a whole. The high-level language applications program is commonly called the *source code* or program text, while the translated version is called the *object code* or *object program*. The BASICA language program itself is an interpreter.

HOW BASIC WORKS

In decoding the source program, BASIC "reads" the applications program statement by statement (the meaning of a statement will be explained in the next section) following certain preset rules. BASIC moves automatically from one program statement to another in sequence (unless specifically told to do otherwise, known as *branching*). If a language rule is violated or if the source text is not understandable to BASIC, then BASIC will display an error message on the CRT (the screen) so that the programmer can correct the mistake.

In executing the source program, BASIC follows the procedure delineated below:

1. For each source program instruction, known as a program *statement* and analogous to a sentence in English, BASIC looks for a statement number. If a legitimate statement number is found, then BASIC will proceed to look for a keyword. This is done by scanning an internally maintained keyword list.
2. If a keyword is found, then BASIC will examine the ensuing text to see if the associated language rules are adhered to.
3. If all is well, then BASIC will translate the source program statement and/or execute it. Otherwise, an associated error message will be displayed, and BASIC will proceed no further.

To learn to program in BASIC, we must therefore first learn the language rules.

THE LANGUAGE RULES

The rules associated with a BASIC program are actually very simple:

1. If only one statement is to be executed, known as programming in the *immediate mode,* then the statement is simply issued without a statement number.
2. If a program is to be constructed with more than one statement, then the statements must begin with statement numbers.
3. After the statement numbers, a keyword must follow either explicitly or implicitly.
4. After the keyword, the rest of the instruction must be constructed according to the language rules, known as syntax, applicable to the particular keyword.

The statement number must be an integer (that is, a whole number) such as 1, 10, or 15.

The keyword may be typed in capital or lowercase letters. BASICA will automatically change it to all capitals.

The statement must end with the <Enter> key being typed.

The BASIC program thus constructed from the statements must be entered into the computer.

CREATING A PROGRAM

In creating a program, the source text must first be entered into the computer so that it can be worked on. If so desired, this source program can also be saved for future use. The procedure for doing all this must be perfected before you can learn to program successfully. Thus, this section discusses the programmer's interaction with the system.

The source text is entered into the computer and held in a section of the memory called the *program text area.* The placement of this source text in the text area is handled by a part of BASIC known as the *text editor.* When BASIC is first activated, this text editor is in control. It signals the programmer to enter the program text with a prompt—the word **Ok**. This prompt has the same function as the system prompt >, which signals to the programmer that it is time for him or her to type something.

If you are in front of a computer, and it is powered, activate BASIC now by typing:

```
basica<Enter>
```

after the system prompt >, or:

```
BASICA<Enter>
```

if the Caps Lock key is first pressed (see Figure 1.1).

At this point BASIC is resident in the computer memory and the BASIC prompt will appear:

```
Ok
_
```

This means BASIC is now ready to accept a program instruction.

BASIC program texts are customarily entered in capitals. Even if they are entered in the lowercase, the BASIC internal text editor will upshift them to capitals automatically. You may cause all keyboard input to be in capital letters automatically by first pressing the Caps Lock key. The Caps Lock key reverses capitals and lowercase.

Notice the little underscore character below **Ok**:

```
>BASICA
Ok
_
```

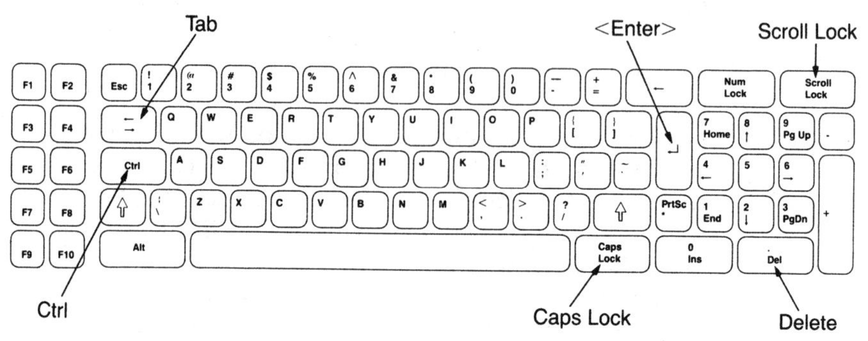

FIGURE 1.1 The IBM PC Keyboard

This is called the *cursor*. A cursor is a symbol displayed on the CRT that marks where the next character typed will be displayed.

A BASIC statement cannot have more than 255 characters. All statements can be entered through the keyboard by typing continuously up to slightly more than three screen lines.

IMMEDIATE MODE

As a first demonstration, key in (type) the following exactly:

```
PRINT "LESSON ONE"<Enter>
```

The CRT should respond with:

```
LESSON ONE
```

You have just completed your first interaction with BASIC.

First, the BASIC text editor obtains the program text from the keyboard. It senses the end of the text entry by the pressing of the <Enter> key. At this point the text editor relinquishes its control, and the interpreter takes over.

The first thing the interpreter does is look for a statement number. Since the program text was entered without a statement number, the BASIC interpreter concludes that the program is to be executed in the immediate mode, and it proceeds to invoke the **PRINT** keyword support routine, which displays **LESSON ONE** on the CRT.

PROGRAM MODE

As a second demonstration, type the following exactly:

```
10 PRINT "LESSON TWO"<Enter>
```

This time nothing will be displayed on the CRT, except for the cursor.

When BASIC detects the presence of a statement number, the interpreter will not execute the statement immediately. Instead, the text editor remains in control and awaits more input from the keyboard.

Program Execution. To activate the interpreter to execute the program, we must issue the systems command **RUN**. Type:

```
RUN<Enter>
```

The CRT should now respond with:

```
LESSON TWO
```

RUN
Form: RUN
Function: To activate the BASIC interpreter to execute all the numbered program statements currently present in the program text area.

Due to the statement number, a program statement is not executed until the **RUN** command is issued. This is known as the *program mode.* A program is thus designed with multiple statements first entered and then executed.

Now type exactly:

```
20 PRINT "LESSON THREE"<Enter>
RUN<Enter>
```

The following display should result:

```
LESSON TWO
LESSON THREE
```

Two statements are presently in the program:

```
10 PRINT "LESSON TWO"
20 PRINT "LESSON THREE"
```

They reside in the program text area and will remain there until erased or changed, or until the system is turned off. As long as the program text is present, it can be executed as often as desired. **RUN** the program several times to become acquainted with this fact.

Listing a Program. To view the program text currently held in the program text area, issue the systems command **LIST**:

```
LIST<Enter>
```

The complete program text is displayed.

To view only a select portion of the program text, **LIST** can be issued with statement number specifications. For instance, to view only statement 20, type:

```
LIST 20<Enter>
```

Statement 20 will be displayed.

To view statements 10 to 20 inclusively, type:

```
LIST 10-20<Enter>
```

The program text from statement 10 to statement 20 will be displayed.

A program stored on a disk or diskette can also be **LIST**ed if the stored filespec (defined later) is specified.

LIST
Form: LIST [start statement] [-end statement] [,filespec]
Function: To display program text.

Clearing a Program. To clear, or get rid of, the program text currently held in the program text area, issue the systems command **NEW**:

```
NEW<Enter>
```

If you **RUN** now, nothing will occur.

If you **LIST**, you will find that no program text exists.

```
NEW
```

```
Form:
NEW
```

```
Function: To initialize the program text area by
erasing all currently present program text.
```

Because **NEW** clears all existing program text in the program text area, it should be used with care. Later you will learn to save the program text before clearing a program. But if a new program is to be entered into the computer, then the program text area should be reinitialized (erased) with the **NEW** command, or both old and new programs will be commingled. A good practice is to issue the **LIST** and **NEW** commands in tandem:

```
LIST<Enter>
```

Inspect the program code listed, then:

```
NEW<Enter>
```

LIST reveals the current program text, allowing you to inspect the current contents of the program text area. If the current program is deemed useless, then **NEW** is issued to release the space it now occupies.

Statement Numbering. Program statements can be entered into the program text area in any order. Although BASIC executes a program by following an ascending order of the program statements, it does not demand that they be entered in the same order, or that the statement numbers be consecutive. For this reason, program statements are best numbered in increments, usually of 10 (that is, 10, 20, 30, and so on). This method of statement numbering reserves enough room between statements so that any missing statement can be restored. Programmers usually select an increment size of 10, which allows nine more statements to be inserted between each statement pair, while the highest statement number is not likely to exceed BASIC's upper limit of 65529.

> The highest statement number permissible is 65529.

To facilitate program text entry, the **AUTO** systems command may be used to generate statement numbers automatically. It is recommended that you always use it for new program text entries. Type:

```
AUTO<Enter>
```

The CRT will respond with:

```
AUTO
10 _
```

You may key in statement 10 at this point without having to type the 10.

After statement 10 is entered, **AUTO** will continue to furnish each consecutive statement number, in increments of 10:

```
10 PRINT "LESSON TWO"
20 _
```

An entire program can be entered through **AUTO**, with proper statement numbering assured.

If for some reason the new program text is designed with statement number increments of 1, starting at statement 100, then this can be specified with **AUTO** as:

```
AUTO 100, 1<Enter>
```

AUTO
Form: AUTO [starting statement number] [,increment]
Function: To generate automatic statement numbering.

At the end of a program text entry, the **AUTO** effect can be canceled by pressing the Scroll Lock key while holding down the Ctrl key.

Reenter the previous program example using **AUTO**, and **LIST** to make sure the program is entered correctly. If it is, **RUN** it again for further verification.

Editing a Program. Often mistakes are made during program text entering, or the program needs to be altered to integrate improvements. BASIC also provides facilities for program text editing. This is achieved through BASICA's built-in screen editor.

The program currently held in the program text area is:

```
10 PRINT "LESSON TWO"
20 PRINT "LESSON THREE"
```

Suppose the following mistake was made:

```
10 PTIBBT "LESSON TWO"
```

To correct the mistake by editing statement 10, follow this procedure:

1. **LIST**.
2. Use the up-arrow key (positioned on the numeric keypad at key 8) to move the cursor to statement 10.
3. Then use the right-arrow key (at key 6 on the keypad) to move the cursor to the letter T.
4. Type the correct letter R.
5. Use the right arrow to move the cursor to the first B occurrence.
6. Press the Del key, which deletes this extra B.
7. Type the correct N in place of the remaining B.
8. Press the <Enter> key.
9. Use the down arrow key to move the cursor below the program.
10. **LIST**.

Statement 10 is now properly edited.

Program statements can be erased, replaced, or duplicated as well as edited through BASICA's screen editor.

To replace a statement, simply type the new statement with the proper statement number. Thus, if you type:

```
10 PRINT "BEGIN"<Enter>
```

and **LIST**, you will see:

```
10 PRINT "BEGIN"
20 PRINT "LESSON THREE"
```

The original statement 10 will have been replaced.

New statements replace old statements with the same statement numbers.

To erase an existing statement, simply type the statement number and press <Enter>:

```
10<Enter>
```

A **LIST** will now show:

```
20 PRINT "LESSON THREE"
```

without statement 10.

A statement number without text erases the current program statement with the same statement number.

To duplicate a statement, first **LIST** the statement to be duplicated, move the cursor to the start of the statement number, and type in the statement number of the duplicate statement:

```
LIST<Enter>
```

The CRT shows:

```
20 PRINT "LESSON THREE"
_
```

Move the cursor under the 2 and press 1. The CRT shows:

```
10 PRINT "LESSON THREE"
```

Press <Enter> and **LIST**. The CRT shows:

```
10 PRINT "LESSON THREE"
20 PRINT "LESSON THREE"
```

You may now edit statement 10 to restore the program.

> Typing a new statement number over an old one duplicates a program statement.

Saving a Program. A program text can be saved on disk or diskette for future use. A saved program text in storage is known as a *program file*. The systems command for program file saving is **SAVE**. Assuming a formatted diskette is in the right-hand disk drive B, type:

```
SAVE "B:1PROGRAM"
```

The current program text is now saved on the diskette in drive B.

To save a program in storage, BASIC must know where the diskette is or which disk drive is holding the disk. This is specified by the drive specification, which is a letter and a colon, such as **B:**, that precedes a stored program filespec (defined below). If the drive specification (**B:** in this case) is omitted, then the program will be saved on the diskette in the *default drive*. The default drive is the drive that the computer is currently communicating with, which is most likely the drive that is holding the BASIC language diskette.

All stored files are identified by a *filespec*. A filespec is a name with miscellaneous specifications designed by the programmer. The setting of the filespec must follow the file-naming convention:

1. A filespec is made up of a file name and an optional extension.
2. The file name cannot be longer than eight characters.
3. The extension cannot be longer than three characters.
4. The file name and extension are separated by a period (.).
5. A filespec without an extension is simply a file name and does not carry a trailing period.
6. The characters you can use to form file names and extensions are:

   ```
   A through Z
   0 through 9
   <>{}()!@#$%^&-_''\~|
   ```

The extension is normally used to categorize the stored file. For example, .BAS may be used to indicate that the stored file is a BASIC program.

```
SAVE "1PROGRAM"
```

and

```
SAVE "1PROGRAM.BAS"
```

do the same thing, as BASIC automatically appends the extension .BAS to a BASIC program file when **SAVE**d.

However, if the program file is **SAVE**d with:

```
SAVE "1PROGRAM.EX"
```

then .EX will be the extension. BASIC will not change the extension to .BAS in such a case. You are, however, encouraged not to do this.

SAVE
Form: SAVE "drive spec:file name [.extension][″]
Function: To save program source text on storage disk or diskette.

It should be pointed out that **SAVE** does not destroy the program text currently residing in the program text area in memory.

The Directory. The program file thus **SAVE**d is logged at an area called the directory on the disk or diskette. The contents of the directory can be displayed either at the systems level or under BASIC control.

At the systems level (that is, before BASIC is activated), the systems command **DIR** can be used:

```
>DIR<Enter>
```

will display the directory of the current (default) disk drive.

```
>DIR drive spec<Enter>
```

will display the directory of the drive specified.

```
>DIR /W<Enter>
```

will display the directory across the CRT. This is used if there are too many filespecs for one screen.

```
>DIR /P<Enter>
```

will display the directory one screenful at a time, to be continued by the pressing of any key.

When BASIC has been activated, the directory is displayed through the **FILES** command:

```
FILES "B:<Enter>
```

will cause the file directory for the diskette in drive B: to be displayed. **FILES** by itself will cause the directory for the default drive, usually drive A:, to be displayed.

FILES works exactly like **DIR**.

Retrieving a Program. To retrieve a stored file from storage, you use the **LOAD** command. Thus:

```
LOAD "1PROGRAM"
```

will retrieve the program "1PROGRAM.BAS" and place it in the program text area, as if it had just been keyed in.

If the stored program has an extension other than .BAS, then the extension must also be typed.

Note that **LOAD** erases any program text that existed in the program text area before the **LOAD** command was issued.

PROGRAM DOCUMENTATION: REM

As you progress in learning BASIC programming, your programs will become longer and longer because the logic usually will become more and more involved. Also, your programs will start to accumulate. For future reference, you should document your program texts. BASIC permits program annotations or comments to be included as part of the program text, which it will overlook and not execute if the annotation is preceded by the keyword **REM**. For example:

```
10 REM MY FIRST PROGRAM
20 PRINT "LESSON THREE"
30 PRINT "LESSON THREE"
```

is to BASIC the same as:

```
20 PRINT "LESSON THREE"
30 PRINT "LESSON THREE"
```

In other words, BASIC interprets the program as if the **REM** statement were not there.

For convenience, BASIC also permits **REM** to be replaced by the apostrophe ('), as:

```
10 'MY FIRST PROGRAM
20 PRINT "LESSON THREE"
30 PRINT "LESSON THREE"
```

You should form the habit of documenting your programs, beginning with chapter 2.

From the next chapter on, we assume that you understand that the <Enter> key is used to signal the end of a keyboard entry. <Enter> will therefore no longer be provided with the examples.

Chapter Exercises

1. What is the difference between immediate mode and program mode?
2. What are the rules associated with statement numbers?
3. What is the function of the <Enter> key?
4. What does **NEW** do?
5. What does **LIST** do?
6. What does **RUN** do?

2 / OUTPUTTING TO THE CRT: PRINT

We shall begin our study of BASIC programming by learning how to display data or results on the CRT. Not only is obtaining results the main reason for programming but displaying data also allows us to see the results of the programs we design—a particularly important function for beginning programming students.

The keyword to produce a display on the CRT is **PRINT**.

CRT DISPLAY

In chapter 1 we used **PRINT** to illustrate the fundamental workings of the BASIC language, so we already know that **PRINT** causes a display to occur on the CRT. This chapter explains the detailed behavior of **PRINT** and its associated rules.

THE LITERAL

The **PRINT** statement causes a data item or items following the keyword **PRINT** to be displayed on the CRT. If this data item is a group of characters enclosed by a pair of double quotation marks, the character group will be displayed on the CRT as spelled out within the quotation marks. In the next example, the phrase **LESSON ONE** is enclosed within a pair of double quotation marks and therefore is displayed on the CRT at the current cursor position. Such a group of characters is known as a *literal,* as it is literally displayed.

Example 2.1

```
10 'PRINT LITERAL
20 '
30 PRINT "Lesson One"
```

producing:

```
Lesson One
```

Unlike the program text, the literal can be made up of lowercase characters. Lowercase characters in literals are not upshifted by BASIC. Also, just about any character on the keyboard can be used to form literals, including the blank character.

Example 2.2

```
10 'BLANK CHARACTERS
20 '
30 PRINT "      Lesson One"
```

producing:

```
      Lesson One
```

However, because the double quotation mark is used to form the literal, it cannot be included in the literal.

Example 2.3

```
10 'DOUBLE QUOTE AS LITERAL CHARACTER
20 '
30 PRINT "     "Lesson One""
```

will produce:

```
      0 0
```

The point is, if quotation marks are required in the display, you should use the single-quote character instead, since the single-quote character is treated by BASIC just like any other displayable character. Thus, the following example is valid.

Example 2.4

```
10 'USE SINGLE QUOTE IN LITERALS
20 '
30 PRINT "'Lesson One'"
```

produces:

```
'Lesson One'
```

Other than the restriction on the double quotation mark, and the keys that normally do not produce display images (such as the Function keys on the left-hand side of the keyboard and the arrow keys on the right), all other symbols are acceptable as literal characters.

In executing a program statement, BASIC first looks for a keyword. Once it finds this keyword, it will proceed to execute the statement. The keyword does not include blanks; hence, blanks in the program statements generally have no effect on the program execution. Thus,

Example 2.5

```
10 'SPACES DO NOT MATTER
20 '
30 PRINT"Literal"
40 PRINT                "Literal"
```

displays:

```
Literal
Literal
```

as if statements 30 and 40 were exactly alike.

It is, of course, senseless to space the keyword **PRINT** and the literal far apart as in statement 40, but it also serves no good purpose to compact the program code as in statement 30. Thus, in coding a program, you should maintain a space after a keyword or between keywords, so that reading the program will not be difficult.

Some programmers may argue that one space saved is one memory byte saved. With the large amount of memory space available for our use in today's computers, the one extra byte is well worth spending for the sake of readability and program maintainability.

In executing a **PRINT** statement, BASIC first identifies the data type to be displayed. There are two types of data recognized by BASIC in a **PRINT** statement. They are:

1. A constant
    a. An alphanumeric constant (a literal)
    b. A numeric constant
2. A variable

The subject of the variable will be addressed in chapter 3.

When BASIC encounters a double quotation mark, it concludes that the data item is a literal and displays it as is.

A literal is a group of characters that begins with a double quotation mark and ends with another double quotation mark. The trailing double quotation mark can be absent if there are no following display items.

Example 2.6

```
10 'OPEN-ENDED LITERAL
20 '
30 PRINT "Missing end quote OK
```

This program is perfectly acceptable. The literal will be displayed as if the ending double quotation mark were present.

More than one display item may follow the **PRINT** statement, as in this example.

Example 2.7

```
10 'MULTIPLE LITERALS
20 '
30 PRINT "Item 1", "Item 2", "Item 3"
```

displaying:

```
Item 1        Item 2        Item 3
```

PRINT **ZONES**

If you **RUN** the following program:

Example 2.8

```
10 'PRINT ZONES
20 '
30 PRINT "Zone 1", "Zone 2", "Zone 3", "Zone 4",
"Zone 5", "Zone 6"
```

you will see the display:

```
Zone 1        Zone 2        Zone 3        Zone 4        Zone 5
Zone 6
```

BASIC looks at the CRT as lines with preset display *zones,* or built-in tab positions. For the IBM PC, there are twenty-four screen lines, with each line made up of eighty character positions segregated into five display zones per line.

Although each line has five distinct **PRINT** zones, they appear to BASIC as a continuous linear series of preset display positions. Thus, in Example 2.8, even though statement 30 appears ready to display beyond the CRT edge with six display items specified, BASIC automatically places the sixth item at the start of a new screen line, which serves as zone number 6 in this case.

How wide is a **PRINT** zone? The next example program will provide the answer.

Example 2.9

```
10 'Zone WIDTH
20 '
30 PRINT "123456789012345678901234567890"
40 PRINT "Zone 1", "Zone 2", "Zone 3", "Zone 4",
"Zone 5", "Zone 6"
```

The following display will be generated:

```
123456789012345678901234567890
Zone 1        Zone 2        Zone 3        Zone 4        Zone 5
Zone 6
```

From this display you can see that each zone is made up of fourteen character positions. Some day you may work with another computer, which may have different zone settings. Example 2.9 is therefore very useful in determining the zone settings quickly without having to resort to the handbook or manual.

BASIC does not display the **PRINT** items at zones simply because they are separate display items. The zone positions are actually specified by the comma (,), which separates the **PRINT** items. The comma is often called the *data delimiter* when its function is merely to separate data, as you will learn later. In the **PRINT** statement, however, it is not a delimiter but a *cursor control code* that causes the cursor position to advance to the next available display zone (with emphasis on the word *available*).

The comma does not always advance the cursor from one zone to another. It specifically advances the cursor to the next zone that is not occupied. For instance, suppose a literal is so long that it spans two **PRINT** zones. An ensuing comma will advance the cursor to the third zone—the one that is available.

Example 2.10

```
10 'AVAILABLE ZONE
20 '
25 PRINT "1", "2", "3", "4", "5"
30 PRINT "This zone is occupied", "This is the next zone"
```

will display:

```
1             2             3             4             5
This zone is occupied       This is the next zone
```

with the phrase **This is the next zone** beginning at **PRINT** line position 29—the third zone.

If the literal is exactly the same size as a zone, or a multiple of it, then it appears that the next **PRINT** item would be displayed immediately next to it at the start of the new zone, as:

```
10 PRINT "12345678901234", "abcdefgh"
```

You would think the display would be:

```
12345678901234abcdefgh
```

But this is not the case. In fact, the following display will result:

```
12345678901234              abcdefgh
```

leaving an entire zone unused. This strange effect can be explained as follows.

After the first **PRINT** item is displayed, the cursor is positioned at character 15, the first character position of zone 2. When the comma is encountered, BASIC moves it to the next available zone. Zone 2 is not available because it is occupied by the cursor, which is one character long.

The cursor-positioning effect due to the comma can be seen clearly with the next example.

Example 2.11

```
10 'THE EFFECT OF THE COMMA
20 '
30 PRINT "Zone 1",
40 PRINT "Zone 2",
50 PRINT "Zone 3",
60 PRINT "Zone 4",
70 PRINT "Zone 5",
80 PRINT "Zone 6"
```

The display appears as:

```
Zone 1        Zone 2        Zone 3        Zone 4        Zone 5
Zone 6
```

which is the same as that in Example 2.8.

Although there are six **PRINT** statements in this example, six display lines are not produced. After each **PRINT** statement, the ending comma moves the cursor to a new display zone, and the next **PRINT** effect takes place at that cursor position. This demonstrates that the comma is not used to separate the display items. In this program, there are no items to be separated in each **PRINT** statement. The comma has the specific function of tabbing.

In fact, the only time BASIC will begin a display at a new line is when the previous **PRINT** statement ends with the <Enter> key being pressed and without an ending cursor-positioning code, such as the comma.

Example 2.12

```
10 'THE EFFECT OF <Enter> ENDING
20 '
30 PRINT "Zone 1",
40 PRINT "Zone 2",
50 PRINT "Zone 3"
60 PRINT "New Line"
```

This program produces the display:

```
Zone 1        Zone 2        Zone 3
New Line
```

There is no comma or other cursor control code at the end of statement 50. BASIC therefore begins statement 60 at the start of a new screen line, which is the new zone 1 position.

Because of the unique zone-positioning function of the comma, it can be used to position the cursor in a variety of screen output designs. Like the typewriter tab key, the comma can cause the advancement of the cursor even before any data is **PRINT**ed.

Example 2.13

```
10 'HORIZONTAL POSITIONING
20 '
30 PRINT,,, "Item"
```

The commas in statement 30 will cause the cursor to move to zone 4 first before **Item** is displayed:

```
                                                  Item
```

From now on, you should think of the comma specifically as a cursor-advancing code, as distinct an entity in the **PRINT** statement as the other items and codes you are to learn soon. Thus, the statement:

```
10 PRINT "Item 1",,, "Item 2"
```

should be read as: First display the literal **Item 1**, move the cursor to zone 2, 3, and 4, then display the literal **Item 2**. (Be aware, however, that this may not be true for BASIC dialects used by other computers.)

Because **PRINT** is so often used in BASIC programming, you may avoid typing the keyword **PRINT** by typing a question mark (?) instead, as:

Example 2.14

```
10 'USING ? AS PRINT
20 '
30 ? "Lesson One"
```

Even though the question mark may be used in place of **PRINT** in the preparation of program code, BASIC automatically replaces all such question marks with the proper **PRINT** keyword, which will be shown when the program is **LIST**ed.

CURSOR-ADVANCEMENT SUPPRESSION

While the comma as a cursor-positioning control code moves the cursor according to preset **PRINT** zones, the semicolon causes the cursor to remain one position following the last item printed on the line. This effect can be demonstrated with an example:

Example 2.15

```
10 'EFFECT OF ; 1
20 '
30 PRINT "Item"; "Item"; "Item"; "Item"
```

The display looks like this:

```
ItemItemItemItem
```

After the first **Item** is displayed, the cursor is at **PRINT** line position 5:

```
Item_
```

The following semicolon holds the cursor at that position, which is where the next **PRINT** action will take place.

Just like the comma, the semicolon is a *functional code* and not a data delimiter. The next example highlights this point:

Example 2.16

```
10 'EFFECT OF ; 2
20 '
30 PRINT "Item";
40 PRINT "Item"
```

The ending semicolon in statement 30 freezes the cursor. Thus, statements 30 and 40 produce the **PRINT** effect of:

```
ItemItem
```

But, unlike the comma, because the semicolon does not move the cursor, statement 30 of the following program is totally meaningless:

Example 2.17

```
10 '; TO BE USED ONLY AS DELIMITER
20 '
30 PRINT ;;;;;;; "Item"
```

In fact, statement 30 of this program can be replaced with:

```
30 PRINT "Item"
```

If neither a comma nor a semicolon is used to separate the display items, then the effect is as if the semicolon were used.

Example 2.18

```
10 'NO SEPARATORS
20 '
30 PRINT "A" "B" "C"
```

displays:

```
ABC
```

PRINT
Form: PRINT [,] [item] [,] [;] [item list]
Function: To display specified items on the CRT according to cursor control code specifications.

Exercise Set 2.1 PRINT literal, comma, semicolon

A. Correct the errors, if any, in the following programs:

1.
```
10 PRINT "            "Exercise Al."            "
```

Answer: ____

____

2.
```
10 PRINT "Page";;; "1", "Report No. 2"
```

Answer: ____

____

B. What does the following program do?

3.
```
10 PRINT "Club Membership"
20 PRINT "=================================="
30 PRINT, "Alan:"
```

```
40 PRINT, "Bonnie:"
50 PRINT, "Chuck:"
```

Answer: ______________________________

____

C. Write a program to produce the following CRT display:

4.
```
Exercise 1                     Date:
Programmer:
```

CRT DISPLAY DESIGN

The literal is most often used for messages. It is also used to produce the headings that help make the program output meaningful. For instance, a literal can be used to produce a simple message to the user of the program, such as:

Example 2.19

```
10 'LITERALS USED AS MESSAGES
20 '
30 PRINT "To the User: Press the <Enter> key after data er
```

displaying the instruction:

```
To the User: Press the <Enter> key after data entry.
```

Or it can be used to produce report headings:

Example 2.20

```
10 'LITERALS USED AS TITLES AND HEADINGS
20 '
30 PRINT "Student Grades"
40 PRINT "______________"
```

displaying:

```
Student Grades
______________

Ok
```

Blank lines are generated on the screen with bare **PRINT** statements—that is, **PRINT** statements that contain only the keyword **PRINT** and nothing else.

Example 2.21

```
10 'PRINT BLANK LINES
20 '
30 PRINT "Student Grades"
40 PRINT "______________"
50 PRINT
```

displaying:

```
Student Grades
______________

Ok
```

Compare Examples 2.20 and 2.21. What is the difference?

Blank lines should be used generously in CRT display designs to render the displays more attractive. In Example 2.22, two blank lines are used to separate the report heading from the report contents:

Example 2.22

```
10 'PRINT BLANK LINES
20 '
30 PRINT "Class Roster"
40 PRINT "____________"
50 PRINT
60 PRINT
70 PRINT "Susan"
80 PRINT
90 PRINT
```

producing:

```
Class Roster
____________


Susan


Ok
```

But just because a **PRINT** exists alone in a program does not mean a blank line will automatically be produced. The previous **PRINT** effect also influences the display design. For instance, if the previous **PRINT** statement causes the cursor to remain in the **PRINT** line, such as with an ending comma or semicolon, then the effect of a single **PRINT** is merely to nullify the previous cursor control effect and to advance the cursor to the start of a new line. The single **PRINT** in this case merely cancels the last cursor control—it **PRINT**s nothing at the current cursor position, but it advances the cursor because it ends without a cursor control code.

Example 2.23

```
10 'CANCEL CURSOR CONTROL CODE
20 '
30 PRINT "Item 1",
40 PRINT
50 PRINT "Item 2"
```

has the same effect as:

```
30 PRINT "Item 1"
50 PRINT "Item 2"
```

SCREEN CLEARING

Because **PRINT** by itself generates a blank line, the CRT can be cleared with twenty-four **PRINT**s, such as:

```
10 PRINT
20 PRINT
30 PRINT
40 PRINT
:
240 PRINT
```

Although this method clears the CRT, it nevertheless leaves the cursor at the bottom of the screen. In BASIC, a different keyword is used to erase the screen, and it positions the cursor in the upper left-hand corner (this position is referred to as *home*). This is the **CLS** statement.

The **CLS** statement is made up of only the keyword **CLS**, with no further specifications. For example,

Example 2.24

```
10 'CLEAR SCREEN
20 '
30 CLS
40 PRINT "Class Roster"
50 PRINT "____________"
60 PRINT
70 PRINT
80 PRINT "Susan"
90 PRINT
```

will start the roster display at the top of the screen with a full screen available below.

CLS
Form: CLS
Function: To clear the CRT screen and position the cursor at home.

THE END STATEMENT

Up to now we have been permitting BASIC to terminate when it has reached the statement with the highest statement number in the program text area. This is perfectly acceptable, and no rule has been violated. However, if you are not careful in creating a new program (for example, if there are other old program statements left behind and the command **NEW** has not been issued), then the remaining old program statements may merge with the new program and interfere with it.

For example, if Example 2.23 is entered immediately after Example 2.22 without the program text area being cleared, then the following will result:

```
10 'CANCEL CURSOR CONTROL CODE
20 '
30 PRINT "Item 1",
40 PRINT
50 PRINT "Item 2"
60 PRINT
70 PRINT "Susan"
80 PRINT
90 PRINT
```

From now on, always terminate your programs with the **END** statement, as:

Example 2.25

```
10 'END STATEMENT
20 '
30 CLS
40 PRINT "Class Roster"
50 PRINT "____________"
60 PRINT
70 PRINT
80 PRINT "Susan"
90 PRINT
100 END
```

In later chapters you will learn that there are other reasons why **END** is needed to terminate a program. But for now, simply form the habit of making **END** the last statement executed by your programs.

END
Form: END
Function: To stop BASIC program execution and maintain stored-file overhead data.

Exercise Set 2.2 PRINT messages, headings, **CLS, END**

A. Correct the errors, if any, in the following programs:

1.

```
10 PRINT 'Cursor Advancement'
```

Answer: ______________________________

____

2.

```
10 PRINT "User instructions:";
20 PRINT "1";
30 PRINT
40 PRINT "========================================:
50 PRINT
```

Answer: ______________________________

____

B. Write a program to produce the following CRT displays:

3.

```
Grades:
===================================

Test 1.
Test 2.
Test 3.
Test 4.

                            Total:
```

4.

```
1. Remove seal at top of package.
2. Open package carefully.
3. Remove slicer with both hands.
4. Place slicer on flat surface.


              IMPORTANT

5. Fill in warranty and mail it promptly.
```

PRINTING NUMERICS

A literal is a group of characters. It has individual characters but does not possess any inherent numeric value. *Numerics,* on the other hand, have values—for example, the symbol 5 represents the value of the decimal number five. When a **PRINT** item is a numeric, this value will be displayed. A numeric is thus a number and is not enclosed by double quotation marks.

Example 2.26

```
10 'PRINT NUMERIC CONSTANT
20 '
30 PRINT 5
40 END
```

displays:

```
 5
```

Compare this example with:

```
30 PRINT "5"
```

Is there any difference in the resulting display, and, if so, what is the difference?

Answer: ______________________________

Numerics carry either a positive or a negative sign. The positive sign, however, is suppressed, thus:

Example 2.27

```
10 'NUMERIC SIGNS
20 '
30 PRINT 5
40 PRINT -5
50 END
```

will display:

```
 5
-5
```

The first **5** has a leading space, the space for the implied positive sign.

If you attempt to specify numerics in a **PRINT** statement without a cursor control code as separator, as in:

Example 2.28

```
10 'NUMERIC SPACES
20 '
30 PRINT 3    5
40 END
```

then BASIC will ignore the spaces and restore the two numerics to:

```
30 PRINT 35
```

Thus, the numbers **3** and **5** in the **PRINT** statement must be stated as:

Example 2.29

either

```
10 'NUMERIC SPACES
20 '
30 PRINT 3, 5
40 END
```

with the resultant display of:

```
 3             5
```

or

```
10 'NUMERIC SPACES
20 '
30 PRINT 3; 5
40 END
```

displaying:

```
 3  5
```

Exercise Set 2.3 Numerics (Using **PRINT, CLS, END**)

A. Correct the errors, if any, in the following programs:

1.
```
10 PRINT ,,"User instructions:"
20 PRINT
30 PRINT "Enter the following choices:"
40 PRINT "1" "2" "3" "4"
```

Answer: ______________________________

____

2.
```
10 PRINT 2 + 4;
20 PRINT " =";
30 PRINT 6
```

Answer: ______________________________

____

B. Modifying Programs

3. Modify problem 2 in Exercise Set 2.1 by using numerics.
4. Modify problem 1 in Exercise Set 2.3 by using numerics.

PERFORMING ARITHMETIC

For numerics, it is the value and not the character image that is **PRINT**ed. This allows arithmetic operations to be performed within **PRINT** statements. For example:

Example 2.30

```
10 'ARITHMETIC
20 '
30 PRINT 10 + 15
40 END
```

displays:

```
 25
```

For the **PRINT** statement, the plus (+) sign is not a data separator. The plus sign is an *arithmetic operator,* which will be introduced in the next chapter. Thus, **10 + 15** is regarded as one data item, with a value of 25, which is 10 plus 15.

As another example, the caret symbol (^), which is the *exponentiation operator,* raises a base number to a power. So:

Example 2.31

```
10 'ARITHMETIC
20 '
30 PRINT 10 ^ 2
40 END
```

generates:

```
 100
```

which is 10 to the second power, or 10 squared.

Example 2.32

```
10 'ARITHMETIC
20 '
30 PRINT ( 10 + 3 ) * 2
40 END
```

This example displays 26, which is 13 times 2.

In contrast to ordinary arithmetic, all arithmetic operators must be specified concisely in BASIC programming. For example, the next program will not perform 10 plus 3 multiplied by 2. Instead, BASIC considers **10 + 3**, surrounded by a pair of parentheses, one value, and the **2** another.

Example 2.33

```
10 'ARITHMETIC
20 '
30 PRINT ( 10 + 3 ) 2
40 END
```

will display:

```
 13 2
```

SENDING RESULTS TO THE PRINTER: LPRINT

The **LPRINT** statement sends the output to the printer. **LPRINT** works exactly like **PRINT**; all the **PRINT** statements in the examples above can be changed to **LPRINT**, and the results will be produced at the printer—provided that there is a printer hooked up to the computer, that it is turned on, and that it has paper in it.

One thing must be mentioned, though. Printers come in many designs; they do not all have the same line width, but, almost certainly, they have line widths of more than eighty characters. It is therefore advised that you check your printer before you perform any printer outputting.

Chapter Exercises (Using PRINT, CLS, END)

1. Design a program to compute and output the total and average of the data 2.86, 98.05, 1.17, and 103.2.
2. Dress up the last program with appropriate **PRINT** statements to report the results.
3. Modify the program to send the results to the printer.
4. Design another program to compute the product of the first three data items and then divide the product by the last data item and report the results on the CRT.

3 / ASSIGNING DATA TO VARIABLES

DATA ASSIGNMENT: LET

While arithmetic can be performed through the **PRINT** statement as demonstrated in chapter 2, neither the operands in the arithmetic operations nor the results are really kept in the computer's memory. This is because the arithmetic expression is program text when made a part of the **PRINT** statement, and the results are directly displayed. If data are to be kept in the computer for further processing, then they must be kept specifically as data in the memory. In BASIC, data are kept in memory under *variables*. A variable is a name used to identify a specific data item. The process of storing data in variables is known as *data assignment.*

In short, data are assigned to variables. In BASIC, data assignment is performed through the **LET** statement. Example 3.1 shows how a data item is assigned to a variable.

Example 3.1

```
10 'DATA ASSIGNMENT 1
20 '
30 LET A = 10
40 PRINT A
50 END
```

In this example, the value 10 is assigned to the variable A in statement 30 by the keyword **LET**. The content of variable A is subsequently displayed due to statement 40. When BASIC sees a data item following **PRINT** that is not enclosed within double quotation marks and that is not a numeral, BASIC assumes that the data item is a variable and **PRINT**s its contents.

It must be pointed out that a data assignment operation does not display the data. **PRINT** is responsible for all CRT output. The following program assigns the data, but nothing is displayed on the CRT.

Example 3.2

```
10 'DATA ASSIGNMENT 1
20 '
30 LET A = 10
40 END
```

A data item must be assigned to a variable before it can be output. If no data are assigned to a variable, then BASIC will assume that the variable value is 0. In the next example, the content of the variable A is displayed before a data item is assigned to it; thus, a 0 is displayed.

Example 3.3

```
10 'STATEMENT SEQUENCE LOGIC
20 '
30 PRINT A
40 LET A = 10
50 END
```

Example 3.4

```
10 'CHANGING VARIABLE CONTENTS
20 '
30 PRINT A
40 LET A = 10
50 PRINT A
60 END
```

In this program, first a 0 is displayed. Then, after the data item 10 is assigned to it, the 10 is displayed. Consequently, although the two **PRINT** statements are identical, they produce different displays because the variable contents have been changed between the first **PRINT** and the second.

This means the same variable can hold different data at different times. Each variable, however, can only hold one data item at a time, as shown by the next example.

Example 3.5

```
10 'CHANGING VARIABLE CONTENTS
20 '
30 LET A = 5
40 PRINT A
50 LET A = 10
60 PRINT A
70 END
```

The numbers 5 and 10 are in turn displayed.

When statement 50 is executed, the data item 5 is no longer in the memory. It has been replaced by 10.

When many data items are thus stored by the program in memory, it may become difficult for the programmer to keep track of them all, especially if the variable contents undergo changes. It is therefore sensible for the programmer to jot down the contents of the variables in a notebook during program design. For example, when the following statement is designed, an accompanying notation should be made:

```
                                        X
                                    +--------+
50 LET X = 12.5                     |  12.5  |
                                    +--------+
```

Once a box for a variable is drawn, all subsequent program logic involving this variable will be expressed in this same box. Thus, if a subsequent statement is:

```
80 LET X = 30
```

then the following notation should be made to reflect the up-to-date status of variable X:

```
      X
+----------+
|    30    |
|          |
|   12.5   |
+----------+
```

LET
Form: LET variable = expression
Function: To assign the value of the expression to the named variable.

Exercise Set 3.1 PRINT arithmetic, **LET**, change variable contents (Using **PRINT**, **CLS**, **END**, **LET**)

A. Correct the errors, if any, in the following programs:

1.

```
10 LET 3.7 = A
20 PRINT A
30 END
```

Answer: ______________________

____

2.

```
10 LET C = 6
20 LET C = 7
30 LET C = 9
40 PRINT C
50 END
```

Answer: ______________________

____

B. What does the following program do?

3.

```
10 PRINT A
20 PRINT C
30 LET A = 5
40 LET C = 15
50 END
```

Answer: ______________________

C. Write a program to:

4. Assign the data 12.6, 7.98, 32, and 56.95 to the variables A, B, C, and D, respectively, and then display their contents.
5. Assign the data item 100.65 to the variable A, display it, and then change the contents of A to 12.88 and verify (through **PRINT**) that the change indeed has taken place.

ARITHMETIC OPERATIONS

By combining the data assignment operation with **PRINT**, arithmetic can be performed in a meaningful manner.

Example 3.6

In this example, the data 3 and 4 are kept in memory under different variables. Statement 50 says: Take what is in B and add it to what is in A, then assign the result to C. When this is done, then statement 60 **PRINT**s it.

```
10 'ARITHMETIC WITH LET
20 '
30 LET A = 3
40 LET B = 4
50 LET C = A + B
60 PRINT C
70 END
```

In BASIC, all the fundamental arithmetic operations can be carried out. Some operators and notations, however, are slightly different. The corresponding arithmetic and BASIC operators are listed below:

In Arithmetic	*In BASIC*
+	+
−	-
×	*
÷	/
x^y	X ^ Y
( )	( )

The use of these symbols in programming is illustrated below.

Example 3.7

In this example, statement 50 shows how an ordinary arithmetic operation looks in program code. The asterisk (*) means multiply.

```
10 'ARITHMETIC WITH LET
20 '
30 LET A = 3
40 LET B = 4
50 LET C = A * ( B + 14 )
60 PRINT C
70 END
```

Ordinarily, the equal sign (=) stands for equal. In programming, however, it is the data assignment symbol. Thus, in statement 50, the result of the arithmetic operation on the right-hand side is assigned to the variable C on the left side, although the two sides of the equal sign are indeed equal in this case. Example 3.8 shows, however, that the numeric quantities on both sides of the equal sign need not be equal. In this case, the value on the right replaces the current content of the variable on the left. The uniqueness of it is that the original data in the variable are used in the arithmetic operation and are then replaced.

In performing data assignment, BASIC first evaluates the data on the right-hand side of the equal sign, then stores it in the variable on the left. Statement 50 of Example 3.8 therefore first computes the value of 10 (held in variable A) multiplied by 2, and then stores the result back in A.

Example 3.8

```
10 '= MEANS STORE
20 '
30 LET A = 10
40 PRINT A
50 LET A = A * 2
60 PRINT A
70 END
```

The numbers 10 and 20 are displayed.

Exercise Set 3.2 LET arithmetic (Using **PRINT**, **CLS**, **END**, **LET**)

A. Correct the errors, if any, in the following programs:

1.

```
10 PRINT A
20 LET A = 3
30 END
```

Answer: ______________________________

____

2.

```
10 LET A = 6
20 LET B = 7
30 LET A + B = C
40 PRINT C
50 END
```

Answer: ______________________________

____

3.

```
10 LET X = Y = 15
20 PRINT Z = X * Y
30 END
```

Answer: ______________________________

____

B. Write a program to:

4. Compute the square of a number.
5. Convert measurements in inches into feet.
6. Compute the interest paid on a deposit of $1,000 for five years. The annual simple interest rate is 6.75 percent.

VARIABLE NAMING

In BASIC exactly two kinds of data can be assigned: *numeric* and *alphanumeric* data. A numeric data item is one that has a numeric value, as in the examples above. An alphanumeric data item is a group of characters;

it does not possess any numeric value, nor can it enter into an arithmetic process.

Numeric data are further classified according to their accuracy. Real numbers commonly encountered are known as *single-precision numbers*. Those that carry large numbers of significant figures are called *double-precision numbers* and are normally used by scientists and mathematicians in highly accurate computations. They are seldom required in business. Finally, whole numbers are called *integers*.

All these data types are stored in the memory differently, so BASIC must be informed of the data types that it will be dealing with. This is done through the particular way variable names are formed.

First of all, variable names are basically made up of letters, numbers, and the decimal point. For the IBM PC, each variable name may be up to forty characters long. The first character must be one of the twenty-six English letters.

This variable name is then followed by a data type declaration suffix, which is a special symbol indicating what kind of data the variable is to hold. These codes are listed below:

Data Type	*Suffix*	*Example*
Single precision	!	FIGURE!
Double precision	#	NUMBER#
Integer	%	COUNTER%
Alphanumeric	$	NAME$

When no suffix is present, BASIC understands that the programmer means single precision, and this form is normally used in programming for single-precision variables.

Example 3.9

```
10 'VARIABLE NAMES
20 '
30 LET DOLLARS = 100.56
40 PRINT DOLLARS
50 END
```

The number 100.56 is assigned and displayed.

Example 3.10

```
10 'VARIABLE NAMES
20 '
```

```
30 LET DOLLARS = 100.56
40 LET CENTS = 66
50 PRINT DOLLARS, CENTS
60 END
```

100.56 and 66 are both assigned and displayed. 66 is an integer, but an integer is also a real number.

With **LET** and **PRINT**, meaningful arithmetic operations and display can be achieved. Example 3.11 combines dollars and cents into a single dollar unit and displays the conversion results in meaningful sentences. Study statements 60 through 80 with the displayed results to understand how the display is achieved.

Example 3.11

```
10 'PRINT RESULTS
20 '
30 LET DOLLARS = 100.56
40 LET CENTS = 66
50 LET TOTAL = DOLLARS + CENTS * .01
60 PRINT "Dollars = "; DOLLARS
70 PRINT "Cents = "; CENTS
80 PRINT "Total = "; TOTAL
90 END
```

The displayed result is:

```
Dollars = 100.56
Cents = 66
Total = 101.22
```

Because the **LET** statement is so frequently used, it is implied even when it is omitted in the program. This is to say that, when a statement begins without a keyword, BASIC understands that the **LET** keyword is implied. Example 3.12 demonstrates this use.

Example 3.12

```
10 'IMPLIED LET
20 '
30 DOLLARS = 100.56
40 CENTS = 66
50 TOTAL = DOLLARS + CENTS * .01
60 PRINT "Dollars = "; DOLLARS
```

```
70 PRINT "Cents = "; CENTS
80 PRINT "Total = "; TOTAL
90 END
```

This program can be designed differently to produce a different display appearance, demonstrating the distinct separation between arithmetic operations (processing) and output.

Example 3.13

```
10 'COLUMN DISPLAY
20 '
30 DOLLARS = 100.56
40 CENTS = 66
50 TOTAL = DOLLARS + CENTS * .01
60 PRINT "Dollars :", DOLLARS
70 PRINT "Cents :", CENTS
80 PRINT "Total :", TOTAL
90 END
```

The results are displayed as:

```
Dollars :        100.56
Cents :          66
Total :          101.22
```

ALPHANUMERIC DATA

Alphanumeric data are also known as *strings*. In program code, strings must be enclosed within double quotation marks as in the case of literals. The rules governing literal formation are also applicable to alphanumeric data, or strings.

Example 3.14

This program produces the same results as in the last two examples. The names **Dollars, Cents**, and **Total**, however, are stored in memory and can be used again in the same program if needed.

```
10 'ALPHANUMERIC DATA
20 '
30 DOLLARS = 100.56
40 CENTS = 66
```

```
50 DOLLARS$ = "Dollars"
60 CENTS$ = "Cents"
70 TOTAL$ = "Total"
80 TOTAL = DOLLARS + CENTS * .01
90 PRINT DOLLARS$; " :", DOLLARS
100 PRINT CENTS$; " :", CENTS
110 PRINT TOTAL$; " :", TOTAL
120 END
```

Exercise Set 3.3 Variable naming, general arithmetic, arithmetic with display (Using **PRINT**, **CLS**, **END**, **LET**)

A. Creating variable names:

1. Create five valid integer variable names:

Answer: ______________________________

____

2. Create five valid single-precision numeric variable names:

Answer: ______________________________

____

3. Convert the variable names in question 2 to double precision:

Answer: ______________________________

____

4. Create five valid alphanumeric variable names:

Answer: ______________________________

____

B. Correct the errors, if any, in the following programs:

5.

```
10 LET A% = 3
20 LET B = 12.8
30 LET C$ = 5.5
40 PRINT;;; A%, B, C$
50 END
```

Answer: ______________________________

____

____

6.

```
10 PRINT A%, B%
20 LET 15 = A%
30 LET 20 = B%
40 LET C% = A% - B%
50 PRINT C%
60 END
```

Answer: ______________________________

____

____

C. Write a program to:

7. Convert 1,000 millimeters into inches and display the result meaningfully. (1 inch = 2.54 centimeters)
8. Establish the alphanumeric data item "Entry no." in memory and display it in a column on the CRT ten times.
9. Establish the first, middle, and last name of a person as data in memory separately, and display them in orders of:
   a. First, middle, and last name
   b. Last name, a comma, first and middle names
   c. First name and middle name

   all in the same program.

INTEGERS: TRUNCATION

Integer variables, unlike real number variables, can take on only whole numbers.

Example 3.15

```
10 'INTEGERS
20 '
30 LET A% = 50
40 PRINT A%
50 END
```

The whole number 50 is assigned to the integer variable A% and displayed.

Example 3.16

In this example, however, even though 50 divided by 3 is 16.6666666667, the rounded number 17 is kept.

```
10 'INTEGERS
20 '
30 LET A% = 50
40 LET B% = A% / 3
50 PRINT A%, B%
60 END
```

displaying:

```
 50              17
```

Example 3.17

If this program is **RUN**, you will see that 16 instead of 17 is kept. Using the backslash (\) in division produces integers without rounding.

```
10 'THE \ DIVISION
20 '
30 LET A% = 50
40 LET B% = A% \ 3
50 PRINT A%, B%
60 END
```

What is displayed by the next example?

Example 3.18

```
10 'TRUNCATION
20 '
30 LET A = 50
40 LET B% = A \ 3
50 PRINT A, B%
60 END
```

Answer: ______________________________

The dropping of the decimal portion of a real number is known as *truncation*. Sometimes truncation is useful if only the integer part of a number is needed. One use is in reestablishing the significant figure of a real number.

Example 3.19

In this example, two places of decimal accuracy are sought. The real number is first multiplied by 100 to force the two places after the decimal to move to the left-hand side of the decimal point; then the number is truncated. The resultant whole number is then divided by 100 to move the decimal point back to its original position.

Notice that the truncation operation must be coordinated with the variable type used, or the wrong data type will be stored during the operation. Again, separately drawn variable boxes will help in the logic analysis.

```
10 'SETTING SIGNIFICANT FIGURE
20 '
                                          A
30 LET A = 50                           [ 50       ]

                                          B
40 LET B = A / 3                        [ 16.66666 ]

                                          C%
50 LET C% = B * 100                     [ 1667     ]

                                          D
60 LET D = C% / 100                     [ 16.67    ]

70 PRINT A, B, C%, D
80 END
```

Such an operation can be used to produce better-looking displays.

Notice that, in statement 50, BASIC rounds the value of **C%** before truncating the decimal portion. This is because the variable name **C%** specifies the integer data type.

Example 3.20 again illustrates how meaningful output is designed.

Example 3.20

```
10 'PRODUCING MEANINGFUL DISPLAY
20 '
30 LET A = 50
40 LET D = 3
50 LET B = A / D
60 LET C% = B * 100
70 LET E% = C% / 100
80 PRINT A; "/"; D; " = "; E%
90 END
```

The displayed result is:

```
 50 / 3 = 17
```

One thing always to remember is that BASIC, as in arithmetic, does not know how to handle divisions by zero. If such an operation is attempted, an error message will be produced.

Example 3.21

```
10 'DIVISION BY 0
20 '
30 LET A = 5 / 0
40 PRINT A
50 END
```

producing:

```
Division by 0
```

The programmer should therefore always ensure that such an event does not occur, either by making sure that the known divisor is not a zero or by some protection mechanism constructed using the **IF** statement (which will be discussed in chapter 6).

Exercise Set 3.4 Integers, truncation, \ (Using **PRINT**, **CLS**, **END**, **LET**)

A. What do the following programs do?

1.

```
10 LET A = 3.14159265
20 LET B% = A * 100
30 LET A = B% * 0.01
```

Answer: ______________________________

____

____

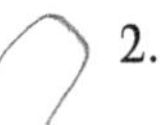

2.

```
10 LET A = 67.8842
20 LET B% = A \ 1
30 LET C = A - B%
40 PRINT C
50 END
```

Answer: ______________________________

____

____

B. Write a program to:

3. Extract the cents of the dollar amount $100.64.
4. Express the same amount above in terms of dollars, quarters, dimes, nickels, and cents.
5. Compute the radian equivalents of angles expressed in degrees (1 degree = π / 180; 1 π = 3.1416) from 1 to 20 degrees at increments of 1 degree and display the results meaningfully with all output rounded to two places after the decimal.

INTRINSIC FUNCTIONS

Arithmetic operations are perhaps the most often performed activity in data processing. Many popular operations have been included by BASIC's designers and are offered for our use as *functions*. A function is a name that represents an entire arithmetic operation, behaving in such a way that it resembles a simple quantity. A function is always a function name followed by a pair of parentheses, which enclose an arithmetic quantity or expression called the **argument**. The argument is then converted into a resultant value according to the operation represented by the function. Such functions that come with BASIC are known as *intrinsic functions*. Some of the more popular functions and their uses are illustrated here.

Example 3.22

An *absolute value* of a number is the magnitude of the number, or the positive-signed version of the number. The function **ABS** provides the absolute value.

```
10 'ABSOLUTE VALUE
20 '
30 LET A = ABS( -6.33 )
40 PRINT A
50 END
```

The number 6.33 without the minus sign is displayed.

This intrinsic function is useful in solving problems where the sign of a number is of no concern (only the magnitude is of importance) or where the result must be reported without the minus sign, as in the next example.

Example 3.23

```
10 'ABSOLUTE VALUE
20 '
30 LET A = ABS( 16.88 + 27.42 - 85.94 )
40 PRINT "The magnitude of the number is "; A
50 END
```

displaying:

```
The magnitude of the number is 41.62
```

For trigonometry and the like, there are the trigonometric functions such as sine and cosine (**SIN** and **COS**), which work on arguments expressed in the unit radian. Cosine is illustrated here:

Example 3.24

```
10 'COSINE FUNCTION
20 '
30 LET A = 3.141593 / 3
```

```
40 LET C = COS( A )
50 PRINT C
60 END
```

Example 3.25

The truncation operation demonstrated earlier with the integer variables is also available in function form. The **FIX** function truncates a real number.

```
10 'TRUNCATION FUNCTION
20 '
30 LET A = 7.777777
40 LET B = FIX( A )
50 PRINT A, B
60 END
```

displaying:

```
 7.777777       7
```

Example 3.26

```
10 'TRUNCATION FUNCTION
20 '
30 LET A = -7.777777
40 LET B = FIX( A )
50 PRINT A, B
60 END
```

displaying:

```
-7.777777      -7
```

Another function, **INT**, also turns a real number into an integer. **INT**, however, returns the lower integer value and does not perform a pure truncation.

Example 3.27

```
10 'INTEGER FUNCTION
20 '
30 LET A = 7.777777
40 LET B = INT( A )
50 PRINT A, B
60 END
```

displays:

```
 7
```

while

```
10 'INTEGER FUNCTION
20 '
30 LET A = -7.777777
40 LET B = INT( A )
50 PRINT A, B
60 END
```

displays:

```
-8
```

Notice that the lower integer from −7.777777 is −8.

Why does BASIC provide integer functions when you can obtain the same results through assigning data to an integer variable? The answer is that an integer variable can only handle numbers between −32,768 and 32,767, while an integer function can produce numbers much beyond this range.

USER-DEFINED FUNCTIONS

If the need arises, you can form your own functions as well. Such a "home-made" function is called a *user-defined function*. A user-defined function is achieved through the **DEF FN** statement.

In the **DEF FN** statement, a function name must follow the **DEF FN** keywords. The naming of a function follows the rules of variable naming, except that the data-type declaration is unnecessary. After the function name is a pair of parentheses.

This function name is then followed by the equal sign and the arithmetic expression for the function. The value to be converted, the argument, is enclosed in the parentheses.

Once the user-defined function is defined, then the program may use it as if it were an intrinsic function. The designing of user-defined functions is illustrated below.

Example 3.28

In this example, a function that converts a centigrade temperature into Fahrenheit is defined and used.

```
10 'USER-DEFINED FUNCTION
20 '
30 DEF FN F( C ) = C * 9 / 5 + 32
40 LET T = FN F( 100 )
50 PRINT T
60 END
```

Pay attention to the form of statement 40, which shows how a user-defined function is invoked.

The argument of a function serves only to inform BASIC of the parameter to be used. It does not have to be in the exact form as when the function is defined. Therefore, in Example 3.28, the number 100 is directly used, even though the argument C was used to define the function. Likewise, a variable can be used, as long as it has a valid value.

The reverse of Example 3.28, converting from Fahrenheit to centigrade, is shown below.

Example 3.29

```
10 'USER-DEFINED FUNCTION
20 '
30 DEF FN F( F ) = ( F - 32 ) * 5 / 9
40 LET T = 212
50 LET T = FN F( T )
60 PRINT T
70 END
```

Notice in this case that the argument is a variable whose contents are preassigned.

Multiple arguments can also be used, as demonstrated in Example 3.30.

Example 3.30

This function calculates the simple interest generated over a term for a principle at a preset rate.

```
10 'MULTIPLE PARAMETERS
20 '
30 DEF FN NTRST( P, R, T ) = P * R * T
```

```
40 LET PRIN = 100
50 LET RATE = .05
60 LET TERM = 5
70 PRINT FN NTRST( PRIN, RATE, TERM )
80 END
```

Because a function produces a single value, it can be treated in programming as merely a data item. Thus, a function can be used by another function.

In Example 3.31, only whole number temperatures are dealt with. Examine statement 50 to understand how the values are passed from one function to another.

Example 3.31

```
10 'FUNCTION WITHIN FUNCTION
20 '
30 DEF FN F( C ) = C * 9 / 5 + 32
40 LET T = 100 / 3
50 LET T = FN F( INT( T ) )
60 PRINT T
70 END
```

DEF FN
Form: DEF FN name [(argument[, argument] ...)] = expression
Function: To define an algorithm that generates a single return value.

Exercise Set 3.5 Functions, user-defined functions (Using **PRINT**, **CLS**, **END**, **LET**, functions, **DEF FN**)

A. Define functions:

1. Write a function definition of the equation:

tan(a) = sin(a) / cos(a)

Answer: ______________________________

2. Write a function to define the relationship:

   yield = principle (1 + rate) to the power term

Answer: ______________________________

3. Define the formula as a function:

   x = center + radius * cos(angle)

Answer: ______________________________

B. Write a program to:

4. Compute the hypotenuse of right-angle triangles with the two short sides being:
   a. 3, 4
   b. 5, 12
   c. 70, 80
   all in the same program.
5. Compute the sales taxes, the subtotal, and the grand total of the three sales amounts $100.75, $24.97, and $36.00, and display all quantities in a sales-receipt form. Sales tax is assessed at 5 percent.
6. First assign appropriate data to variables, perform the necessary computations, and then produce the following purchasing order:

```
                                        Unit
Part #    Description          Qty      Price     Total
=======================================================

A2044     Boots                200      12.55
A2047     Socks                500      2.45
C3101     Belts                50       7.23



                               Total Purchase:
```

and display them as above.

Chapter Exercises (Using **PRINT**, **CLS**, **END**, **LET**, functions, **DEF FN**)

1. Design a CRT display for a list of courses offered by a school department. The courses offered are: CS001, CS004, CS102, CS212, CS356, CS401. Along with the courses, list the corresponding credit units.
2. Design a general CRT display for an experiment report for Advanced Engineering, Inc. The test specimens involved in the experiment are: round rod, T-bar, I-bar, and tube. Assume you know the experimental results (as numbers).
3. Design a program to produce a sales receipt for Quickie Hardware accommodating five sale items. Assume the programmer will be given the five sales amounts. Include Quickie's address and phone number.
4. Write a program to compute and report the final numeric grade average of twelve tests administered in one school term by Professor Meanie. Assume the numeric test grades are given.
5. Design a customer statement for Hardwork, Inc. Items to be included are: heading, credit and debit, their subtotals, and the final balance. Each statement is to contain three credits and five debits at appropriate dates. (For each credit, the corresponding debit is zero, and vice versa.)

4 / INPUTTING DATA AND DESIGNING PROGRAMS

In chapter 3 we learned that **LET** permits the programmer to store data under variables. But data values are not always known to the programmer during programming. Usually, real data are only known after a program is completed or when the program is executed. In most programming cases, the program only expresses a method by which data are converted into output; the working data must be supplied to the program after it is finished. In BASIC, the most common way to supply data to a finished program is through the keyboard.

ENTERING DATA: INPUT

A *user* is a person who uses an established program to produce a desired result, as opposed to the person designing the program. In BASIC, user data input is achieved through the **INPUT** statement.

The **INPUT** statement begins with the keyword **INPUT**. When an **INPUT** statement is reached in a program, BASIC suspends the program execution and awaits data to be assigned to variables, in much the same way as with the **LET** statement. The data, however, are obtained from the keyboard. Example 4.1 illustrates the simplest form of the **INPUT** statement.

Example 4.1

```
10 'INPUT WITH ?
20 '
30 INPUT A
40 END
```

In this example, program statement 30 says **INPUT A**, which means: Hold all operations, go to the keyboard, and wait for a data item. When a data item is entered via the keyboard, assign it to the variable **A.**

If this example program is **RUN**, then a question mark will appear on the CRT. The user may at this point type in a data item for the variable **A** and press the <Enter> key to signal the end of the data entry. Upon sensing the <Enter> key being pressed, BASIC will then assign the data item just typed to the variable **A** as if the statement:

```
LET A = data item
```

had been executed.

The difference in this case, of course, is that the data item is assigned to the variable **A** only when the program is executed.

If the user does not respond to the **INPUT** request during program execution, then BASIC will continue to hold up operation until some sort of response from the user is detected.

As with **LET**, **INPUT** also requires that the data item supplied be of consistent data type with the variable requesting the data. **RUN** Example 4.1 again. This time type a string data (such as "ABC") and press the <Enter> key to signal the end of the data entry. You should get the error message:

```
?Redo From Start
```

?Redo From Start indicates that the **INPUT** statement has no syntax error but that the input data are unacceptable. A string data item that is input for a numeric data request is unacceptable. To satisfy the program, you must enter a numeric data item, or the program will not proceed.

On the other hand, numerals are acceptable for string data requests, as BASIC simply regards the numeric digits typed as a string.

Example 4.2

```
10 'INPUT STRING
20 '
30 INPUT A$
40 END
```

For this program, an input such as "123.45" is perfectly all right, and no error message will be triggered. This is not to say that the number 123.45 has been assigned to the variable **A$**. Rather, the string made up of the six symbols 123.45 has been assigned; as far as BASIC is concerned, the data item held at **A$** possesses no numeric value, just the six characters that make up the string. A subsequent statement such as:

```
LET B = A$ + 3
```

will not yield 126.45.

Because data assigned through the **INPUT** statement begin with the first key pressed and end with the <Enter> key, string data entered from the keyboard do not need to be enclosed within double quotation marks. So string data accepted by the program, such as the 123.45 above, must not be misconstrued to be the same as 123.45 accepted under a numeric variable.

Unlike **LET**, **INPUT** is not restricted to single data assignments. More than one data entry may be accomplished through the same **INPUT** statement, as long as the variables and the input data are separated by commas (which, in this case, serve as delimiters and not cursor control codes as in a **PRINT** statement).

Example 4.3

```
10 'MULTIPLE INPUT
20 '
30 INPUT A, B, C
40 END
```

RUN this example program and enter three numeric data items through the keyboard, all separated by commas as:

```
1.2, 3, 4.05
```

If the input data are not separated by commas, then a **?Redo From Start** error message will be invoked.

In the **INPUT** statement, a minimum of one space must be used to separate the keyword **INPUT** from the variables, or the syntax error message is again triggered. Statement 30 in Example 4.4 is thus unacceptable.

Example 4.4

```
10 'SPACE MUST FOLLOW INPUT
20 '
```

```
30 INPUTA,B,C
40 END
```

In each of the example programs above, data items were supposedly assigned to the variables named in the **INPUT** statements. As the user types in the input data, the data are displayed on the CRT. This is known as *echoing*. Recall that with the **LET** statement the data assigned are not automatically displayed, unless the variable contents are subsequently displayed through **PRINT** statements. The echo feature for **INPUT** statements is designed to indicate immediately to the user the data typed. To verify that the input data are assigned to the respective variables, the **PRINT** statement must still be used, as demonstrated in the next example.

Example 4.5

```
10 'DATA ASSIGNMENT WITH INPUT
20 '
30 INPUT A
40 PRINT A
50 END
```

If you **RUN** this program, you will first get a question mark, then the typed input data item will be echoed on the CRT immediately followed by the data item displayed by the **PRINT** statement.

Example 4.6

```
10 'DATA ASSIGNMENT WITH INPUT
20 '
30 INPUT A, B, C
40 PRINT A, B, C
50 END
```

Example 4.6 demands three input data to be entered, separated by commas. The combined display from the input echo and the ensuing **PRINT** statement is:

```
?12.4, 3.55, 7.08
 12.4          3.55          7.08
```

This example also clearly shows the different functional roles of the comma in the **INPUT** and **PRINT** statements.

The **INPUT** statement assigns the input data to the variables requested according to the sequence of the variable list. **INPUT** also requires that the input data match the requesting variables by data type. Consequently, as long as these two requirements are met, mixing data types within the same **INPUT** variable list is perfectly acceptable—but the input data must be arranged in exactly the same data-type sequence. In Example 4.7, both numeric and string data are requested through the same **INPUT** statement and then displayed for verification purposes.

Example 4.7

```
10 'DATA ASSIGNMENT WITH INPUT
20 '
30 INPUT A, B, C$
40 PRINT A, B, C$
50 END
```

RUN the program and supply the **INPUT** requests with appropriate input data. Also try mismatching the data types and note the result.

Result: ____

____

If an **INPUT** request is responded to by pressing the <Enter> key, then BASIC will assume one of two input data values depending on the data type requested:

1. If numeric data are asked for, then the pressing of the <Enter> key is the same as inputting a zero.
2. If a string is expected, then a null string entry is assumed. A null string is equivalent to "", namely, a no-character string enclosed by a pair of double quotation marks.

Try the next two example programs by pressing the <Enter> key to satisfy the **INPUT** requests. In the first case, a 0 will be displayed. In the second case, nothing will be displayed—that is, nothing visible. However, a carriage return and a line feed will be produced.

Example 4.8

```
10 'DATA ENTRY WITH ENTER
20 '
30 INPUT A
40 PRINT A
50 END
```

Example 4.9

```
10 'DATA ENTRY WITH ENTER
20 '
30 INPUT A$
40 PRINT A$
50 END
```

INPUT
Form: INPUT[;] ["prompt";] variable[, variable] . . .
Function: To request input value(s) from the user for the named variable(s).

Exercise Set 4.1 INPUT with **?** (Using **END**, **LET**, functions, **DEF FN**, **INPUT**)

A. Correct the errors, if any, in the following programs:

1.

```
10 INPUT A,
20 PRINT A
30 END
```

Answer: ______________________________

____

2.

```
10 INPUT A B C
20 PRINT A B C
30 END
```

Answer: ______________________________

____

3. What does the following program do?

```
10 CLS
20 INPUT A, B
```

```
30 LET C = A * B + 3
40 PRINT A, B, C
50 END
```

Answer: ______________________________

____

____

B. Program Design:

4. Obtain three single-precision numbers to be entered through the keyboard, total them, compute their average, and output them meaningfully on the CRT.
5. Report the magnitude of the difference between two numbers entered from the keyboard.
6. Reduce each of three keyboard-entered numbers to integers. No rounding is desired.
7. Write a program asking a ski instructor computer user for three team-member names and display them.

PRODUCING PROMPT MESSAGES

As demonstrated, **INPUT** provides a great variety of data entry possibilities. From the programmer's standpoint, these possibilities do not seem overwhelming, as the **INPUT** specifications are clearly stated in the program code. But the user, who is not privy to the program design process, may not find data entry all that straightforward. Suppose, as the user, you are confronted by the following display:

```
?
```

You probably would not know whether you are being asked to enter one or several data items, or whether they are to be numerics or strings. In such situations, some form of instruction would be desirable. An instruction for guiding the user of a program is known as a *prompt*. Prompts can be provided for the user through the **INPUT** statements.

A prompt in an **INPUT** statement is a literal, as in a **PRINT** statement, that precedes the **INPUT** variables and is separated from the variables by either a semicolon or a comma.

Example 4.10

```
10 'INPUT WITH PROMPT
20 '
30 INPUT "What is the input number"; A
40 PRINT A
50 END
```

RUN this example program. The following display will be produced:

```
What is the input number?
```

At this point, BASIC is awaiting a data item to be entered to be assigned to the variable **A**. Enter this data, and see that it is displayed again due to statement 40.

The only difference between this example and the previous ones is the display of the phrase: **What is the input number**. This phrase is the prompt, designed by the programmer, and is displayed through the **INPUT** statement prior to any **INPUT** action as if a **PRINT** statement had been issued. After the prompt is displayed, the normal **INPUT** action then resumes, and a question mark is generated to signal to the user that BASIC is waiting for a data entry.

To be meaningful, the prompt should always be designed to be brief and yet informative. This depends on two factors. First, the prompt must correctly specify the type of data requested and the manner in which they are to be entered; and second, the phrasing of the prompt should correspond to the level of the user's technical competency. And most of all, the prompt should be meaningful in terms of clear English. Let us examine the next example.

Example 4.11

```
10 'THE OBJECTIONABLE ?
20 '
30 INPUT "Enter data"; A
40 PRINT A
50 END
```

For this program, the following display will be generated:

```
Enter data?
```

The programmer has designed the prompt to be an order: **Enter data**! However, BASIC automatically supplies a question mark with the prompt, causing the prompt to appear as a question of unclear purpose. A user may perceive the prompt to mean "Do you want to enter data?" and is likely to respond with yes or no.

Such a prompt in the form of an order is desirable. For this, BASIC permits the use of the comma after the prompt literal to suppress the question mark, as demonstrated in the next example.

Example 4.12

```
10 'SUPPRESSING THE ?
20 '
30 INPUT "Enter data : ", A
40 PRINT A
50 END
```

In this case, the displayed prompt is:

```
Enter data :
```

much more meaningful than **Enter data?**

With the prompt, the computer is made to "converse" or interact with the user. This is known as *interactive programming*. For interactive programming, often the prompt alone is not sufficient to create complex and extensive dialogues. The **PRINT** statement may be brought in to help out. For instance, the next example program uses both **INPUT** and **PRINT** to produce a meaningful dialogue. The **PRINT** statement is used to make a meaningful report after the data input.

Example 4.13

```
10 'DATA ENTRY BY NONTECHNICALLY ORIENTED USERS
20 '
30 INPUT "Please enter a number and then press the
   ENTER key : ", A
40 PRINT "The number entered is"; A
50 END
```

The display on the CRT is:

```
Please enter a number and then press the ENTER key : 4.55
The number entered is 4.55
```

Example 4.14 uses **PRINT** statements to produce an elaborate set of instructions for a nontechnically oriented user:

Example 4.14

```
10 'INTERACTIVE PROGRAMMING
20 '
30 CLS
40 PRINT "Please enter a number and press the ENTER
   key when done."
50 PRINT "The ?Redo From Start message means you have
   made an error,"
60 INPUT "and you should try again : ", A
70 PRINT A
80 END
```

A detailed display of instructions is produced:

```
Please enter a number and press the ENTER key when done.
The ?Redo From Start message means you have made an error
and you should try again :
```

Exercise Set 4.2 Prompt message, **INPUT** without **?,** interactive programming (Using **PRINT**, **CLS**, **END**, **LET**, functions, **DEF FN**, **INPUT**)

A. Correct the errors, if any, in the following programs:

1.

```
10 INPUT "Enter data : "; A
20 PRINT
30 END
```

Answer: ____

____

2.

```
10 INPUT "Enter sales : "; A
20 PRINT "Please enter the sales amount.
30 PRINT Press the ENTER key when done.
40 PRINT The ?Redo From Start message means you
   have made an error,
50 PRINT and you should try again."
60 PRINT
70 PRINT "THE SALES AMOUNT IS $"; B
80 END
```

Answer: ______________________________

____

____

B. Write a program to:

3. Instruct a seasoned computer user to enter three integers from the keyboard.
4. Obtain three inventory amounts from a seasoned data entry clerk by providing the three corresponding part numbers.
5. a. Write a program segment to input three real numbers from the keyboard using three **INPUT** statements. The user is an occasional computer user, so the program should prompt the user for the numbers.
   b. Write a program segment to obtain the same data as in 5a using one **INPUT** statement. The user is knowledgeable about computers.

THE ALGORITHM

A program is generally made up of three distinct components: input, processing, and output. During input, data are supplied to the program. During processing, the input data are converted into the results sought. The results produced are then presented for people to read during output. In designing a program, you must recognize these three components and attempt to separate them whenever possible.

Because the processing component of a program is the link between a variety of input and the corresponding results, its processing logic (expressed as computer instructions) must be general. Such a general set of program instructions is called an *algorithm*. An algorithm is thus a well-defined procedure that takes an input and produces an output. For instance, the formula for converting a Fahrenheit temperature into centigrade is an algorithm, as it can take any input temperature and turn it into the corresponding output temperature through a series of mathematical computations.

As an illustration, let us design a program that computes the total of any three sales amounts.

Example 4.15

Because at the time of program design we do not yet know what the sales amounts are, these amounts will simply be called A, B, and C. These three sales amounts are to be totaled into a quantity that shall be called D. D is thus obtained from A, B, and C summed; that is, D = A + B + C. This is the algorithm, the relationship between A, B, C, and D, without the data being defined explicitly.

A program that will compute the total of the three sales amounts must then follow these logical steps:

1. Obtain the data from the user, which can be achieved through the **INPUT** mechanism.
2. The input data are then processed to produce the total according to D = A + B + C.
3. The three sales amounts and the total are then output.

In designing the program, we should deal with these three major actions separately. With a little thought, the data input action can be expressed in program code as:

```
PRINT "Enter 3 sales amounts separated by commas,"
PRINT "and press the ENTER key when finished."
PRINT "A ?Redo From Start message means you should try
      again."
PRINT
INPUT "Enter data : ", A, B, C
```

The three numbers thus obtained are used to produce the total through the statement:

```
LET D = A + B + C
```

The results are then output with:

```
PRINT "Sales item 1", "$"; A
PRINT "Sales item 2", "$"; B
PRINT "Sales item 3", "$"; C
PRINT
PRINT , "Total : $"; D
```

When the three sections are combined, the complete program code is arrived at:

```
10 'THE ALGORITHM
20 '
30 'DATA ENTRY:
40 '
50 CLS
60 PRINT "Enter 3 sales amounts separated by commas,"
70 PRINT "and press the ENTER key when finished."
80 PRINT "A ?Redo From Start message means you should
   try again."
90 PRINT
100 INPUT "Enter data : ", A, B, C
110 PRINT
120 '
130 'TOTALING:
140 '
150 LET D = A + B + C
160 '
170 'DISPLAYING RESULTS:
180 '
190 PRINT "Sales item 1", "$"; A
200 PRINT "Sales item 2", "$"; B
210 PRINT "Sales item 3", "$"; C
220 PRINT
230 PRINT , "Total : $"; D
240 END
```

RUN the program and try it with various input sales amounts.

As another example, let us write a program to compute the grade average for a student.

Example 4.16

Assuming there are four grades to be averaged, we shall call them A, B, C, and D. The grade average for any four grades is obtained from the following algorithm: average $E = (A + B + C + D)/4$. The program to accomplish this is:

```
10 'ALGORITHM EXAMPLE 2
20 '
```

Input section:

```
30 'DATA ENTRY:
40 '
```

```
50 CLS
60 PRINT "Enter 4 test grades separated by commas,"
70 PRINT "and press the ENTER key when done."
80 PRINT "A ?Redo From Start message means you should
   try again."
90 PRINT
100 INPUT "Enter grades : ", A, B, C, D
```

Processing section (algorithm):

```
110 'GRADE AVERAGING:
120 '
130 LET E = ( A + B + C + D ) / 4
140 '
```

Output section:

```
150 'OUTPUTTING:
160 '
170 PRINT
180 '
190 PRINT "Grade 1 : "; A
200 PRINT "Grade 2 : "; B
210 PRINT "Grade 3 : "; C
220 PRINT "Grade 4 : "; D
230 PRINT
240 PRINT , "Grade average : "; E
250 END
```

THE PARAMETER

Let us take a closer look at the two algorithms presented above:

1. $D = A + B + C$
2. $E = (A + B + C + D) / 4$

In each of these two algorithms, letters are used to denote quantities that are unknown at the time of program design. Once the program designs are finished, however, these quantities can take on practically any value at all. Thus they are called *variables*. Specifically, the variables on the left-hand side of the equations obtain their values only after the values on the right-hand side of the equal sign are defined. Therefore, the variables on the left-hand side are called *dependent variables*, and the ones on the right-hand side are called *independent variables*.

But in these algorithms there are other values as well, such as the 4 in algorithm 2, used to average the total. Such numbers are fixed as far as the algorithms are concerned and thus are called *constants*.

Variables and constants used in algorithms are called the *parameters* of the algorithms. The question, of course, is: When is a parameter a variable, and when is it a constant? Usually, those quantities that can take on various values are variables, and those used to define the relationships are constants. There exists, however, a group of parameters that are semi-variables, as illustrated in the following example.

Example 4.17

Suppose Example 4.15 is expanded to include the computation of the sales tax as well. In this case, the program code is:

```
10 'PARAMETER
20 '
30 'INPUT:
40 '
50 CLS
60 INPUT "Enter 3 sales amounts separated by commas :
   ", A, B, C
70 '
80 'TOTALING:
90 '
100 LET SUB.TOTAL = A + B + C
110 LET TAX = SUB.TOTAL * 0.065
120 LET TOTAL = SUB.TOTAL + TAX
130 '
140 'OUTPUT:
150 '
160 PRINT
170 PRINT "Sale 1 : $"; A
180 PRINT "Sale 2 : $"; B
190 PRINT "Sale 3 : $"; C
200 PRINT
210 PRINT , "Subtotal : $"; SUB.TOTAL
220 PRINT
230 PRINT , "Sales tax : $"; TAX
240 PRINT
250 PRINT , "Total : $"; TOTAL
260 END
```

Here we find the extra parameter of 0.065, which is the sales tax rate and in this case clearly a constant. But conceivably this tax rate may change from time to time, depending on the current and foreseeable government policies. The way the program is designed, it does not lend itself readily to updating should the tax rate change some time after the program's completion. In fact, to make such a change, the programmer (who may be different from the programmer who designed the program originally) must locate this 0.065 among the program statements and make the correction—not a very convenient procedure.

To anticipate such possible program updating (an activity known as *program maintenance*), the program designer ought to set this tax rate as a variable, even though as far as the algorithm is concerned, it is a constant. Thus, we consider the following a better program version:

```
10 'SETTING PARAMETER
20 '
25 LET TAX.RATE = 0.065
26 '
30 'INPUT:
40 '
50 CLS
60 INPUT "Enter 3 sales amounts separated by commas :
   ", A, B, C
70 '
80 'TOTALING:
90 '
100 LET SUB.TOTAL = A + B + C
110 LET TAX = SUB.TOTAL * TAX.RATE
120 LET TOTAL = SUB.TOTAL + TAX
 ⋮  (The body of the program remains the same.)
260 END
```

With the **TAX.RATE** set at the very beginning of the program, any change involving it will be accomplished easily.

Exercise Set 4.3 Algorithm, parameter (Using **PRINT**, **CLS**, **END**, **LET**, functions, **DEF FN**, **INPUT**)

Write a program to:

1. Compute and report the gross pay for an employee if the total hours worked and the hourly rate are provided by the user.
2. Report the total sales of three car models if the user provides the three sales volumes and the corresponding unit prices.

PROGRAM DESIGN PROCEDURES

In writing a program to solve a problem, you do not begin immediately with coding. Instead, the problem must first be understood thoroughly. Obviously, you must know what the results sought are (the output requirements) and what the data are that must be provided in order to arrive at those results (the input requirements). Then a solution method must be designed. This series of activities is known as *problem analysis*. When all three are determined, then the thought process is expressed by a *flowchart*. A flowchart is the thought process documented in a pictorial form, with standardized symbols intended to make the flowchart easy to follow. To learn to flowchart, you must begin with the fundamental symbols and then apply them to thought expression. When the flowchart is finished, then it must be retraced to make sure that the solution logic has been correctly expressed. This is known as the *stepping-through* phase or the *desk check*. It is only when the flowchart is thoroughly checked that the coding is *transcribed*. This entire series of program development activities beginning with an understanding of the problem to the transcription of coding is known as the *top-down approach*.

In flowcharting, program actions are represented by the following symbols:

Processing:

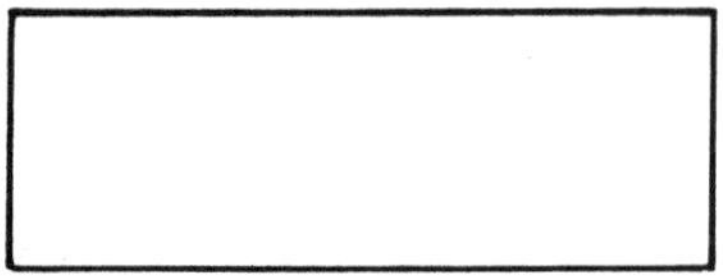

Input/output:

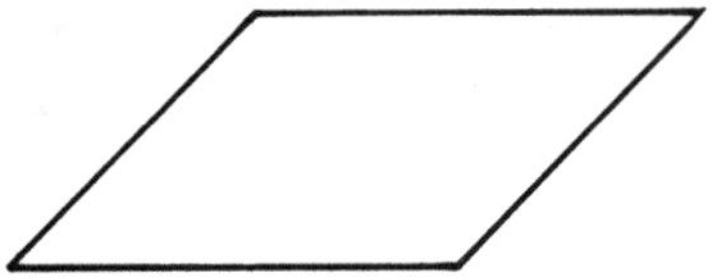

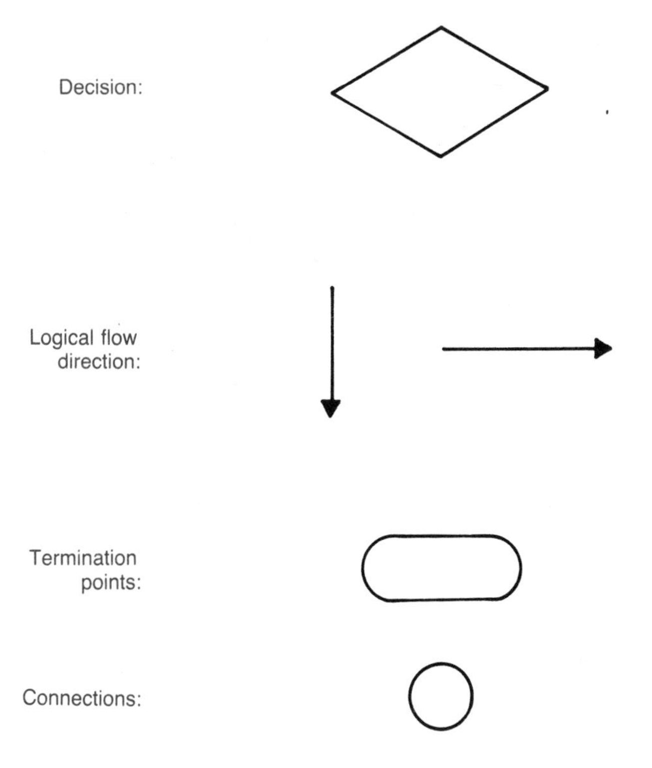

The program logic actions are expressed within the flowcharting symbols (sometimes called "boxes"), and the sequence of the logic follows the direction of the arrows. As an example, let us show the flowchart for Example 4.17. First of all, recall that this program is made up of three major components:

1. Input the necessary sales data A, B, C.
2. Compute the subtotal, the sales tax, and the total.
3. Display the results.

Expressing these thoughts in diagram form, we arrive at the following flowchart.

First, data entry:

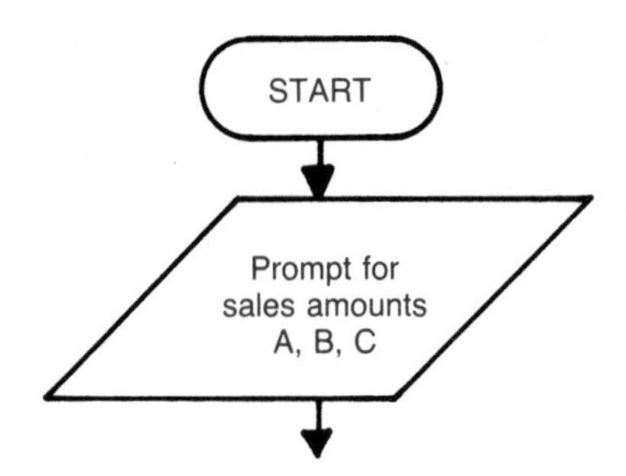

Then perform the necessary computations:

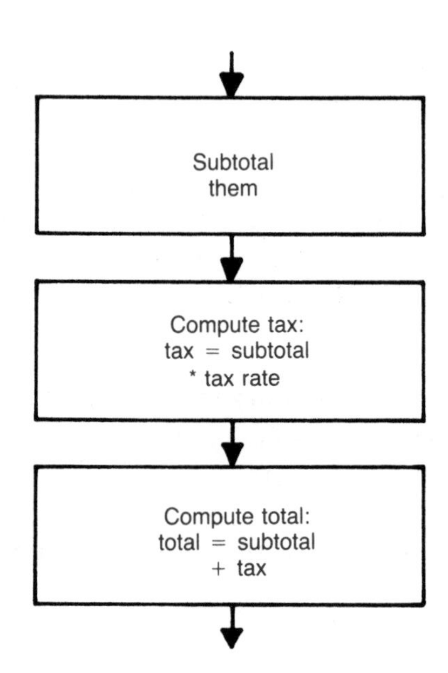

And finally, design the output based on the following design pattern:

```
SALE 1 : $ sales amount
SALE 2 : $ sales amount
SALE 3 : $ sales amount
             SUBTOTAL : $ subtotal amount
             SALES TAX : $ tax amount
             TOTAL : $ total amount
```

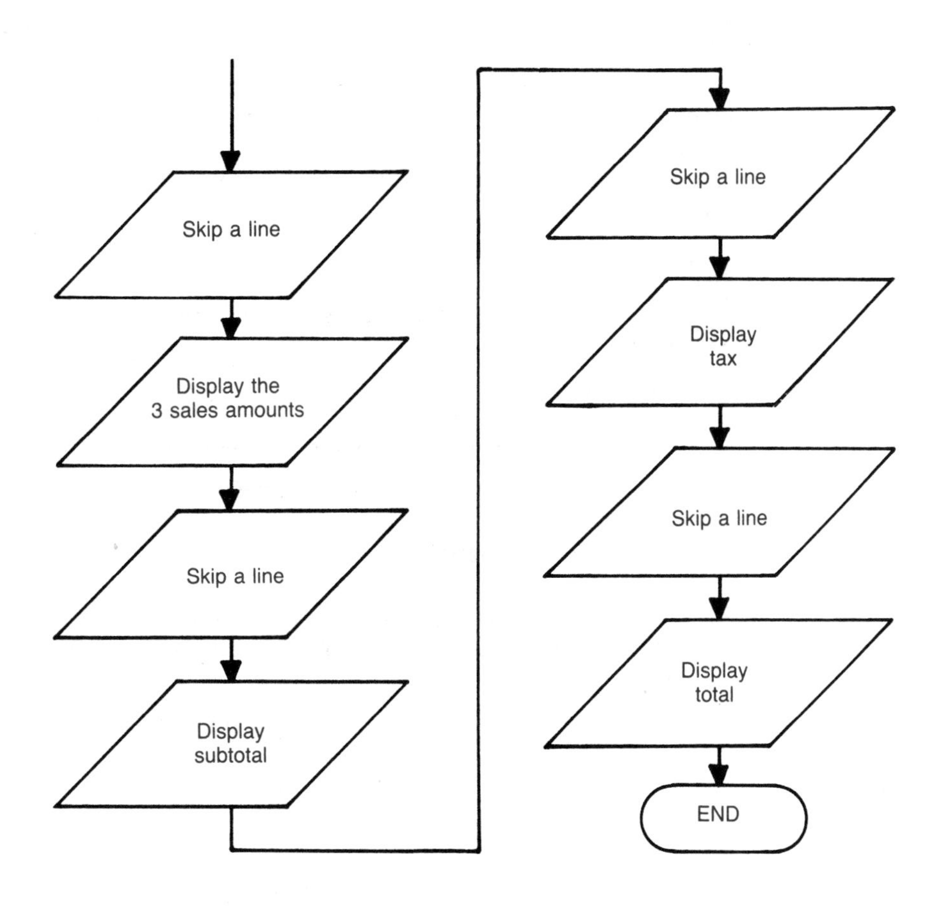

When the preliminary thought process has thus been formulated, the flowchart must be reviewed to make sure that the whole process makes sense. This is known as stepping through or the desk check. In this illustration, it is soon discovered that the tax rate was never defined. So we return to the start of the flowchart and restore the missing step; Figure 4.1 shows the complete flowchart.

The flowchart is then transcribed into code as shown in Figure 4.2.

After the program code is transcribed and program documentation is added, then the program must be keyed into the computer and **RUN** with various input data until a high degree of confidence in the program is attained. At this point, any missing blank lines or screen clearing may be added to clarify the final display.

The flowchart is a very useful program logic developmental tool. Not only does it help with the program development, but it also serves as the basis of communication between colleagues and fellow programmers, as well as a reference for future program updating. It should therefore be concise and expressive and directly reflect the coding. Programming with flowcharting actually results in fewer errors. In this book, all programming techniques will be introduced with flowcharts. Standardized flowcharting methods will also be presented that will greatly increase the code transcription efficiency.

Chapter Exercises Top-down approach, flowcharting, code transcription (Using **PRINT**, **CLS**, **END**, **LET**, functions, **DEF FN**, **INPUT**)

A. Flowcharting

1. Flowchart problems 1, 4, and 5 of the chapter exercises for chapter 3.
2. Flowchart problems 1 and 2 for Exercise Set 4.3.

B. Flowchart and transcribe into code:

3. Design a program for a football coach, an occasional user of the computer, to enter five scores, list them, and report their average on the CRT.
4. Design a program for the same coach to report the scoring differentials between the consecutive games.

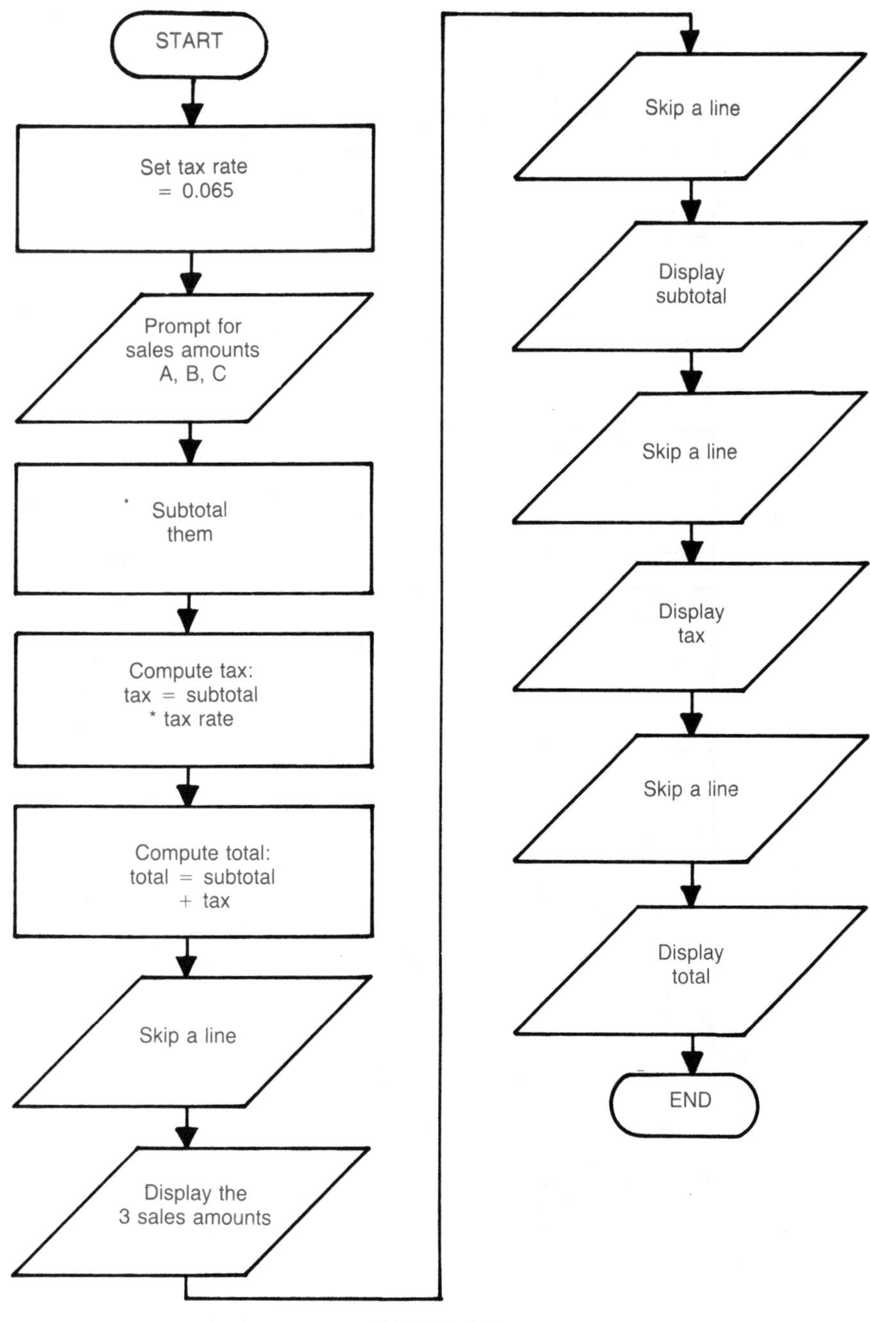
START
Set tax rate
= 0.065
Prompt for
sales amounts
A, B, C
Subtotal
them
Compute tax:
tax = subtotal
* tax rate
Compute total:
total = subtotal
+ tax
Skip a line
Display the
3 sales amounts
Skip a line
Display
subtotal
Skip a line
Display
tax
Skip a line
Display
total
END

FIGURE 4.1

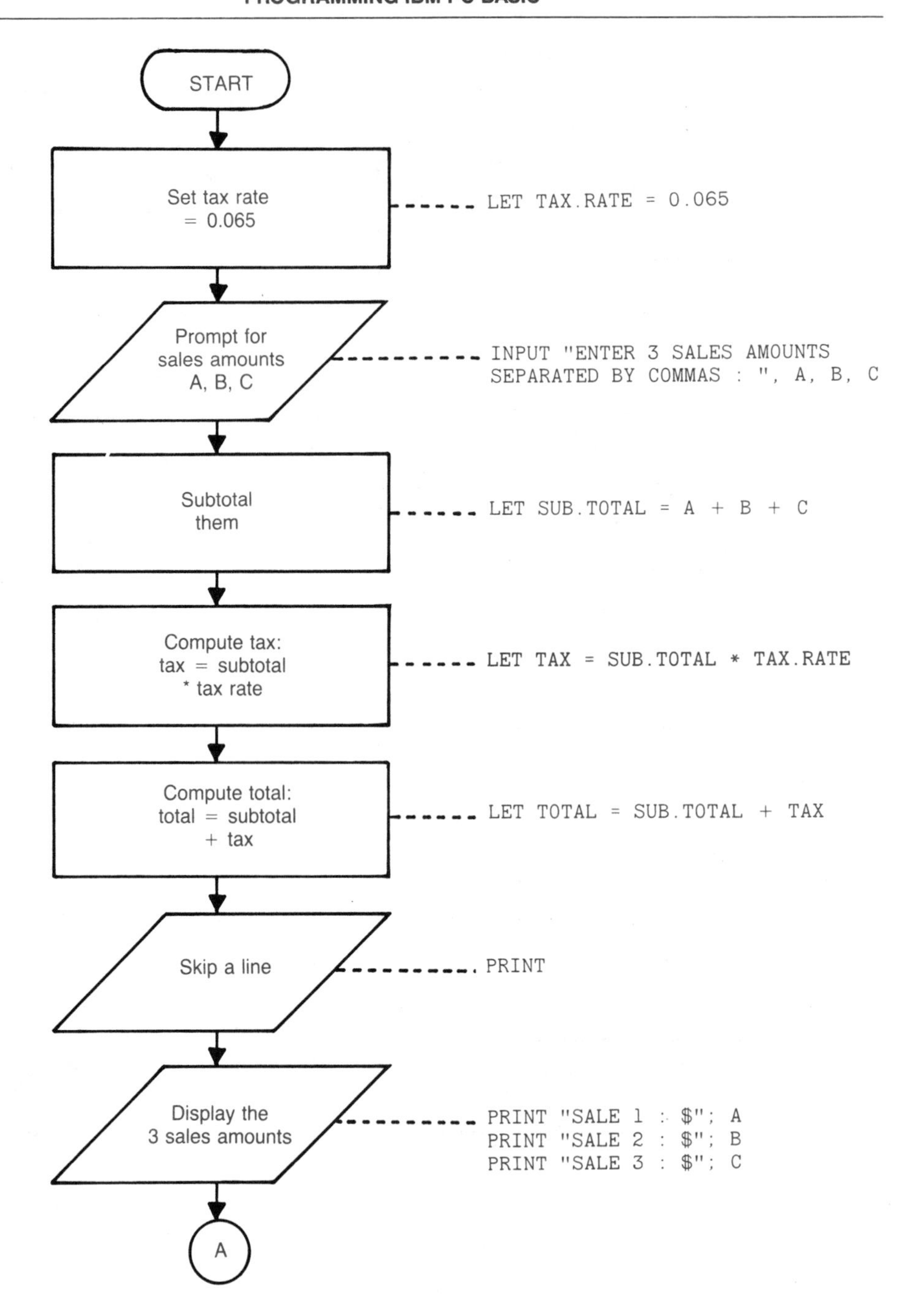
START
Set tax rate
= 0.065
LET TAX.RATE = 0.065
Prompt for
sales amounts
A, B, C
INPUT "ENTER 3 SALES AMOUNTS
SEPARATED BY COMMAS : ", A, B, C
Subtotal
them
LET SUB.TOTAL = A + B + C
Compute tax:
tax = subtotal
* tax rate
LET TAX = SUB.TOTAL * TAX.RATE
Compute total:
total = subtotal
+ tax
LET TOTAL = SUB.TOTAL + TAX
Skip a line
PRINT
Display the
3 sales amounts
PRINT "SALE 1 : $"; A
PRINT "SALE 2 : $"; B
PRINT "SALE 3 : $"; C
A

FIGURE 4.2

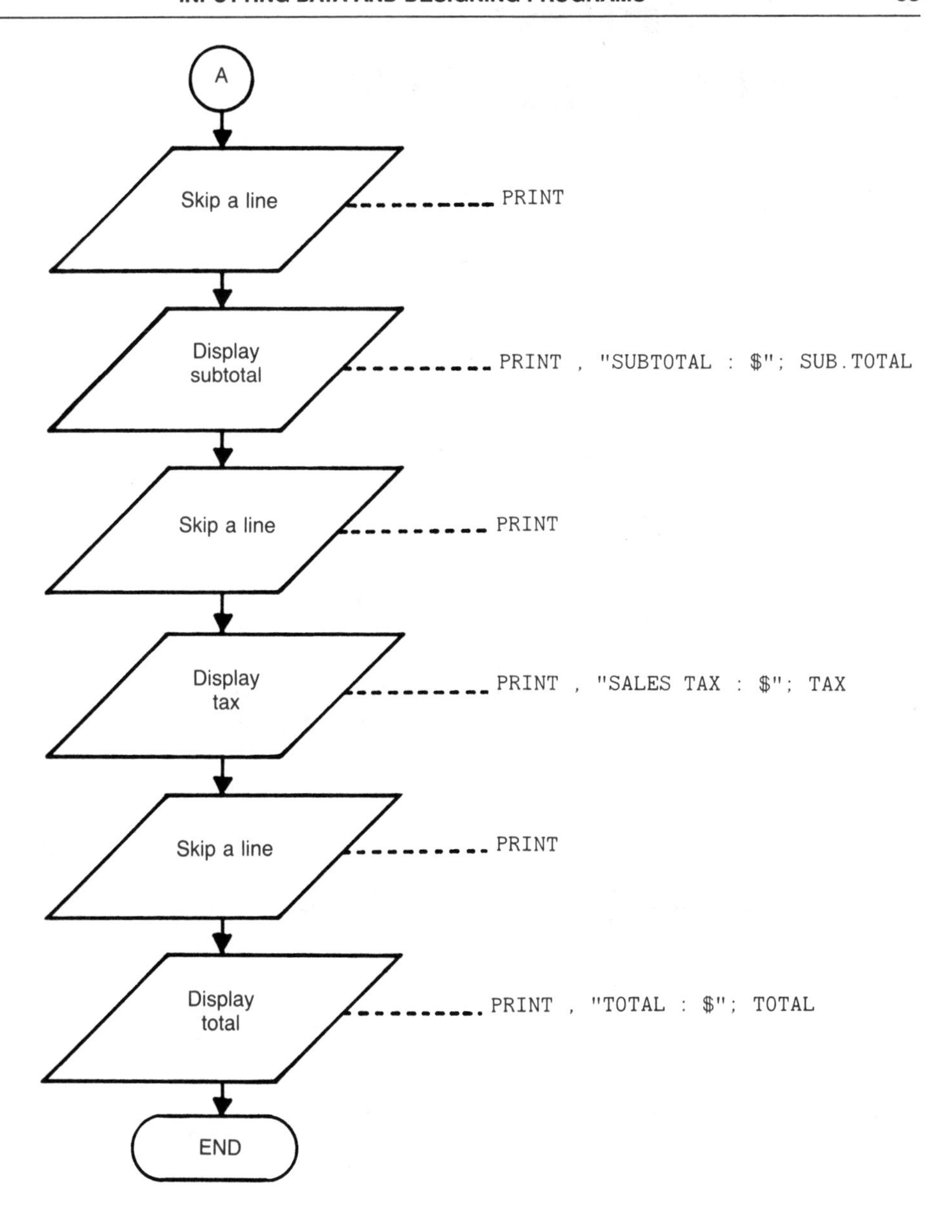

FIGURE 4.2 (continued)

5 / LOOPING WITH FOR/NEXT

There are three major reasons why the computer is such a valuable computational tool. First of all, the computer is extremely accurate (provided the program generating the results is logically correct). Second, the computer performs at an extremely high speed. And third, the computer is far superior to human beings in performing repetitive operations. Consequently, a major function of any language is to provide for program logic iteration, which means performing repeatedly. (Technically, a repeat is the second occurrence of an event. Each occurrence in a repeated series of events is known as an *iteration*.) The programming implementation of iteration is called *looping*. In BASIC, there are two ways to iterate: through the **FOR/NEXT** statements, and the **WHILE/WEND** statements. BASIC looping with **FOR/NEXT** is the subject of this chapter; **WHILE/WEND** will be discussed in chapter 6.

FOR/NEXT

In programming, logic represented by a group of program statements often needs to be performed a number of times, as you have already experienced when solving some of the exercise problems up to this point. In BASIC, the **FOR/NEXT** statements are designed to provide for this effect. The **FOR/NEXT** statements are characterized by the keywords **FOR** and **NEXT**; each is responsible for actions in different statements, but they must perform in coordination with each other. The **FOR/NEXT** statements maintain a loop counter, which is a numeric variable. Under the control of the **FOR/NEXT** statements, this counter will count in a specified manner, thus governing the looping. The basic function of **FOR/NEXT** is illustrated in this example.

Example 5.1

```
10 'LOOPING
20 '
30 CLS
40 FOR C% = 1 TO 10
50 PRINT "Repeat"
60 NEXT C%
70 END
```

This example program, when **RUN**, will cause ten lines of **Repeat** to be displayed on the CRT. The cause of the display of the word **Repeat**, of course, is statement 50, with which you should be familiar by now. The fact that ten display lines are produced is due to statements 40 and 60: **FOR** and **NEXT**.

In statement 40 (the **FOR** statement), **C%**, an integer variable, is the loop counter mentioned above. The **FOR** statement informs BASIC that this counter is to begin counting at 1 and stop when 10 is exceeded (**FOR C% = 1 TO 10**).

Statement 60 (the **NEXT** statement) manages the counting process in coordination with the **FOR** statement. Essentially, the **FOR/NEXT** statement pair says: Execute all the statements between the **FOR** and **NEXT** statements repeatedly, using the counter to control the number of times this is to be repeated as specified by the **FOR** statement.

When BASIC encounters the **FOR** statement, it will either create the counter as specified or use the counter variable that already exists (that is, if the numeric variable named in the **FOR** statement has been used before in the same program). First, BASIC stores the starting count (1 in Example 5.1) into this counter and marks the ending count as specified (10 in Example 5.1) in the computer memory. After the **FOR** statement is executed, BASIC continues on its sequential program execution. When the **NEXT** statement is eventually reached, BASIC then updates the counter (in this case from 1 to 2) and checks against the preset ending count (10) to see if it has been exceeded. If it has not, then BASIC will return to the statement immediately following the **FOR** statement (statement 50 in this case) and resume its sequential program execution until the **NEXT** statement is reached again. This iterative process continues until finally the preset ending counter value has been exceeded; then BASIC will stop looping and continue program execution sequentially at the statement immediately following **NEXT**.

The counter is a numeric variable just like the variables used in the previous chapters. It is not a special code, and it can be used just like other variables. For instance, the value in the loop counter can be displayed.

Example 5.2

```
10 'THE COUNTER
20 '
30 CLS
40 FOR C% = 1 TO 10
50 PRINT C%
60 NEXT C%
70 PRINT C%
80 END
```

This program will display the numbers 1 through 11 in a column. Notice that, between the **FOR** and **NEXT** statements, there is only one **PRINT** statement, but it causes ten numbers to be displayed, with all ten numbers being different.

When the loop is first entered, **C%** holds 1. During the first pass through the loop, this 1 is displayed due to the **PRINT** statement. When the **NEXT** statement is reached, the value in **C%** is updated to 2, and the next **PRINT** action shows this 2 on the CRT.

At the end of the tenth iteration, when the **NEXT** statement is reached, **NEXT** updates the counter from 10 to 11 and checks against the preset ending count. When BASIC decides that 11 indeed exceeds 10, it exits the loop and executes the **PRINT C%** in statement 70. As a result, the last count displayed is 11.

The last count contained in the loop counter always exceeds the preset ending count, as this is the way BASIC knows when to exit the loop. This loop exit control mechanism is known as *posttesting,* which means the test for the end of the loop is at the end, not the beginning, of the loop. In fact, you must bear in mind that once the **FOR** statement sets up the counter, the **NEXT** statement does not redirect the program execution back to it. The program returns only to the statement immediately following it. **NEXT**, not **FOR**, is the statement that governs the counting and the looping logic.

The **FOR/NEXT** loop governs a distinct logic section within a program. Programmers often indent the looping program section for highlighting purposes. Thus Example 5.2 can also be coded as:

```
10 'THE COUNTER
20 '
```

```
30 CLS
40 FOR C% = 1 TO 10
50   PRINT C%
60 NEXT C%
70 PRINT C%
80 END
```

or

```
10 'THE COUNTER
20 '
30 CLS
40   FOR C% = 1 TO 10
50   PRINT C%
60   NEXT C%
70 PRINT C%
80 END
```

The indentation can be produced by pressing the space bar (thus generating blank characters) or by pressing the tab key, which is the right-arrow key above the Ctrl key.

Unlike most other BASIC statements, the **FOR** and **NEXT** statements function as a pair. One cannot exist without the other. If one exists in a program without the other, error messages will be triggered, and the program execution will be aborted.

Example 5.3

```
10 'FOR without NEXT
20 '
30 FOR C% = 1 TO 5
40      PRINT C%
50 END

RUN

FOR without NEXT in 30
```

This program will trigger the **FOR without NEXT in 30** error message, indicating that the **FOR** in statement 30 has no backup **NEXT**.

Similarly, the next program will trigger the **NEXT without FOR in 40** error message due to the lonesome **NEXT** in statement 40:

Example 5.4

```
10 'NEXT without FOR
20 '
30 PRINT C%
40 NEXT C%
50 END

RUN

NEXT without FOR in 40
```

Even if both **FOR** and **NEXT** exist, if the counter variables do not agree in the two statements, the effect is the same as one existing without the other, as:

```
10 FOR C% = 1 TO 10
20 NEXT D%
```

For the **FOR/NEXT** loop control mechanism to function, the loop counter need not always begin with 1 and count upward, and the ending count need not always indicate the number of loop iterations. In fact, any of the values involved in the **FOR** statement can be set in many different ways.

Example 5.5

```
10 'FOR COUNTER
20 '
30 CLS
40 FOR C% = 5 TO 10
50        PRINT C%,
60 NEXT C%
70 END
```

In this example, the loop counter starts at 5. The display produced is:

```
5             6             7             8             9
10
```

Six numbers are displayed altogether, not ten, which is the ending count value specified.

The **FOR/NEXT** statements also do not always have to count with increments of +1. An increment other than +1 can be specified in the

FOR statement through a **STEP** option. For instance, the program in Example 5.6 will cause the display to be:

```
1             3             5             7             9
```

Example 5.6

```
10 'THE INCREMENT
20 '
30 CLS
40 FOR C% = 1 TO 10 STEP 2
50      PRINT C%,
60 NEXT C%
70 END
```

In this case, BASIC is told to count with increments of 2. Thus, each time the **NEXT** statement is reached, 2 is added to the current counter value. So the counter takes on values of 1, 3 (= 1 + 2), 5 (= 3 + 2), and so on.

When the optional **STEP** specification is absent in the **FOR** statement, BASIC simply assumes the increment to be +1.

If the **STEP** specification is set to be negative, then the **NEXT** statement will add the negative increment to the current counter value, which in effect is the same as subtraction. So if the starting count is higher than the ending count, the loop is made to count backward.

Example 5.7

```
10 'COUNTING BACKWARD
20 '
30 CLS
40 FOR C% = 10 TO 1 STEP -1
50      PRINT C%,
60 NEXT C%
70 END
```

The display from this program is:

```
10            9             8             7             6
5             4             3             2             1
```

What is the current value of the counter **C%** after the loop?

Answer: ______________________________

Of course, when counting backward, you can specify an increment larger in magnitude than 1:

Example 5.8

```
10 'COUNTING BACKWARD
20 '
30 CLS
40 FOR C% = 10 TO 1 STEP -3
50       PRINT C%,
60 NEXT C%
70 END
```

What is the final **C%** value in this case?

Answer: ______________________________

Thus, depending on the counter specifications, the loop counter can be made to count forward, backward, or by an increment, and start and end with practically any count setting. However, you must maintain the sense of the counting; that is, the **FOR** statement must not be specified to count from small to large with a negative **STEP**, or vice versa. If so, then BASIC will simply skip the loop entirely and proceed with the program execution as if the loop did not exist. For instance, in Example 5.9, the program asks BASIC to count from 10 to 1 but with a positive increment of 1. The result is that only the statement after the loop is executed.

Example 5.9

```
10 'COUNTING BACKWARD
20 '
30 CLS
40 FOR C% = 10 TO 1
50       PRINT C%
60 NEXT C%
70 PRINT "Continue . . ."
80 END
```

RUN the program to see the display. Then modify the program to show the current value in **C%** after the loop.

Finding: ______________________________

Counter settings need not be constants. Just as the counter is a variable, the counter settings can be variables as well, with values assigned through any of the available data assignment mechanisms. Example 5.10 shows that the counter settings can be set prior to the entry of the loop. And if the program logic demands, the counter settings can be set by the users as well, as illustrated in Example 5.11.

Example 5.10

```
10 'VARIABLE COUNTER SETTINGS
20 '
30 CLS
40 LET C1% = 1
50 LET C2% = 10
60 LET C3% = 3
70 FOR C% = C1% TO C2% STEP C3%
80      PRINT C%
90 NEXT C%
100 END
```

Example 5.11

```
10 'USER-SET COUNTER SETTINGS
20 '
30 CLS
40 INPUT "Enter start count : ", START%
50 INPUT "Enter end count : ", FINISH%
60 INPUT "Enter counter increment : ", INC%
70 FOR C% = START% TO FINISH% STEP INC%
80      PRINT C%
90 NEXT C%
100 END
```

Furthermore, the counter settings can be arithmetic expressions. In Example 5.12, the ending count value is not set but is computed from the starting count and a user-set range (in statement 70, **START% + RANGE%**).

Example 5.12

```
10 'COMPUTED COUNTER SETTINGS
20 '
30 CLS
40 INPUT "Enter start count : ", START%
50 INPUT "Enter range : ", RANGE%
```

```
60 INPUT "Enter counter increment : ", INC%
70 FOR C% = START% TO START% + RANGE% STEP INC%
80      PRINT C%
90 NEXT C%
100 END
```

Because the counter is simply a numeric variable, it can also be a single-precision variable. In all the previous examples, integer variables were used because, in BASIC, integer arithmetic is much more efficient than single-precision arithmetic. In looping, the use of integers as counters thus results in faster program execution times. If the counter serves more purposes than merely simple counting, such as being used as a mathematical series of coefficients or as a sequence of pricing steps actually used in the looped calculations, then a single-precision variable would be used, and the count specifications will take on decimal points as well.

Example 5.13

This example is designed to produce a temperature conversion table.

```
10 'TEMPERATURE CONVERSION TABLE
20 '
30 PRINT "Fahr.", "Cent."
40 PRINT
50 FOR FAHR = 10 TO 20 STEP 0.5
60   LET CENT = ( FAHR - 32 ) * 5 / 9
70   PRINT FAHR, CENT
80 NEXT FAHR
90 END
```

The general forms of **FOR** and **NEXT** are:

FOR
Form: FOR counter = initial value TO final value [STEP increment]
Function: To specify the loop counter setting.

NEXT
Form: NEXT counter
Function: To control the loop counter.

Loops are created to cause a program segment to iterate. Consequently, in designing a loop, the programmer should pay primary attention to the logic that needs to be iterated, and not to the loop mechanism. For instance, in designing Example 5.1, which displays ten **Repeats**, we established the display of one **Repeat** first, then we designed a loop to make this display iterate. In loop designing, you do not first create a looping mechanism and then decide how the loop contents are to be filled in. Thus, in the chronological development of Example 5.1, first the action "display the word **Repeat** is decided (see Figure 5.1). Then a loop is drawn to indicate that this action is to be iterated ten times (Figure 5.2). Once the loop is designed, then the flowchart may be transcribed as shown in Figure 5.3.

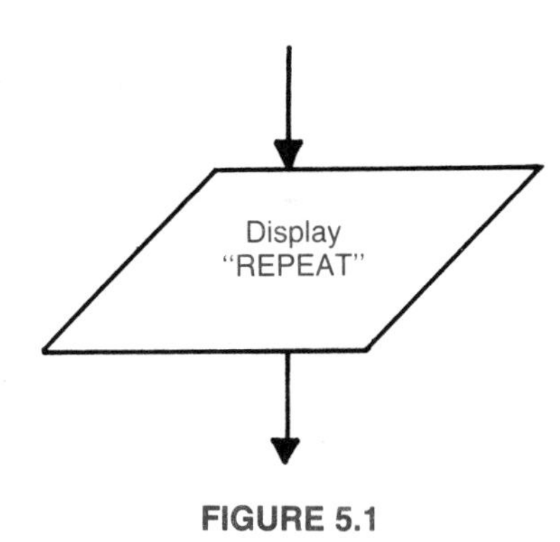

FIGURE 5.1

The rules for **FOR/NEXT** loop transcription are therefore:

1. Design the flowchart.
2. Transcribe all logic symbols into appropriate coding.

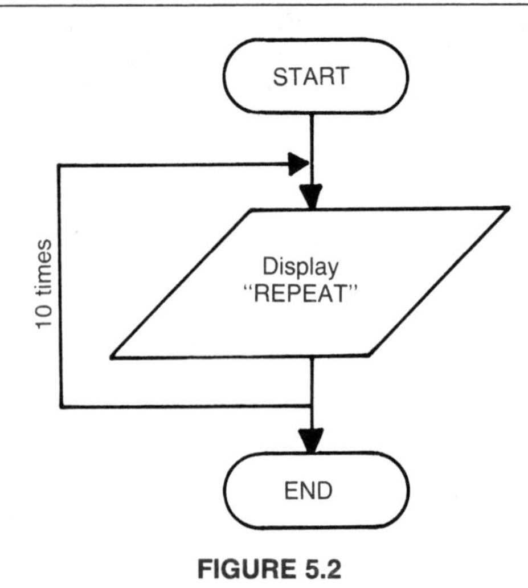

FIGURE 5.2

3. Transcribe loop arrows into corresponding **FOR** and **NEXT** statements. (This way one always accompanies the other.)
4. Assign counter variables. (This way the counter variables are always correct.)
5. Specify counting mode.

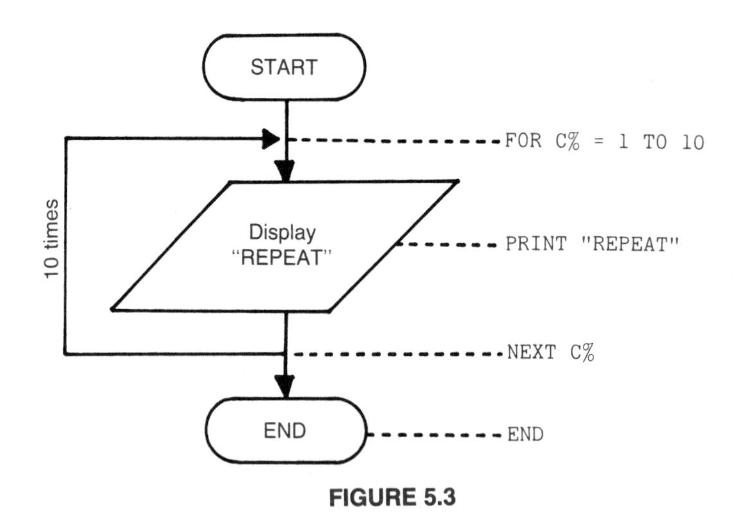

FIGURE 5.3

Exercise Set 5.1 FOR/NEXT, STEP, forward, backward, with variables, and with expressions (Using flowcharting, **PRINT, CLS, END, LET**, functions, **DEF FN, INPUT, FOR/NEXT**)

A. Correct the errors, if any, in the following programs:

1.

```
10 CLS
20 FOR C% = 10 TO 1 STEP 2
30       PRINT C%,
40 NEXT C
50 END
```

Answer: ______________________________

____

2.

```
10 CLS
20 FOR C% = 1 TO 10
30       PRINT C%,
40 PRINT "The last count is: "; C%
50 END
```

Answer: ______________________________

____

B. What do the following programs do?

3.

```
10 CLS
20 FOR C% = 1 TO 100 STEP 10
30       PRINT C%,
40 NEXT C%
50 END
```

Answer: ______________________________

____

____

4.

```
10 CLS
20 FOR C% = 1 TO 10
```

```
30        PRINT C%;
40 NEXT C%
50 PRINT
60 PRINT C%
70 END
```

Answer: ____

____

C. Flowcharting and code transcription:

5. Write separate programs to produce the following CRT displays:
   a. 1, 2, 3, 4, 5, 6, 7, 8, 9,
   b. 1, 2, 3, 4, 5, 6, 7, 8, 9
   c. 1, 2, 3, 4, 5, 6, 7, 8, and 9
6. Write a program to generate a degree-to-radian conversion table starting at 30 degrees and stopping at 90 degrees with an increment of 5 degrees. (Degree = radian * 180 / π)
7. Write a program to compute the squares of the consecutive integer series from 1 to 20.

ACCUMULATION AND COUNTING

A most useful function of the loop is the implementation of the summation of a series of numbers. Let us study the next example.

Example 5.14

```
10 'ACCUMULATION
20 '
30 LET SUM = 0
40 CLS
50 FOR C% = 1 TO 10
60        PRINT "Enter number "; C%;
70        INPUT ": ", NUMBER
80        LET SUM = SUM + NUMBER
90 NEXT C%
100 PRINT
110 PRINT "The sum is "; SUM
120 END
```

RUN this program. The user will be asked to input ten different numbers. At the end of the program, the ten input numbers will be totaled and the sum displayed.

The program logic of interest is embodied by statements 30 and 80. In statement 30 the variable **SUM** is established with an initial value of zero. As each loop is executed, an input data item is added to this variable **SUM** by virtue of statement 80, which says: Add the value in **NUMBER**, which is the input number, to the current value in **SUM**, and assign the result to **SUM** again.

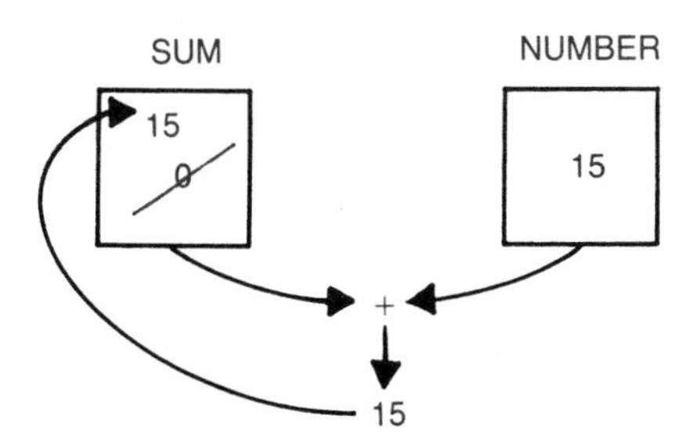

The key to grasping this lies in the understanding of the equal sign in the **LET** statement. As pointed out before, the equal sign in the **LET** statement does not mean equal; it means assign or store. Specifically, the value on the right-hand side of the equal sign is to be assigned to the variable on the left-hand side. Because of this, the same variable may appear on both sides of the equal sign and the **LET** statement will still be perfectly acceptable, as the **LET** statement is not an arithmetic or algebraic statement in the traditional sense.

Likewise, this mechanism can be used for counting purposes.

Example 5.15

```
10 'COUNTING
20 '
30 LET C% = 0
40 FOR LOOP% = 6 TO 16 STEP 4
50      PRINT LOOP%
60      LET C% = C% + 1
70 NEXT LOOP%
80 PRINT "The loop has "; C%; " iterations."
90 END
```

This example program will produce the display of:

```
 6
 10
 14
The loop has 3 iterations.
```

Again the counting effect is produced by statements 30 and 60 in combination with a loop.

Statement 30 in both example programs (**LET SUM = 0** and **LET C% = 0**) is known as a **variable initialization**. Initialization refers to the first time a value is assigned to a variable that will undergo subsequent periodic updatings. Obviously, in the above statements, the same variables are assigned different values many times in the course of looping.

Example 5.14 is known as *accumulation* and has a general form of:

accumulator initialization
FOR
accumulator = accumulator + addend
NEXT

Example 5.15 exemplifies *counting* and has the general form of:

counter initialization
FOR
counter = counter + increment
NEXT

We shall now apply what we have learned above to a practical situation.

Example 5.16

In this example, a sales-receipt tabulation program is to be created. At the end of a transaction, the salesperson will enter the sales amount of the transaction into the computer, and the program will compute the sales tax and the total. Because the program is designed for all similar transactions, it must account for a varying number of sales amounts for each transaction. This is achieved through the salesperson informing the program of the number of sales items at the beginning of the data entry. The program then uses a loop based on this information to control the data entry and summation (accumulation process). Figure 5.4 shows the flowchart for this program.

```
10 'SALES RECEIPT
20 '
30 LET TAX.RATE = .065
40 CLS
50 INPUT "How many sales items do you have"; ITEM%
60 CLS
70 LET SUB.TOTAL = 0
80 FOR C% = 1 TO ITEM%
90       INPUT "Enter sales amount : ", AMOUNT
100      LET SUB.TOTAL = SUB.TOTAL + AMOUNT
110 NEXT C%
120 LET TAX = SUB.TOTAL * TAX.RATE
130 LET TOTAL = SUB.TOTAL + TAX
140 PRINT
150 PRINT , "Subtotal : $"; SUB.TOTAL
160 PRINT
170 PRINT , "Sales tax : $"; TAX
180 PRINT
190 PRINT , "Total : $"; TOTAL
200 END
```

Statement 70 is the accumulator initialization, while statement 100 achieves the accumulation.

Exercise Set 5.2 Accumulation, counting (Using **PRINT**, **CLS**, **END**, **LET**, functions, **DEF FN**, **INPUT**, **FOR/NEXT**)

A. Correct the errors, if any, in the following programs:

1.

```
10 'ACCUMULATION
20 '
30 LET A = 0
40 FOR C% = 1 TO 10
50       INPUT N
60       LET N = N + A
70 NEXT C%
```

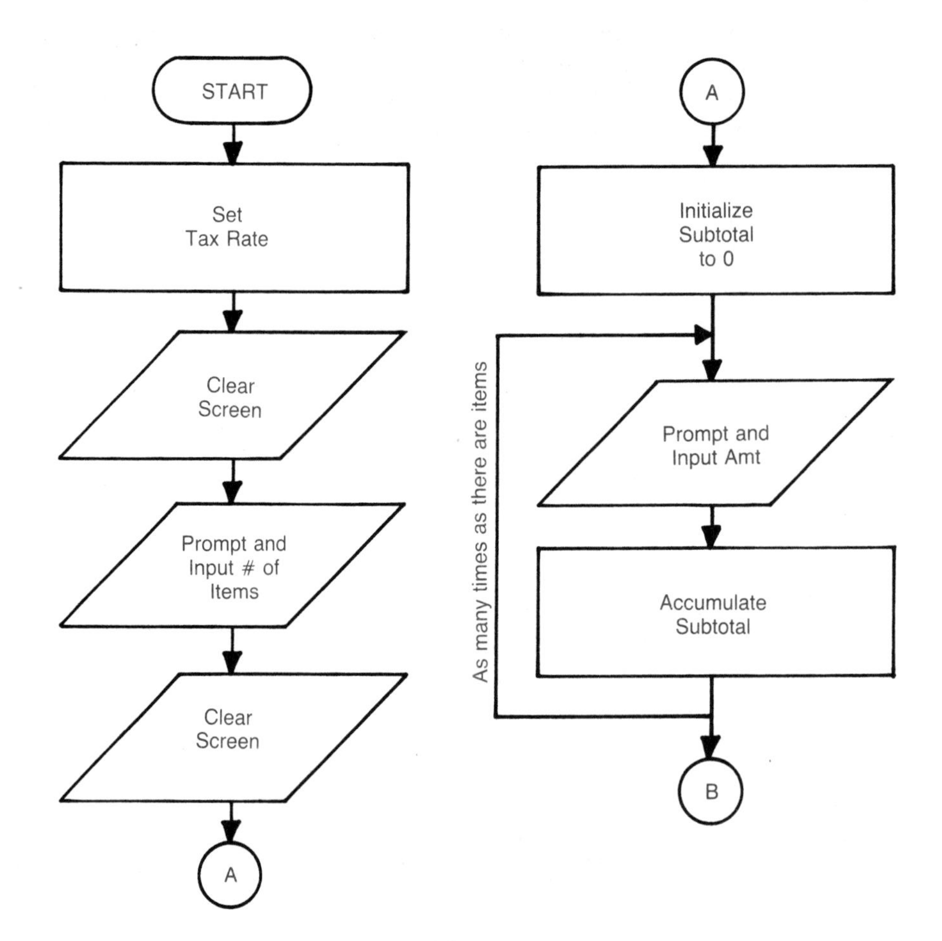
START
Set
Tax Rate
Clear
Screen
Prompt and
Input # of
Items
Clear
Screen
A
A
Initialize
Subtotal
to 0
As many times as there are items
Prompt and
Input Amt
Accumulate
Subtotal
B

FIGURE 5.4

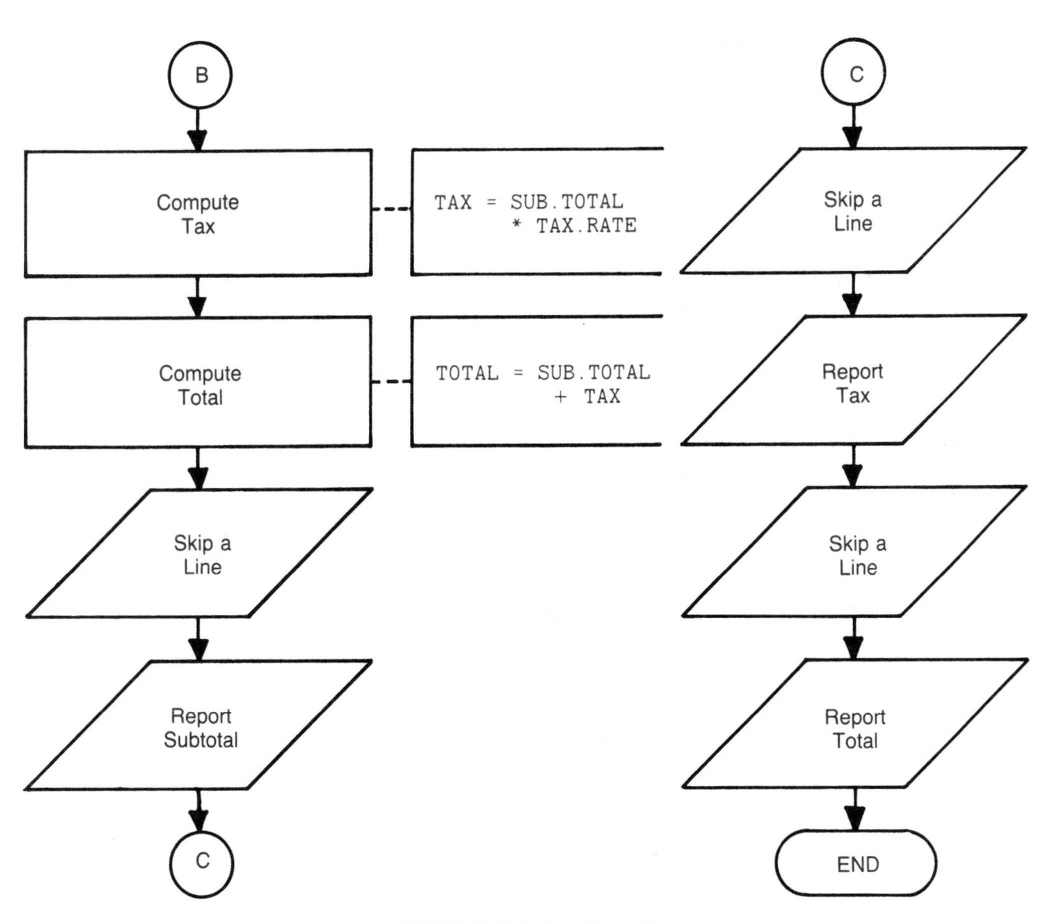

FIGURE 5.4 (continued)

```
80 PRINT
90 PRINT "The sum is "; A
100 END
```

Answer: ______________________________

____

____

2.

```
10 'COUNTING
20 '
30 LET C% = 1
40 FOR LOOP% = 6 TO 16 STEP 4
50      PRINT LOOP%
60      LET C% = C% + 1
70 NEXT LOOP%
80 PRINT "The loop has "; C%; " iterations."
90 END
```

Answer: ______________________________

____

3. What does the following program do?

```
10 LET A% = 0
20 LET C% = 0
30 FOR LOOP% = 1 TO 100 STEP 2
40      LET A% = A% + LOOP%
50      LET C% = C% + 1
60 NEXT LOOP%
70 END
```

Answer: ______________________________

____

____

B. Flowcharting and code transcription:

4. Design a program to produce the following CRT display:

```
L
L
L
L
L
L
L
L
L
LLLLLLLLLLLLLLLL
```

5. Write a program for a fast-food store production manager to tabulate on the CRT, sum, and average ten inventory figures to be entered via the keyboard.
6. Write a program for an architect user to produce the sine of twenty different angles, all different by 10 degrees once the first angle is specified.

NESTED LOOPS

Example 5.17

```
10 'NESTED LOOPS
20 '
30 FOR R% = 1 TO 4
40      FOR C% = 1 TO 5
50              PRINT R%; C%,
60      NEXT C%
70 NEXT R%
80 END
```

Let us analyze this example program:

In this program there are two **FOR/NEXT** statement pairs: statement 30 with 70 and statement 40 with 60. The resultant display is:

```
1 1           1 2           1 3           1 4           1 5
2 1           2 2           2 3           2 4           2 5
3 1           3 2           3 3           3 4           3 5
4 1           4 2           4 3           4 4           4 5
```

When BASIC encounters statement 30, it sets up a counter **R%** and places the initial value 1 in it as specified. Then it proceeds to statement 40, which also happens to be a **FOR** statement. BASIC thus sets up another counter, **C%**, accordingly, and places the initial value 1 in it as specified.

As BASIC continues with the sequential program execution, it finally reaches statement 60, which updates the counter **C%** to 2 and returns to statement 50—the statement immediately following the **FOR** statement corresponding to **NEXT C%**.

This iterative process continues to update the counter **C%**, but it does not affect **R%**, which still holds the initial value of 1. Consequently a row of **1 1**, **1 2**, **1 3**, and so on is displayed due to statement 50.

When the value in **C%** finally exceeds the final **C%** setting, which is 5, BASIC exits the **C%** loop and proceeds to the next statement in sequence. But this next statement is statement 70, **NEXT R%**, which updates the counter **R%** to 2 and returns the program execution to statement 40—the statement immediately following the **FOR** statement corresponding to **NEXT R%**. Statement 40 is the **FOR C%** statement. So BASIC acts as stated: Set up the **C%** counter again with 1, and perform the loop controlled by the **C%** counter.

The net effect of this is the completion of the **C%** loop for every loop pass in the **R%** loop. This loop within another loop is known as a *nested loop*.

In Example 5.17, the nested loop mechanism is employed to generate number pairs. The number pairs are displayed horizontally due to the comma at the end of the **PRINT** statement. It so happens that four neat rows are displayed because each CRT **PRINT** line has five display zones. If the program were:

```
10 'NESTED LOOPS
20 '
30 FOR C% = 1 TO 5
40        FOR R% = 1 TO 4
50                PRINT C%; R%,
60        NEXT R%
70 NEXT C%
80 END
```

then the display would have been:

```
1 1           1 2           1 3           1 4           2 1
2 2           2 3           2 4           3 1           3 2
```

and so on.

To make each row of four number pairs appear on their own lines, the cursor must be advanced at the end of each row loop, as shown in the next example.

Example 5.18

```
10 'CURSOR ADVANCEMENT
20 '
30 FOR C% = 1 TO 5
40        FOR R% = 1 TO 4
50                PRINT C%; R%,
60        NEXT R%
70        PRINT
80 NEXT C%
90 END
```

The display is now:

```
1 1           1 2           1 3           1 4
2 1           2 2           2 3           2 4
3 1           3 2           3 3           3 4
4 1           4 2           4 3           4 4
5 1           5 2           5 3           5 4
```

To demonstrate the use of the nested loop, we can expand the sales-receipt generation program in Example 5.16 so that it will perform for more than one transaction.

Since each receipt generation is basically the same, the only difference between this case and the last is a controlling loop that makes the entire program iterate:

Example 5.19

```
10 'MULTIPLE SALES ACCOUNTING
20 '
30 LET TAX.RATE = .065
40 CLS
50 INPUT "How many customers do you have"; CUSTOMER%
60 CLS
70 FOR RECEIPT% = 1 TO CUSTOMER%
80       CLS
90       PRINT "Receipt"; RECEIPT%
100      PRINT
110      INPUT "How many sales items do you have"; ITEM%
120      PRINT
130      LET SUB.TOTAL = 0
140      FOR C% = 1 TO ITEM%
150              INPUT "Enter sales amount : ", AMOUNT
160              LET SUB.TOTAL = SUB.TOTAL + AMOUNT
170      NEXT C%
180      LET TAX = SUB.TOTAL * TAX.RATE
190      LET TOTAL = SUB.TOTAL + TAX
200      PRINT
210      PRINT , "Subtotal : $"; SUB.TOTAL
220      PRINT
230      PRINT , "Sales tax : $"; TAX
240      PRINT
250      PRINT , "Total : $"; TOTAL
260 NEXT RECEIPT%
270 END
```

To begin with, we can recognize that this program is essentially a repetition of the program in Example 5.16. Hence our first thought can be flowcharted as shown in Figure 5.5.

The double vertical lines in the process box indicate that the process represents a group of program statements. With this flowchart, only one loop is suggested: the iteration of a program logic. It just so happens that

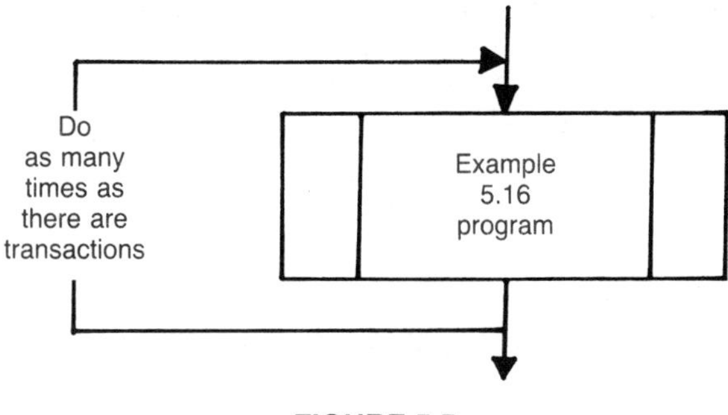

FIGURE 5.5

the program in Example 5.16 contains a loop itself. Thus, the net result is a set of nested loops.

What this all means is that you should not consciously think of nested loops when programming. In other words, you do not program with the thought: "Hmm, let me see how I can engineer a set of nested loops." In programming, you simply proceed with logical thinking. If the logic suggests a loop, then there will be a loop. If a program segment containing a loop demands to be iterated itself, then the result is nested loops.

In loop designing, the thought process is therefore from the inside toward the outside and not from the outside in.

Nested loops must use different counters, as they control different iterative processes. However, certain circumstances do allow them to be related, as demonstrated in the next example.

Example 5.20

```
10 'DEPENDENT NESTED LOOPS
20 '
30 FOR R% = 1 TO 5
40       FOR C% = 1 TO R%
50                 PRINT C%,
60       NEXT C%
70       PRINT
80 NEXT R%
90 END
```

This program produces the display:

```
1
1             2
1             2             3
1             2             3             4
1             2             3             4             5
```

The ending count of the inner loop is controlled by the current counter value of the outer loop. Such nested loops are known as *dependent loops*. Notice the two loops still use different counter variables.

Loop counters must not be reset by the internal logic. In the next program, the loop never ends because the loop counter is continuously reset by the program code it controls.

Example 5.21

```
10 'RESET COUNTER
20 '
30 FOR C% = 1 TO 5
40        PRINT C%
50        LET C% = 3
60 NEXT C%
70 END
```

For this program, an infinite number of **4**s are displayed vertically. The reason: **C%** is never allowed to reach the ending counter value 5. Through each pass of the loop, **C%** is set to 3 due to statement 50. When the **NEXT** statement attempts to update the counter, it is always updating from 3. Program logic in a loop that involves the counter variable must be analyzed carefully to avoid such occurrences. In fact, it is a good policy to forbid the loop counter to be assigned new values within a loop unless absolutely justified.

Exercise Set 5.3 Nested loop, cursor advancement, dependent loops (Using **PRINT**, **CLS**, **END**, **LET**, functions, **DEF FN**, **INPUT**, **FOR/NEXT**)

A. Correct the errors, if any, in the following programs:

1.
```
10 FOR C% = 1 TO 4
20      FOR R% = 1 TO 5
30              PRINT C%; R%,
40              LET R% = 2
50      NEXT C%
60 NEXT R%
70 END
```

Answer: ______________________________

____

2.
```
10 FOR R% = 1 TO C%
20      FOR C% = 1 TO 10
30              PRINT C%,
40      NEXT C%
50 NEXT R%
60 END
```

Answer: ______________________________

____

B. Program logic and analysis

3. What does the following program do?
```
30 FOR R% = 2 TO 6
40      FOR C% = 1 TO R% - 1
50              PRINT C%,
60      NEXT C%
70      PRINT
80 NEXT R%
90 END
```

Answer: ______________________________

____

____

C. Write a program (flowchart and code transcription) to:

4. Produce the following CRT display:

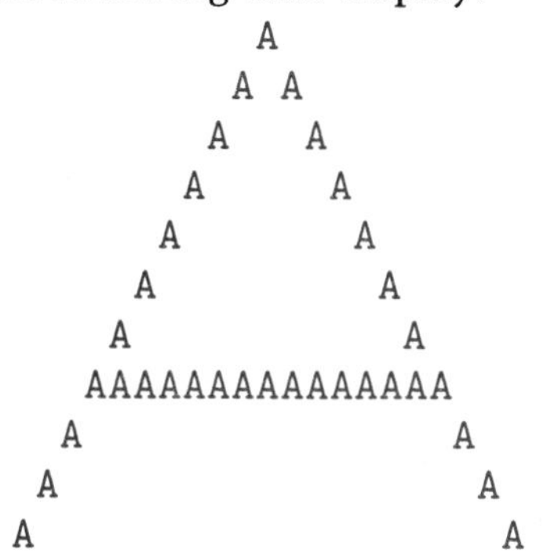

5. Allow a psychologist to enter the personal history data into the computer for five patients. Each history should include: the name, address, phone number, personal physician name, and date of last physical exam.

PROGRAMMING RULES WITH FOR/NEXT LOOPS

Besides the syntax rules, a few other rules must also be observed with **FOR/NEXT** loop programming. They are summarized as follows:

1. While it is permissible to exit a loop before the **NEXT** statement is reached, it is not permissible to enter a loop bypassing the **FOR** statement, which is known as parachuting into a loop (see Figure 5.6).

   The reason for this is that the actual maintenance of the **FOR/NEXT** loop action is controlled by the **NEXT** statement and not the **FOR** statement. When a loop is escaped before the **NEXT** statement is reached, all that happens is that the loop counter is not updated. But when a loop is entered bypassing the **FOR** statement (made permissible by techniques that will be discussed in chapter 7), the loop counter is never set up; thus there is no loop counter for the **NEXT** statement to update and with which to test. (Recall that **NEXT** performs internal testing.)
2. As long as a loop is completely surrounded by an outer loop, there can be no limit to the number of loops contained within another loop. Loop lines that cross, however, are not permissible (see Figure 5.7).

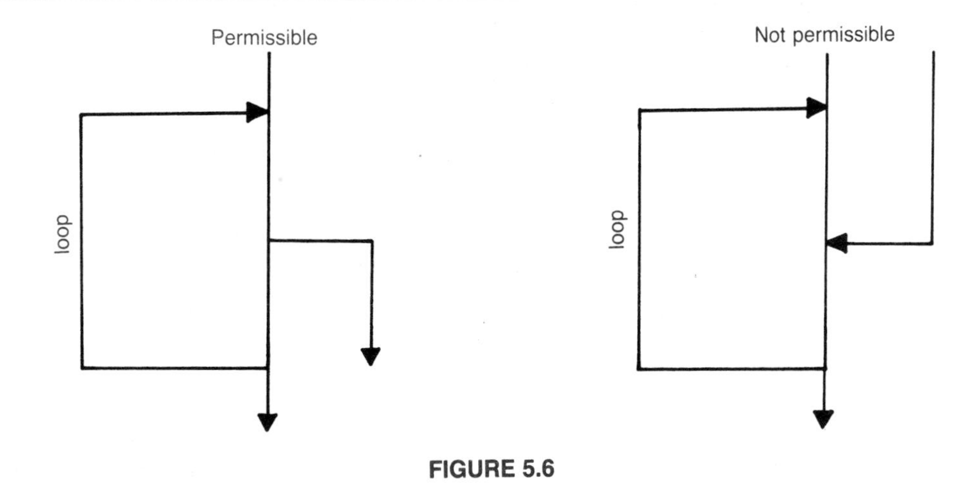

FIGURE 5.6

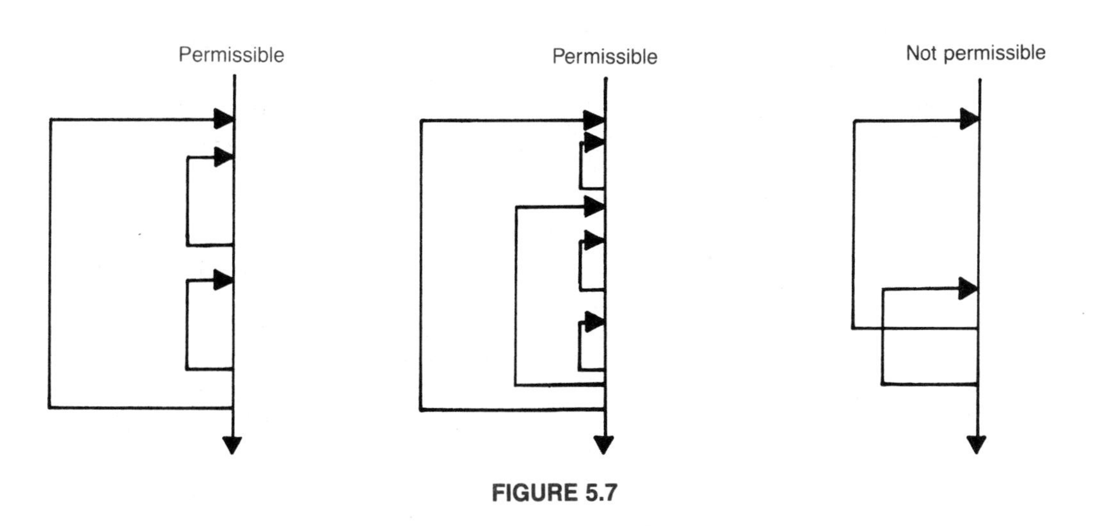

FIGURE 5.7

Chapter Exercises (Using **PRINT**, **CLS**, **END**, **LET**, functions, **DEF FN**, **INPUT**, **FOR/NEXT**)

Flowcharting and code transcription:

1. Design a program to accumulate all debits and credits for an accounts statement for 500 statements. The statement data are to be entered into the computer by a professional bookkeeper. Credit data are entered as positive numbers while debit data are negative.
2. Design a program permitting an aerospace scientist to enter into the computer a list of radio telemetry data one CRT screenful at a time.
3. Design a program that produces a temperature conversion table as follows:

```
C          F               C          F
=======================================

0          32              110        221
5          41              120         .
10         50              130         .
                                       .

           .
           .
           .
100        212
```

   A screenful of display is to be produced.
4. Modify the program for problem 3 to permit a user to set the starting temperature and the computational increment.

6 / LOOPING WITH WHILE/WEND

The **FOR/NEXT** loop employs a loop control mechanism based on a counting scheme. However, in programming, often the number of iterations is not known by either the programmer or the user. In fact, sometimes the number of iterations itself is the answer the program is designed to produce. Under such circumstances, the **FOR/NEXT** mechanism does not function efficiently, and we should resort to the **WHILE/WEND** loop, which bases the looping control on a condition.

WHILE/WEND

The **WHILE/WEND** loop is characterized by the **WHILE** statement working in partnership with the **WEND** statement. They surround the logic that needs to be iterated in much the same manner as **FOR/NEXT**, except that the iterative process continues only when a specified condition holds true. The construct of the **WHILE/WEND** loop is:

```
WHILE/WEND
-----------------------------------------------
Form:
WHILE condition
iterative logic
WEND
-----------------------------------------------
Function: To iterate when the condition is true.
```

Example 6.1 illustrates the working of the **WHILE/WEND** mechanism.

Example 6.1

```
10 'WHILE/WEND
20 '
30 LET C% = 1
40 WHILE C% <= 10
50      PRINT C%;
60      LET C% = C% + 2
70 WEND
80 END
```

This program performs the same duty as:

```
FOR C% = 1 TO 10 STEP 2
     PRINT C%;
NEXT C%
```

which produces the display:

```
 1  3  5  7  9
```

Let us understand how this is achieved.

First of all, statement 30 assigns the number 1 to the variable **C%**. Statement 40 says: **WHILE** the content of **C%** is less than or equal to 10, execute all the program statements up to the **WEND** statement and then return to statement 40. Between the **WHILE** and **WEND** statements, the program displays the contents of **C%** and adds 2 to **C%**. When the program execution returns to statement 40, as long as **C%** holds a number less than or equal to 10, the logic surrounded by **WHILE** and **WEND** is executed anew. This logic can be flowcharted as shown in Figure 6.1.

The diamond symbol in this flowchart represents a condition. This condition is either true or not true (false), and it is responsible for selecting between the two logical paths that can be taken, as represented by the two arrows coming out of the two tips (vertices) of the diamond.

Unlike **FOR/NEXT**, the **WHILE/WEND** loop uses a pretest. That is, the control of the iterative process is performed at the beginning of the loop, and not at the end (as with the **NEXT** statement).

The working of the **WHILE/WEND** mechanism hinges on the truth or fallacy of the condition specified in the **WHILE** statement. The key to understanding the **WHILE/WEND** loop therefore lies in learning how to form conditions.

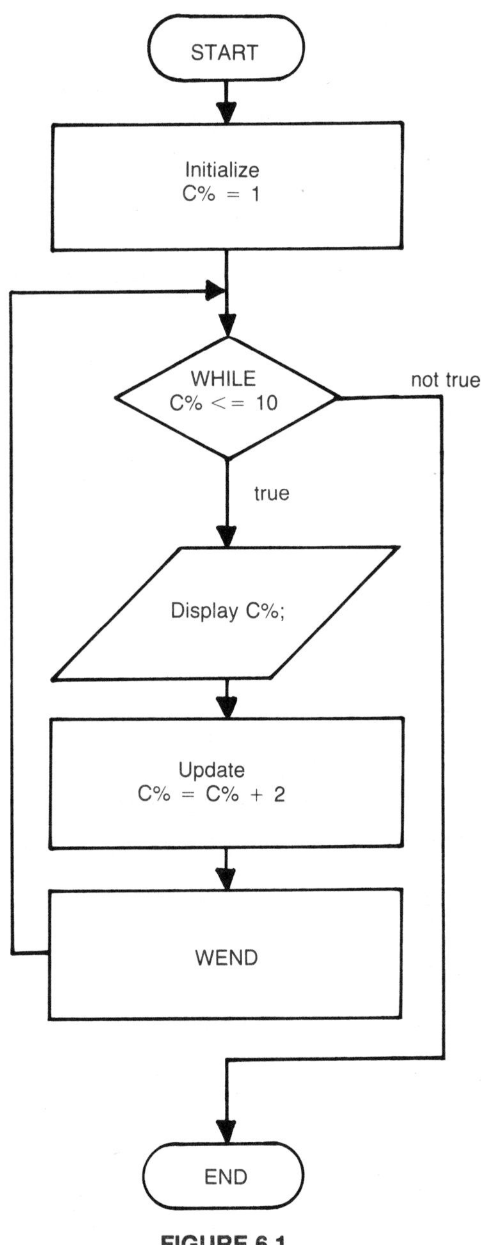
START
Initialize
C% = 1
WHILE
C% <= 10
not true
true
Display C%;
Update
C% = C% + 2
WEND
END

FIGURE 6.1

ARITHMETIC CONDITIONS

In general, there are two types of conditions used in programming: *arithmetic conditions* and *logical conditions* (although, strictly speaking, all conditions are logical). Logical conditions will be discussed fully in Chapter 8. Arithmetic conditions are formed by comparing two data items. They are called arithmetic conditions because the comparison actions are arithmetic in nature. Six possible comparison modes can be constructed using six different relational operators. They are listed below.

Relational Operator	*Meaning*
=	equals
<	is less than
>	is larger than
<=	is less than or equals (i.e., not larger than)
>=	is larger than or equals (i.e., not less than)
<>	is not equal to

(Note: the equal sign here is the same assignment symbol used in **LET** statements, but the function is different.)

These six operators are used to relate two data items, which may be constants, variables, or arithmetic expressions. Thus, in Example 6.1, the condition **C% <= 10** demands that the content in **C%** be less than or at the most equal to 10. If the number held in **C%** is 10 or below, then the condition is satisfied, and the state of the condition is deemed true. Otherwise, the state of the condition is not true, or false.

Similarly, the condition:

```
Z = 100
```

is true only if the content of **Z** is exactly 100.

The condition:

```
SALES > 10000
```

is true for all numbers larger than 10,000, but not 10,000 itself.

And the condition:

```
B <> D * 3.6
```

is true only if **B** and the product of **D times 3.6** are not the same.

Exercise Set 6.1 WHILE/END loop, arithmetic conditions

Correct the errors, if any, in the following programs:

1.

```
10 LET C% = 1
20 WHILE C% > 1
30        PRINT C%;
40        LET C% = C% + 1
50 WEND
60 END
```

Answer: ______________________________

____

2.

```
10 PRINT "Enter 0 to quit"
20 WHILE C% <> 0
30        INPUT A
40        PRINT A
50 WEND
60 END
```

Answer: ______________________________

____

____

3. Express the following conditions in BASIC:
   a. The break point is over 100,000.

Answer: ______________________________

   b. The average grade is below 70.

Answer: ______________________________

   c. An employee number that is other than 45508.

Answer: ______________________________

d. All credits $2,000 and up.

Answer: ______________________________

____

Because the condition must be true for the iterative process to occur in a **WHILE/WEND** loop, the condition must first be initialized so that the condition is true prior to the entry of the loop. Statement 30 of Example 6.1 ensures that this requirement is met, so that the first iteration will take place. There are other occasions where the loop must not be allowed to happen if a condition is not true; in that case, the initial condition may need to be set up so that it is not true. At any rate, the initial condition must be defined. In the course of the loop action, provisions must be made to permit the condition to change, or the loop will never end. The general form for the **WHILE/WEND** loop construction is therefore:

```
condition initialization
WHILE condition
resetting of condition
WEND
```

Let us now look at various ways the **WHILE/WEND** looping mechanism can be used.

Example 6.2

In this program, a scheme is to be devised whereby a series of positive numbers other than 0 entered via the keyboard is summed. The pressing of the <Enter> key (producing 0) or the entry of a negative number is used to terminate the summation process. Figure 6.2 shows the flowchart for the program logic.

```
 10 'PRESS <ENTER> TO END
 20 '
 30 LET SUM = -1
 40 LET ADDEND = 1
 50 CLS
 60 WHILE ADDEND > 0
 70      LET SUM = SUM + ADDEND
 80      INPUT "Enter addend : ", ADDEND
 90 WEND
100 PRINT "The sum is "; SUM
110 END
```

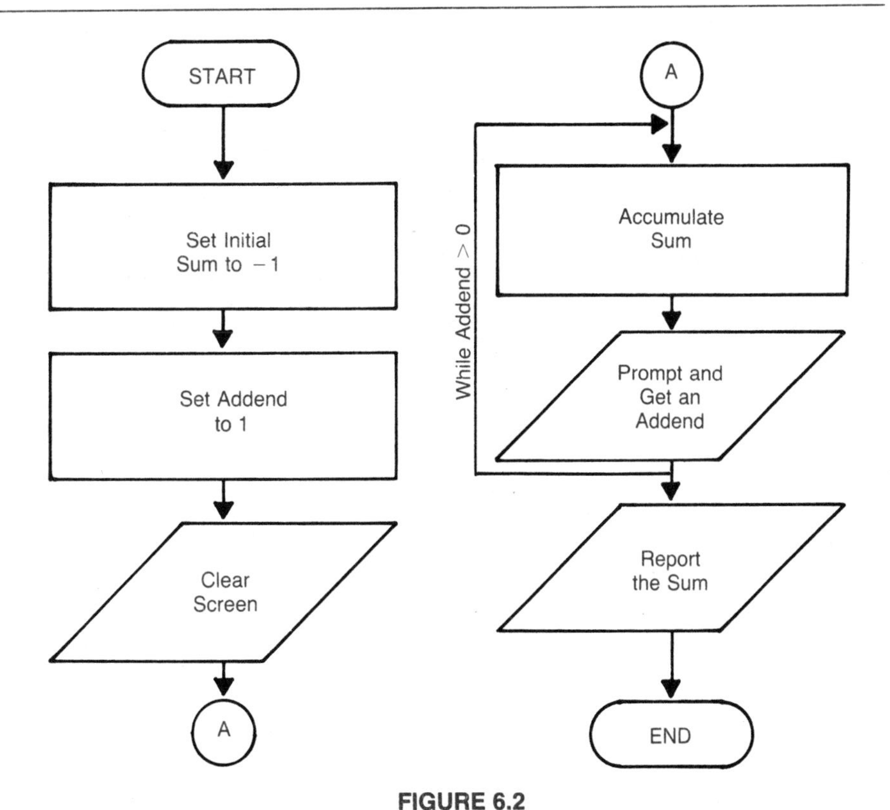

FIGURE 6.2

Notice in this example the elaborate loop initialization. To ensure that the loop will begin, the programmer gives **ADDEND** the initial value of 1, which satisfies the condition **ADDEND > 0**. But, because **ADDEND** is to be added to the running **SUM**, the initial **SUM** is given the value −1 so the first sum is 1 + −1 = 0.

Example 6.3

In this example, the number of times a bettor must win to multiply the original ante by 1,000 is sought. This is a classic case where the number of iterations is the object of the program. Figure 6.3 shows the flowchart for the program.

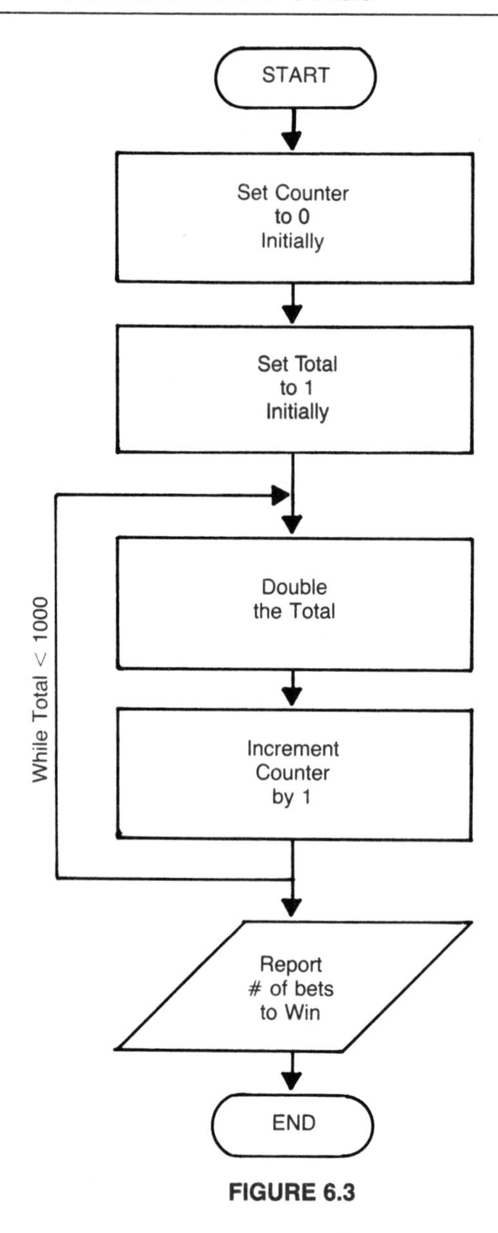

FIGURE 6.3

```
10 'BETTING
20 '
30 LET COUNT = 0
40 LET TOTAL = 1
```

```
50 WHILE TOTAL <= 1000
60       LET TOTAL = TOTAL * 2
70       LET COUNT = COUNT + 1
80 WEND
90 PRINT "To multiply your original investment by 1000,"
100 PRINT "you must win continuously "; COUNT; " times."
110 END
```

RUN the program to see the answer.

Exercise Set 6.2 Programming with **WHILE/WEND** (Using **PRINT**, **CLS**, **END**, **LET**, functions, **DEF FN**, **INPUT**, **WHILE/WEND**)

Flowcharting and code transcription:

1. Design a program to find out how many times a user-supplied number must be halved before it becomes one or less.
2. a. Design a program to report the accumulated annual compound interests for a savings account deposit of $10,000 for all the years from one year to when the accumulated interest is more than double the original deposit. The annual interest rate is 8 percent compounded every six months.
   b. Modify the program so that a user may set the initial deposit amount and the rate of money growth.

STRING COMPARISON

Alphanumeric data, or strings, can also be used in forming conditions, even though they are not regarded as possessing numeric values. The same relational operators are used, but the comparisons thus formed have different meanings.

Relational Operator	*Meaning*
=	is identical to
<	precedes in the ASCII scale
>	follows in the ASCII scale
<=	precedes or is identical to
>=	follows or is identical to
<>	is not the same as

To understand these operators when applied to strings, you must first understand how strings are represented in the computer memory.

Characters, which make up strings, are kept in the computer memory in code form according to a standard known as ASCII—American Standard Code for Information Interchange. Each character or symbol has an assigned binary code pattern that can be viewed as a numeric value. For instance, the capital letter A is represented in memory as 01000001, which is also the numeric value 65. The characters and their assigned ASCII values are listed in appendix B. When strings are used to form conditions, it is the ASCII (and therefore numeric) values that are used in the comparisons. For example, the condition:

```
"A" < "B"
```

is true because the ASCII value for A is 65, and the ASCII value for B is 66. Since 65 is less than 66, "A" is less than "B". But all this merely means that the letter A precedes the letter B in the ASCII scale.

When viewed this way, you can see that the blank character, which has an ASCII value of 32, is ahead of the letter A, so:

```
" " > "A"
```

is false.

Likewise, the condition:

```
"A " = "A"
```

is not true because the first string is made up of two characters, A and the blank, while the second is just A alone. They are not the same. Note that BASIC performs the comparison character by character. If the relational operator is the equal sign, as in this case, BASIC compares the first character in the first string to the first character in the second string. If these two characters are equal, BASIC goes on to compare the second character in the first string to the second character in the second string, and so on, until either it finds two characters that are not equal (in which case the condition is false) or it finds the end of both strings (in which case the condition is true).

Exercise Set 6.3 String comparison

Assess the truthfulness of the following comparisons:

1. "Abel" < "Abbey"

Answer: ______________________________

2. "322-7564" > "ROZ-7758"

Answer: ______________________________

3. A$ = "RS4078", B$ = "RS6221"
   A$ >= B$

Answer: ______________________________

4. "Annie" < "ANNIE"

Answer: ______________________________

With this understanding of the ASCII values for strings, let us see how string conditions can be used in certain situations to control loops.

Example 6.4

In this example, the user is prompted to enter a series of names. The program decides to maintain the loop or terminate it depending on whether the user types a "y" to indicate the desire to continue. Figure 6.4 is the flowchart for this program.

```
10 'STRING COMPARISONS
20 '
30 LET REPEAT$ = "y"
40 CLS
50 WHILE REPEAT$ = "y"
60      INPUT "Enter name : ", NAMES$
70      PRINT NAMES$
80      PRINT
90      INPUT "More? (y/n) ", REPEAT$
100     PRINT
110 WEND
120 END
```

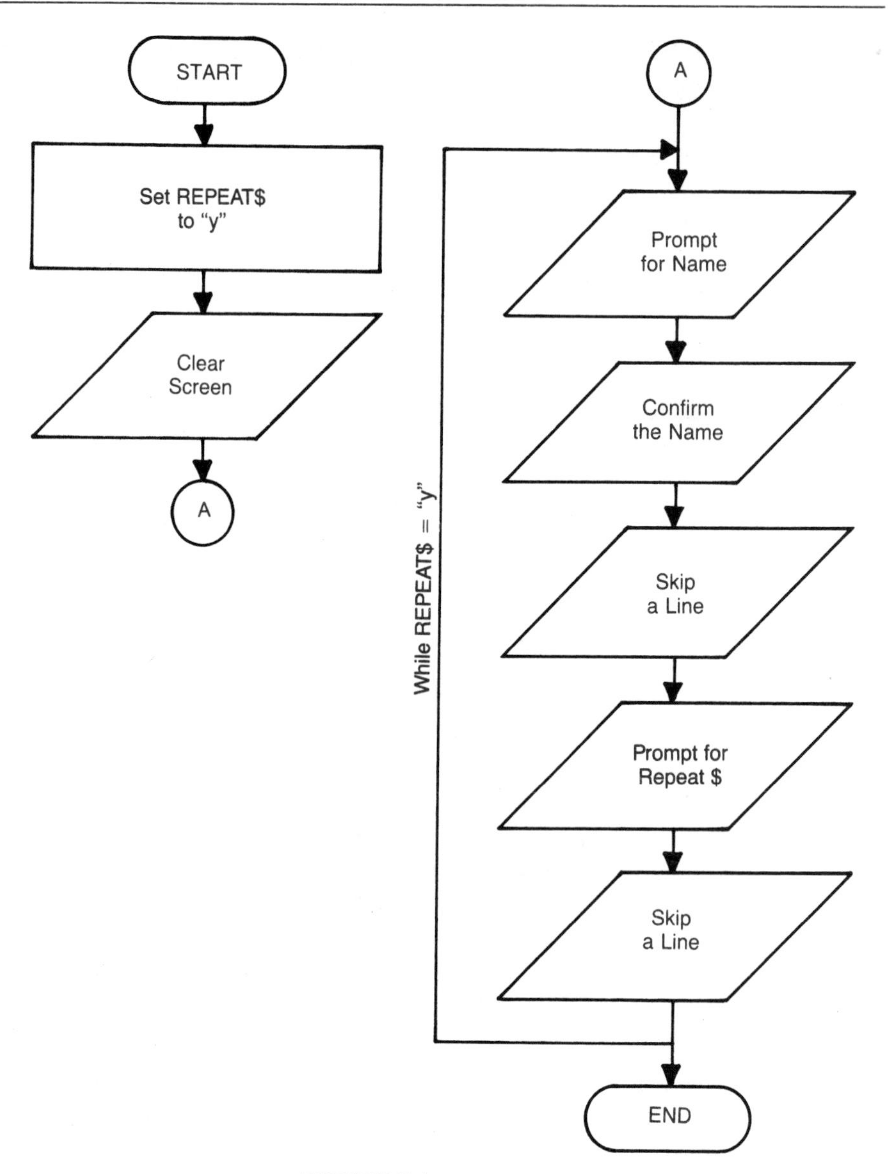
START
Set REPEAT$
to "y"
Clear
Screen
A
A
Prompt
for Name
Confirm
the Name
Skip
a Line
Prompt for
Repeat $
Skip
a Line
While REPEAT$ = "y"
END

FIGURE 6.4

RUN the program to observe the interaction between the program and the user.

Example 6.5

In Example 6.4, the user must respond with "y" to continue the data entry. Any other response terminates the program. If continuous data entry is desired, then the program can be made to continue with all responses from the user except when the letter "n" is entered.

```
10 'STRING COMPARISONS
20 '
30 LET REPEAT$ = "y"
40 CLS
50 WHILE REPEAT$ <> "n"
60       INPUT "Enter name : ", NAMES$
70       PRINT NAMES$
80       PRINT
90       INPUT "More? (y/n) ", REPEAT$
100      PRINT
110 WEND
120 END
```

In this example the condition is:

```
REPEAT$ <> "n"
```

If **REPEAT$** holds the letter "n", then the condition is not true because "n" is indeed the same as "n". Thus, when the letter "n" is entered, the loop terminates.

In the next example (a modified version of Example 5.19 from the last chapter), instead of being asked to express the desire to continue, the salesperson is asked to decide on program termination. This illustrates that a positive response is not always associated with the continuation of program execution. In the next chapter, you will learn how to use this knowledge to provide double protection for the users.

Example 6.6

```
10 'MULTIPLE SALES ACCOUNTING
20 '
30 LET TAX.RATE = .065
```

```
40 CLS
50 LET REPEAT$ = "n"
60 CLS
70 WHILE REPEAT$ <> "y"
80       CLS
90       INPUT "How many sales items do you have"; ITEM%
100      PRINT
110      LET SUB.TOTAL = 0
120      FOR C% = 1 TO ITEM%
130              INPUT "Enter sales amount : ", AMOUNT
140              LET SUB.TOTAL = SUB.TOTAL + AMOUNT
150      NEXT C%
160      LET TAX = SUB.TOTAL * TAX.RATE
170      LET TOTAL = SUB.TOTAL + TAX
180      PRINT
190      PRINT , "Subtotal : $"; SUB.TOTAL
200      PRINT
210      PRINT , "Sales tax : $"; TAX
220      PRINT
230      PRINT , "Total : $"; TOTAL
240      PRINT
250      PRINT
260      PRINT
270      PRINT "Enter y to terminate program."
280      INPUT "Press <ENTER> to continue ...", REPEAT$
290 WEND
300 END
```

Step through the program to understand the logic.

Exercise Set 6.4 "y" or "n" to quit (Using **PRINT**, **CLS**, **END**, **LET**, functions, **DEF FN**, **INPUT**, **FOR/NEXT**, **WHILE/WEND**)

Flowcharting and code transcription:

1. Design a program to report the accumulated annual compound interests for a savings account deposit of $10,000 annually. The annual interest rate is 8 percent compounded every six months. The program shall continue to compute as long as a user wishes to see the results of the computation.

2. Design a program for a retail sales clerk to produce sales receipts. Each receipt shall report the product names, price, the subtotal, a sales tax assessed at 4.5 percent, a grand total, and the final phrase of THANK YOU FOR SHOPPING AT RUBEN'S. This program shall be operating every day until the store's closing time.
3. Design a program to display the figures that are over 500 from a series of results entered into the computer by a pollster based on a survey conducted. The program shall end when the results are exhausted.

Chapter Exercises (Using **PRINT**, **CLS**, **END**, **LET**, functions, **DEF FN**, **INPUT**, **FOR/NEXT**, **WHILE/WEND**)

Flowcharting and code transcription:

1. Design a program to accumulate all debits and credits for an accounts statement. The statement data are to be entered into the computer by a professional bookkeeper. Credit data are entered as positive numbers while debit data are negative. The program is to stop when there is no further data entry.
2. Design a program permitting an aerospace scientist to enter into the computer a list of radio telemetry data. For aesthetic purposes, after the data entered have filled one full CRT screen, the screen should be cleared for the subsequent data entries. Permit the scientist to terminate the data entry session at will.
3. Design a program that produces a temperature conversion table one screenful at a time as follows:

```
C          F                   C           F
========================================

0          32                  21          69.8
1          33.8                22
            .                               .
            .                               .
            .                               .
20         68                  40
```

The display is to end when indicated by the user.

7 / CONTROLLED BRANCHING: ARITHMETIC CONDITIONS

Although BASIC executes program statements sequentially according to statement numbers, this is by no means the predominant mode of program execution. In fact, the same problem frequently requires that different logic paths be taken in order to respond to different controlling circumstances. For instance, different membership-dues formulas may be applied to adult and minor members for a club. In some problems, such as the computation of square roots, only nonnegative numbers are permitted to run through the calculations. To invoke different algorithms in response to different conditions, the program code must be able to override the normal sequential program execution. Taking logical paths other than that of the normal flow of the program statements, as dictated by controlling conditions, is called *conditional branching*. The mechanism that controls the conditional branching is known as *decision making*. In BASIC, conditional branching is made possible by the **IF/THEN** statement.

IF/THEN

The **IF** statement achieves logic control based on the truth or fallacy of conditions, such as those used in the **WHILE/WEND** statements. But instead of causing a looping action, the **IF** statement directs the program to execute the statement(s) specified after the keyword **THEN** if the condition is met. The next example illustrates this action.

Example 7.1

```
10 'IF/THEN ILLUSTRATION 1
20 '
30 CLS
40 INPUT "Enter a positive number : ", A
50 IF A < 0 THEN PRINT "Number not acceptable."
60 END
```

The objective of this program is to ask the user to enter a positive number only. Should the user enter a negative number, the program will indicate that the data entry is not acceptable. **RUN** the program twice. Enter a positive number the first time and a negative number the second. You should see a warning message displayed the second time only.

Statement 50 says: **IF** the number in **A** is negative (less than zero), **THEN** display the message and continue with the normal sequential program execution. Otherwise, simply continue with the program execution and ignore the statement(s) after the **THEN** keyword.

The flowchart for this program is shown in Figure 7.1.

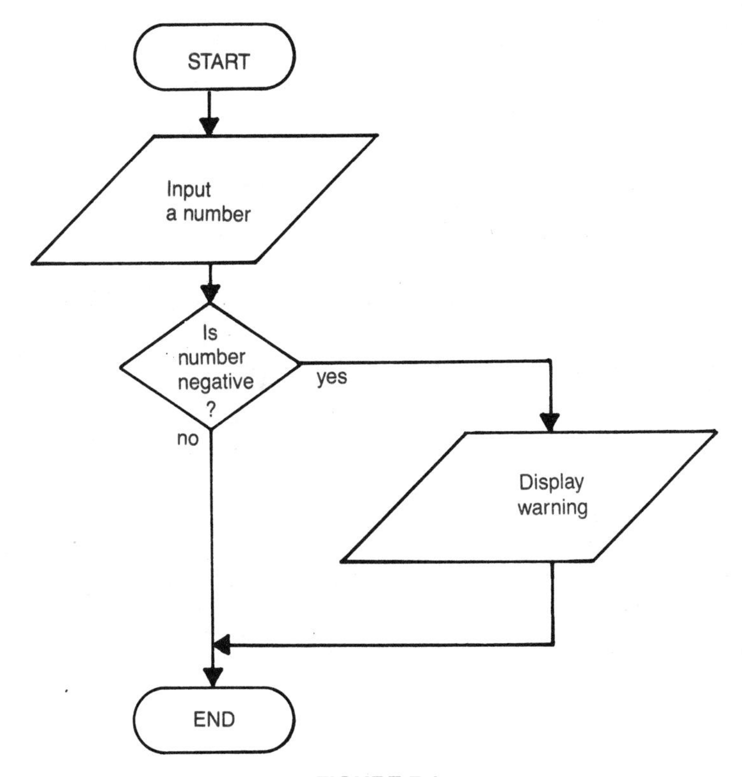

FIGURE 7.1

Notice that the diamond is used to show the condition. With the **IF** statement, which implements *controlled branching,* two arrows always emanate from two of the diamond vertices, representing the two possible logical paths that can be taken.

Statement 60 is called the *default* statement, which means it is the statement to be executed after the control branching mechanism, unless the program is specifically directed to another statement, as illustrated in the next example.

Example 7.2

Figure 7.2 shows the flowchart for this program.

```
10 'IF/THEN ILLUSTRATION 2
20 '
30 CLS
40 INPUT "Enter a positive number : ", A
50 IF A < 0 THEN 40
60 END
```

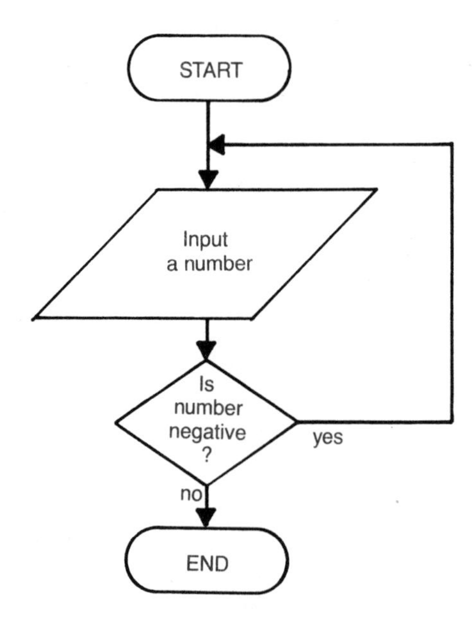

FIGURE 7.2

This example sends the program back to request the input number again if it is negative, instead of displaying a message.

The **IF** statement must begin with the keyword **IF**, followed by a condition and the keyword **THEN**, which specifies the action to be taken if the condition is met. The action can be either a BASIC statement without the statement number (as illustrated in Example 7.1) or a statement number indicating the next statement to be executed (as illustrated in Example 7.2).

IF/THEN
Form: IF condition THEN action
Function: To control the ensuing program logic path.

In controlled branching, the consequences of the decision are represented by the outgoing arrows in the flowchart. If the arrow points to an activity off the main flow of the program logic, then the consequence takes the form of a BASIC statement in the transcribed coding. If the arrow points to an activity along the flow of the program logic, then it will be transcribed as a statement number.

Action transcribed into a BASIC statement:

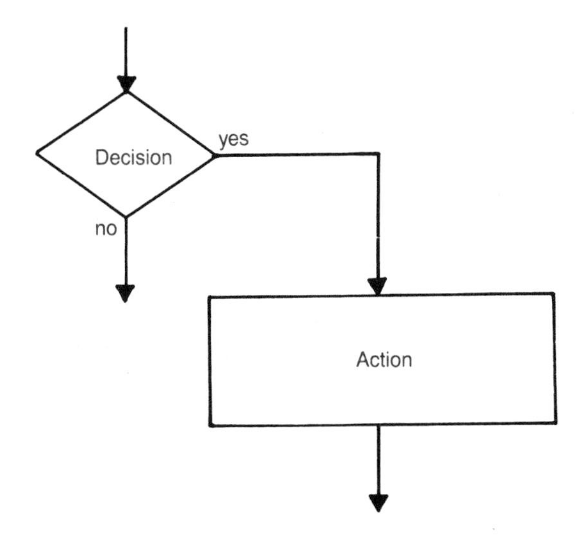

Action transcribed into a statement number:

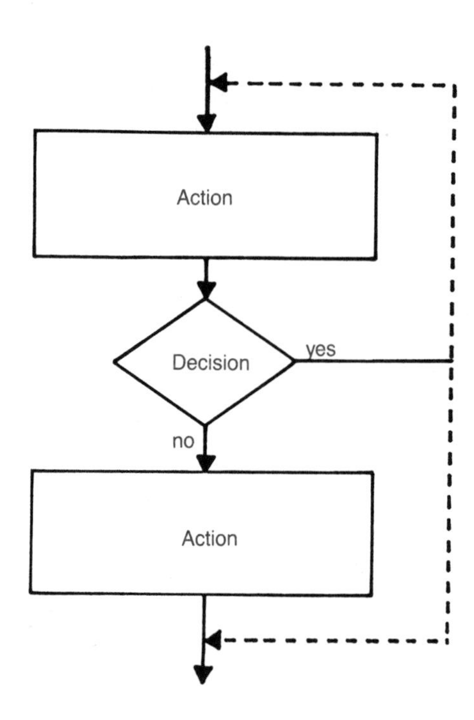

UNCONDITIONAL BRANCHING: GOTO

Frequently, arrows in flowcharts do not follow the main flow of the logic. These arrows represent the *unconditional branches* and are to be transcribed into the **GOTO** statement.

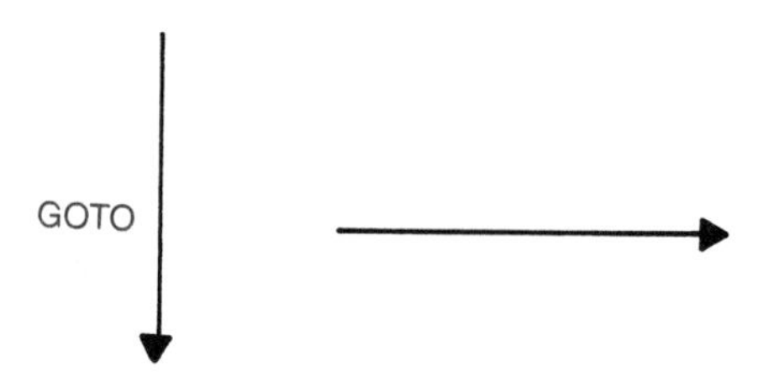

Example 7.3

Suppose that, in developing the logic of the following example program, the programmer arrived at the flowchart in Figure 7.3.

The branching arrow at the bottom will be transcribed into a **GOTO** statement as follows:

```
10 'GOTO
20 '
30 CLS
40 PRINT "Enter a number."
50 INPUT "Enter 999 to quit : ", A
60 IF A = 999 THEN END
70 GOTO 30
```

GOTO, one keyword, breaks the sequential program execution without dependency on a condition and directs the program execution to a statement elsewhere in the program as specified.

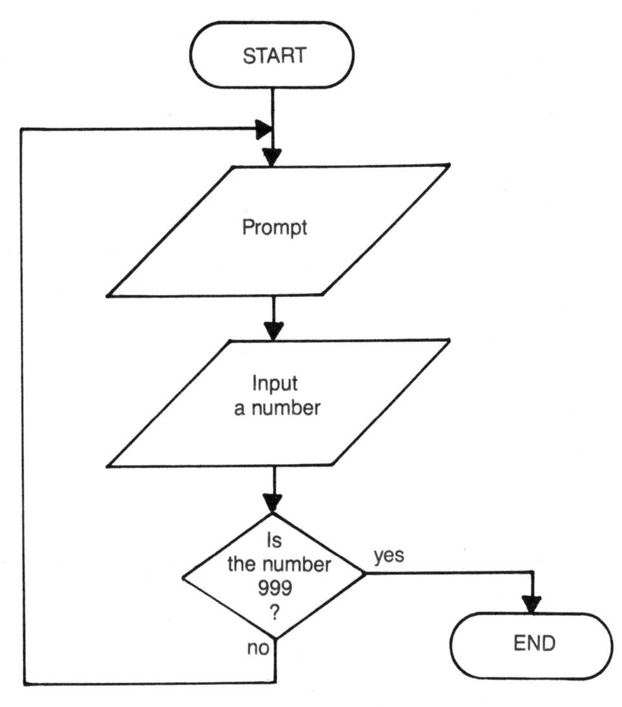

FIGURE 7.3

GOTO
Form: GOTO statement number
Function: To direct the program execution away from the sequential mode unconditionally.

The **GOTO** statement is mainly used to indicate a break from the logic's sequential flow—that is, it is used to transcribe branching flowchart arrows. If the logic design has not been thoroughly thought out and the **GOTO** statement is used arbitrarily, as in the next example, very undesirable effects can result.

Example 7.4

```
10 'ENDLESS LOOP
20 '
30 PRINT "Do again"
40 GOTO 30
50 END
```

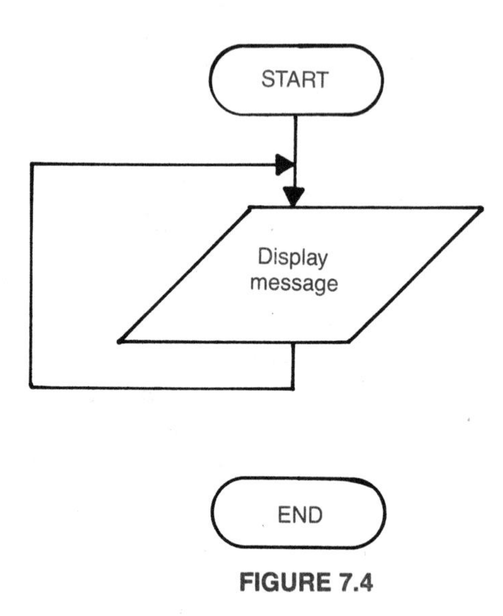

FIGURE 7.4

This program will go on endlessly, as the **GOTO** in statement 40 continually directs the program back to statement 30, resulting in an *endless loop*. If the program had been flowcharted first, then it would have been clear that the **END** statement could never have been reached (see Figure 7.4).

Exercise Set 7.1 IF/THEN with arithmetic conditions (Using **PRINT**, **CLS**, **END**, **LET**, functions, **DEF FN**, **INPUT**, **FOR/NEXT**, **IF/THEN**, **GOTO**)

A. Correct the errors, if any, in the following programs:

1.

```
10 INPUT "Enter a file number : ", FLNO
20 IF FLNO > 10000 PRINT "File does not exist"
30 END
```

Answer: ______________________________________

____

2.

```
10 CLS
20 PRINT "Enter a number."
30 INPUT "Enter 99999 to quit : ", A%
40 IF A% = 99999 THEN 30
50 END
```

Answer: ______________________________________

____

B. (Practice on syntax) Write a program to:

3. At statement 50 direct the program to continue at statement 120 if the value in the variable is not positive.
4. At statement 100 express the logic that, if a value exceeds 200,000, a warning message must be displayed before the program can continue.

C. Flowcharting and code transcription:

5. Design a program permitting a clerk to enter into the computer a list of unfinished projects with associated project numbers. Permit the clerk to terminate the data entry session at will.

6. Design a program that will selectively sum only the credit data among both credit and debit data entered through the keyboard by a financial analyst. Credit data are entered as positive numbers while debit data are entered as negative. The process shall end when there are no more data (you decide how this is indicated).

USER PROGRAM CONTROL

As demonstrated in Example 7.3, the **IF** statement can be used by the user to control the program logic. Example 7.3 employs a particular input data item (999) for such purposes, but that precludes that particular data item from being used in the program logic. This works if the program logic deals only with a small set of input data—for example, a school grading program usually deals with numbers between 0 and 100. Numbers outside of this range can therefore be used for program control. However, this method would fail if all numbers can be valid data. One popular way of forming program controls, therefore, is by using a specially selected string, and the control mechanism is made to be interactive. For instance, the user can be asked to enter either a "yes" or a "no" to indicate the desire to continue with the program execution. We used this technique in the last chapter.

In many applications, for the protection of valuable data, program termination should be permitted only when the user is absolutely sure it is safe. This is typically the case when a program termination will nullify the prior effort of a large quantity of data entry. For these situations, program termination should be allowed only if the user signals it twice, but different responses must be elicited to express the same desire in order to prevent the same user response mistake from occurring twice in succession. For example,

```
100 INPUT "Want to quit? (y/n) : ", ANSWER$
110 IF ANSWER$ <> "y" THEN 10
120 INPUT "Are you sure? (y/n) : ", ANSWER$
130 IF ANSWER$ <> "y" THEN 10
140 END
```

would permit the user to make an irreversible error by entering "y" twice in quick succession. The correct implementation should be:

```
100 INPUT "Continue? (y/n) : ", ANSWER$
110 IF ANSWER$ <> "n" THEN 10
120 INPUT "Are you sure? (y/n) : ", ANSWER$
```

```
130 IF ANSWER$ <> "y" THEN 10
140 END
```

Study these two cases carefully to understand the logic.

Controlled branching, of course, is not used only for purposes of user program control. Complex program logic variations can be accomplished with the use of the **IF** statement. One of the many uses of **IF/THEN** is illustrated in the next example.

Example 7.5

Food sold in the supermarket is often exempt from tax. This program discriminates between food items and other merchandise; it assesses tax only on the latter. The discrimination is based on a predetermined system of product coding: All food items have product codes below 1000. Figure 7.5 provides part of the flowchart for the program.

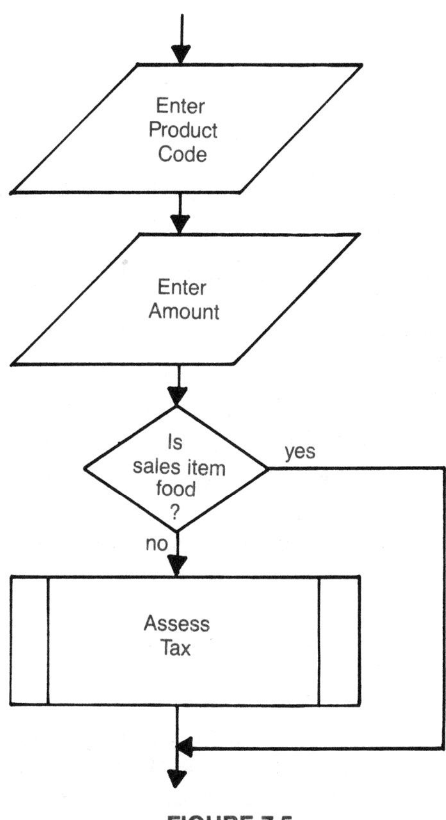

FIGURE 7.5

```
10 'SELECTIVE SALES TAXING
20 '
30 LET SALE = 0
40 LET TAX.TOTAL = 0
50 CLS
60 INPUT "Product code : ", CODE
70 INPUT "Amount : ", AMOUNT
80 IF CODE < 1000 THEN 120
90 LET TAX = AMOUNT * .065
100 LET TAX.TOTAL = TAX.TOTAL + TAX
110 LET SALE = SALE + AMOUNT
120 PRINT
130 INPUT "More? (y/n) ", TRANS$
140 IF TRANS$ = "y" THEN 60
150 LET TOTAL.SALES = SALE + TAX.TOTAL
160 PRINT
170 PRINT
180 PRINT
190 PRINT "Total sales :", "$"; SALE
200 PRINT "Sales tax :", "$"; TAX.TOTAL
210 PRINT "Grand total :", "$"; TOTAL.SALES
220 END
```

Exercise Set 7.2 User program control (Using **PRINT**, **CLS**, **END**, **LET**, functions, **DEF FN**, **INPUT**, **FOR/NEXT**, **WHILE/WEND**, **IF/THEN**)

Flowcharting and code transcription:

1. Redo problem 2 of Exercise Set 6.4 by providing the user with a double protection for program termination.
2. Redo problem 2 of Exercise Set 6.4 by permitting the salesperson to enter either "Y" or "y" to terminate the program.
3. Redo problem 6 of Exercise Set 7.1 by asking the analyst whether it is a credit or a debit item he or she is entering, so that both items can be entered as positive numbers. Also provide double protection for program termination.

CHOICES: IF/THEN/ELSE

Example 7.5 typifies the program logic options of either doing something or not doing something. The **IF** statement in statement 80 is used to skip an activity normally enacted. There are occasions when the control is not to cause a logical path to be skipped but to make possible a choice between two logical paths.

As an example, let us study the programming associated with deciding whether a student is to pass or fail a course. Suppose that, for this teacher, 60 is the pass/fail grade. Students scoring above 60 will pass, while all grades 60 and below fail.

Example 7.6

Figure 7.6 shows the flowchart of the program logic. The transcribed coding is:

```
10 'IF/THEN/ELSE
20 '
30 CLS
40 INPUT "Enter grade : ", GRADE
50 IF GRADE > 60 THEN PRINT "Pass" ELSE PRINT "Fail"
60 END
```

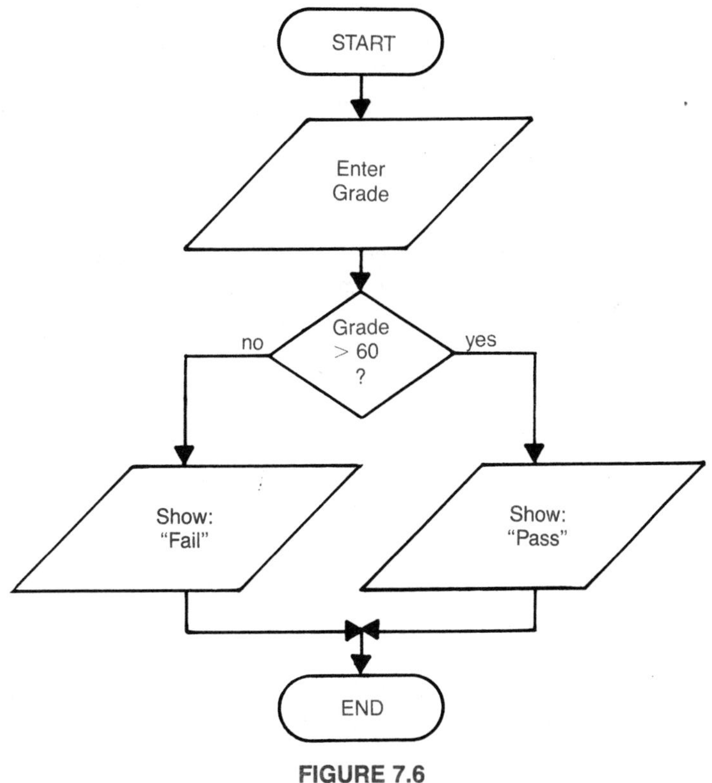

FIGURE 7.6

For conditional branching, both possible consequences of a branching control can be expressed in the same **IF** statement, if the **ELSE** option is invoked.

When the **IF** statement is followed by the keyword **THEN** and then the keyword **ELSE**, the **THEN** statement gives the result if the condition is true, while **ELSE** gives the result if the condition is not true. In fact, **IF/THEN/ELSE** reads just like English: **IF** a condition is met, **THEN** do such and such, **ELSE** do such and such.

ELSE is followed by a consequence that can be either a BASIC statement without the statement number or a statement number, as with **THEN**.

IF/THEN/ELSE
Form: IF condition THEN true consequence ELSE untrue consequence
Function: To effect a choice between two possible results of a decision.

SPAGHETTI CODE

The same result can be obtained using **IF/THEN** alone without the help of **ELSE**. Let us follow a program development process for the same problem arriving at the following coding:

```
10 'CHOICE THROUGH IF/THEN (SPAGHETTI CODE)
20 '
30 CLS
40 INPUT "Enter grade : ", GRADE
50 IF GRADE > 60 THEN 80
60 PRINT "Fail"
70 GOTO 90
80 PRINT "Pass"
90 END
```

In this example, the grades above 60 are tested. If the input grade is not above 60, then the report "Fail" is generated. If the grade is indeed above 60, then "Pass" is shown. However, due to the placement of the two **PRINT** statements in sequence in the program code, "Pass" would be displayed automatically after "Fail" due to the sequential program execution of BASIC unless specifically avoided. Thus a **GOTO** statement is inserted at statement 70 to "go around" the "Pass" display. The corresponding flowchart for this program is shown in Figure 7.7.

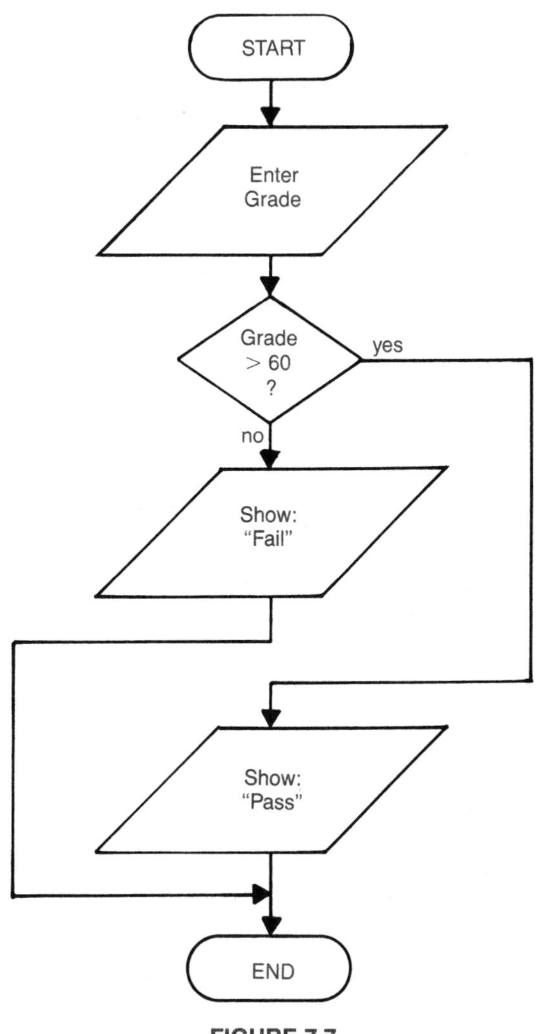

FIGURE 7.7

This flowchart looks awkward because it was created after the coding, which was designed at the keyboard. The result is unnecessary **GOTO** statements in the program coding. This type of program is known as *spaghetti code*. The name is derived from the many twisting arrows (that is, **GOTO**s) in the flowchart.

Three techniques can help you avoid spaghetti code:

1. Develop the logic in flowchart form and not directly in code.
2. Use the **IF/THEN/ELSE** code option if the logic represents a choice.
3. Use the proper flowchart-to-code transcription technique (to be discussed in chapter 8).

Choice implies two logical paths of equal significance. In programming, when logic splits into two paths that rejoin later, a choice is formed. To the human mind, one path may still be considered a preferred case, while the other is an option. Such logical preferences can result in different flowchart representations, even though the resultant program logic may not show any apparent difference. Where the logical paths are of equal importance, the flowchart represents the logic as two off branches (as in Figure 7.6). When one path is the preferred choice, it remains with the main logic flow, while the other path becomes the branch.

MULTISTATEMENT LINES

As an example of the latter case, suppose the "false" path in Example 7.6 is the preferred logical path (the main flow) and the "true" path is considered a branch (which corresponds to the thinking of a really mean teacher, as he or she associates failing with the main flow). The same logic can be flowcharted as shown in Figure 7.8.

Example 7.7

The transcribed coding accordingly is:

```
10 'MULTISTATEMENT LINES
20 '
30 CLS
40 INPUT "Enter grade : ", GRADE
50 IF GRADE > 60 THEN PRINT "Pass" : GOTO 70
60 PRINT "Fail"
70 END
```

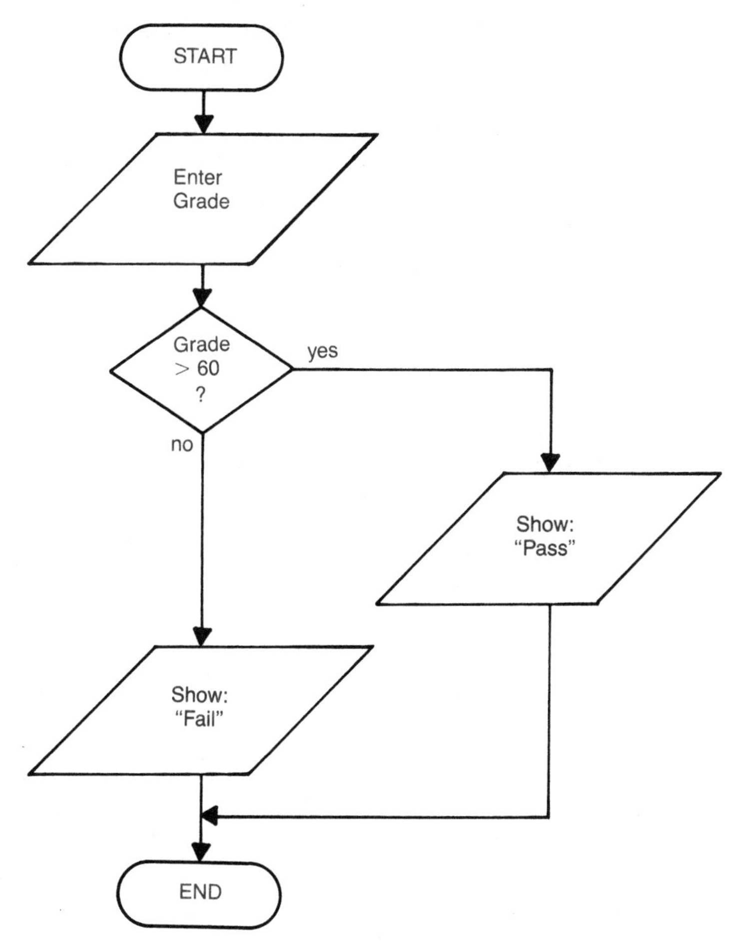

FIGURE 7.8

Pay attention to the extra **GOTO 70** at the end of statement 50. This **GOTO** corresponds to the arrow emerging from the **Show: "Pass"** box in the flowchart. Because this is an off-branch arrow, it becomes a **GOTO** (if a strict flowchart transcription procedure is followed). But because it associates with the "true" consequence of the decision, it also belongs to the **THEN** consequence. However, a BASIC statement cannot have two opening keywords, as would have been the case if the **THEN** consequence were coded as:

```
THEN PRINT "Pass" GOTO 70
```

These two statements are therefore combined into one with the statement delimiter—the colon (:). The resultant "statement" is called a *compound statement.*

Thus, with the colon, multiple statements can be combined into one statement. How many statements can be compounded? As many as are necessary, as long as the total statement length is not over 255 characters.

The next example shows compound statements used in an **IF/THEN/ELSE** statement.

Example 7.8

In this example, the magnitude of the differences between two numbers is of interest, but not the sign (as with the comparison between the forces applied in opposite directions). The flowchart for this program is shown in Figure 7.9.

```
10 'FINDING DIFFERENCE
20 '
30 CLS
40 INPUT "Enter first number : ", A
50 INPUT "Enter second number : ", B
60 IF A > B THEN LET C = A - B : PRINT A, B, C
            ELSE LET C = B - A : PRINT B, A, C
70 END
```

Exercise Set 7.3 IF/THEN/ELSE (Using **PRINT**, **CLS**, **END**, **LET**, functions, **DEF FN**, **INPUT**, **FOR/NEXT**, **WHILE/WEND**, **IF/THEN/ELSE**)

A. Correct the errors, if any, in the following program:

1.

```
10 CLS
20 INPUT "Enter data : ", AMOUNT
30 IF AMOUNT > 10,000 THEN PRINT "Too high"
                      ELSE PRINT "OK"
40 IF AMOUNT < 10,000 THEN PRINT "Too low"
                      ELSE PRINT "OK"
50 END
```

Answer: ____

____

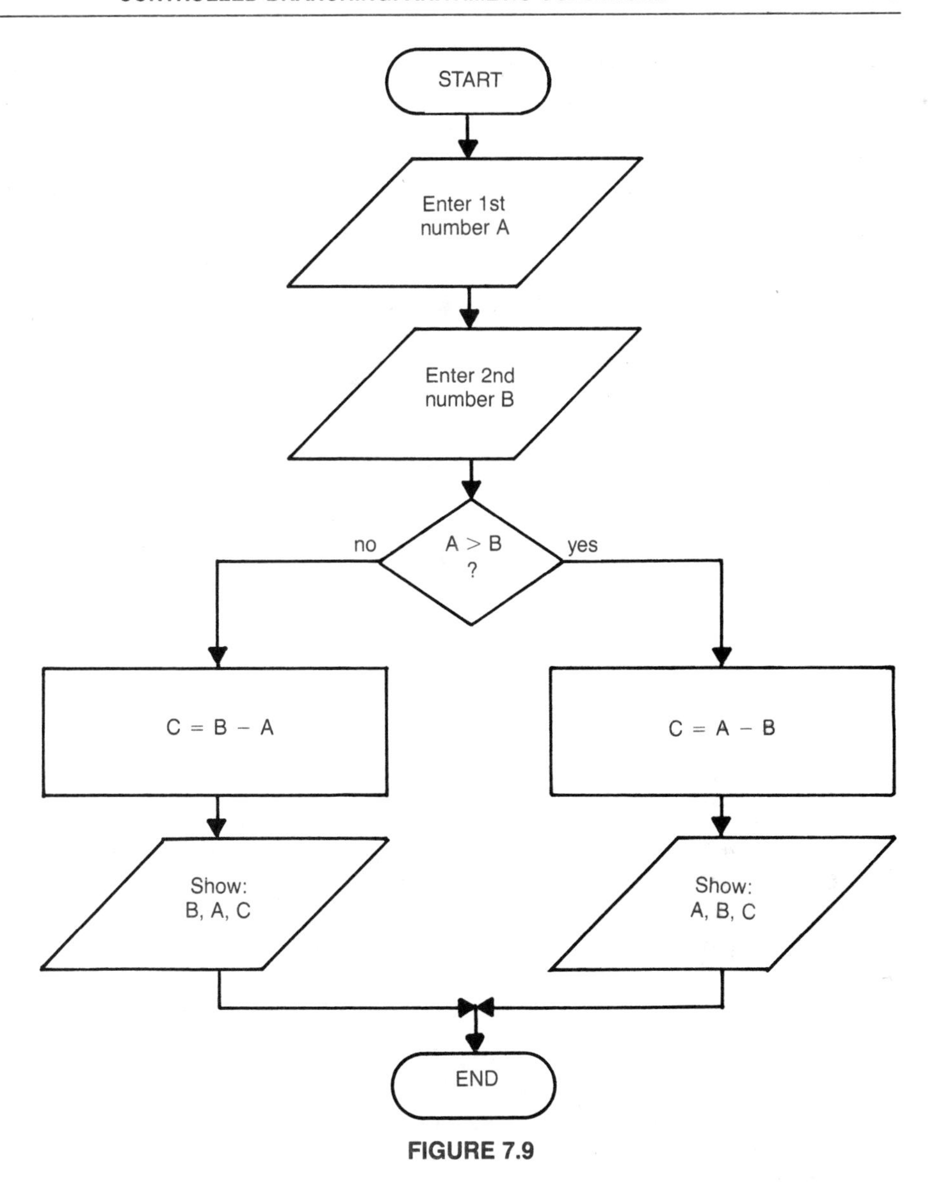

FIGURE 7.9

B. Transcribe the following flowcharts into code:

2. (See Figure 7.10.)
3. (See Figure 7.11.)

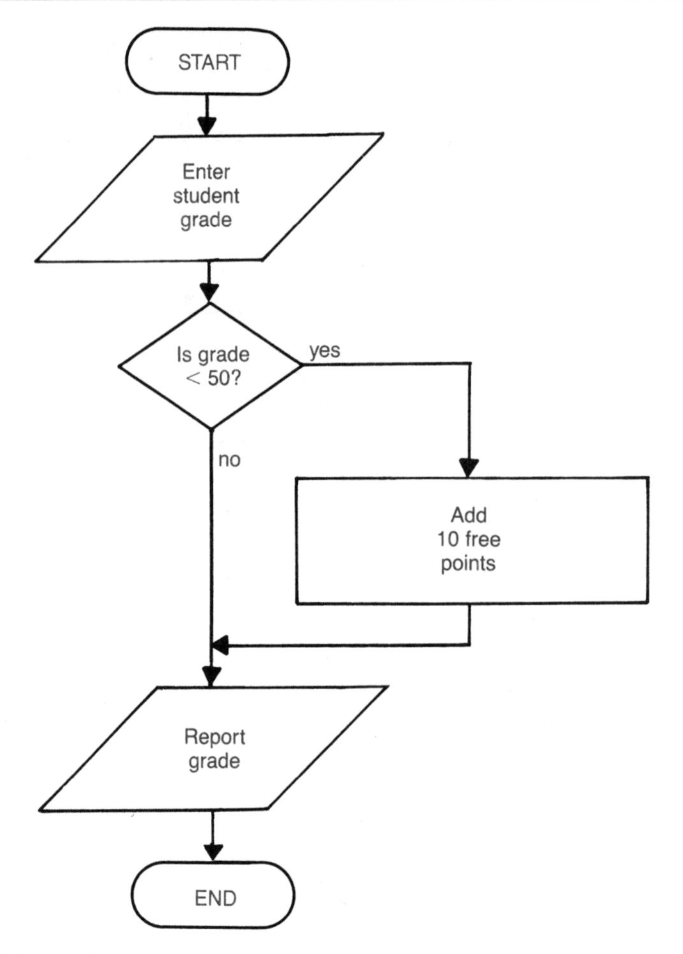

FIGURE 7.10

C. Flowcharting and code transcription:

4. At the end of every day, the maintenance engineer of a nuclear plant enters all turbine operational times in minutes into the computer, which totals all the up- (or on-) and downtimes automatically. Uptimes are entered as positive numbers and downtimes as negative numbers. The two totals are then entered into a logbook. Design a program to accomplish this.
5. Modify the above so that both the up- and downtimes can be entered as positive numbers, and the results are reported as positive numbers as well.

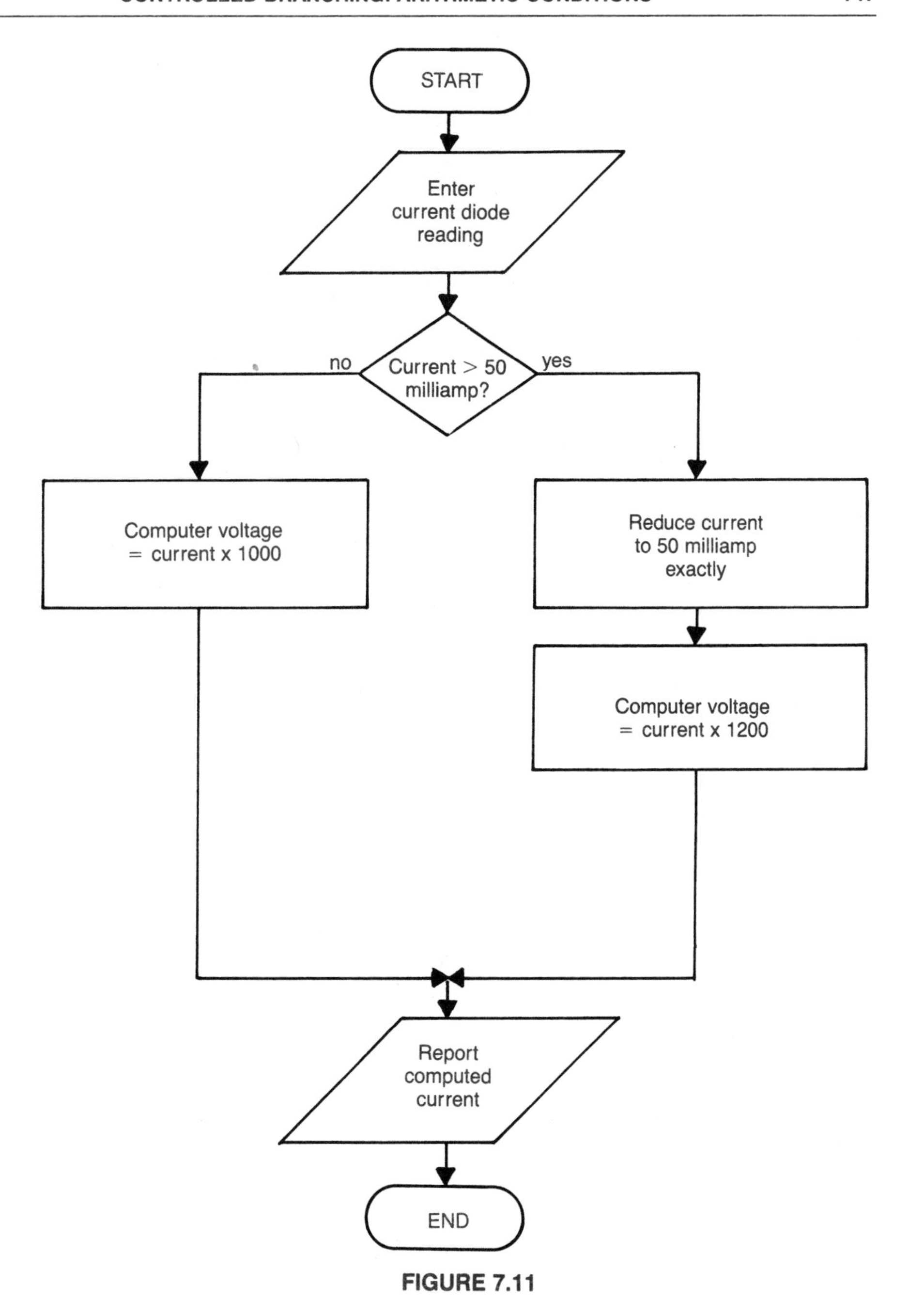
START
Enter
current diode
reading
no
Current > 50
milliamp?
yes
Computer voltage
= current x 1000
Reduce current
to 50 milliamp
exactly
Computer voltage
= current x 1200
Report
computed
current
END

FIGURE 7.11

LOGIC STRUCTURE

In Example 7.8, statement 60 could have been coded as:

```
60 IF A > B THEN LET C = A - B : PRINT A, B, C ELSE LET
   C = B - A : PRINT B, A, C
```

But the resultant coding would not have been easy to read. With the two decision outcomes aligned (achieved by typing blank characters), the program code reflects the structure of the logic.

The next example shows how a relatively complex logic structure can be preserved with well-aligned coding.

Example 7.9

The flowchart for this program is shown in Figure 7.12. The transcripted code is:

```
10 'NESTED IF
20 '
30 CLS
40 INPUT "Enter grade : ", GRADE
50 IF GRADE < 60 THEN PRINT "C"
                 ELSE IF GRADE < 80 THEN PRINT "B"
                                    ELSE PRINT "A"
60 END
```

Again, pay attention to how the coding corresponds to the flowchart.

The structure of the flowchart shows the programmer's analytical point of view. The flowchart in Figure 7.12 reflects one of two things: Either the programmer considers the "C" result as a group opposed to all the rest ("A"s and "B"s), or the logic has been developed by thinking in terms of one little piece at a time. Another way of developing the flowchart is shown in Figure 7.13. The corresponding coding is:

```
10 INPUT "Enter grade : ", GRADE
20 IF GRADE < 60 THEN PRINT "C" : GOTO 50
30 IF GRADE < 80 THEN PRINT "B" : GOTO 50
40 PRINT "A"
50 END
```

The same result is obtained.

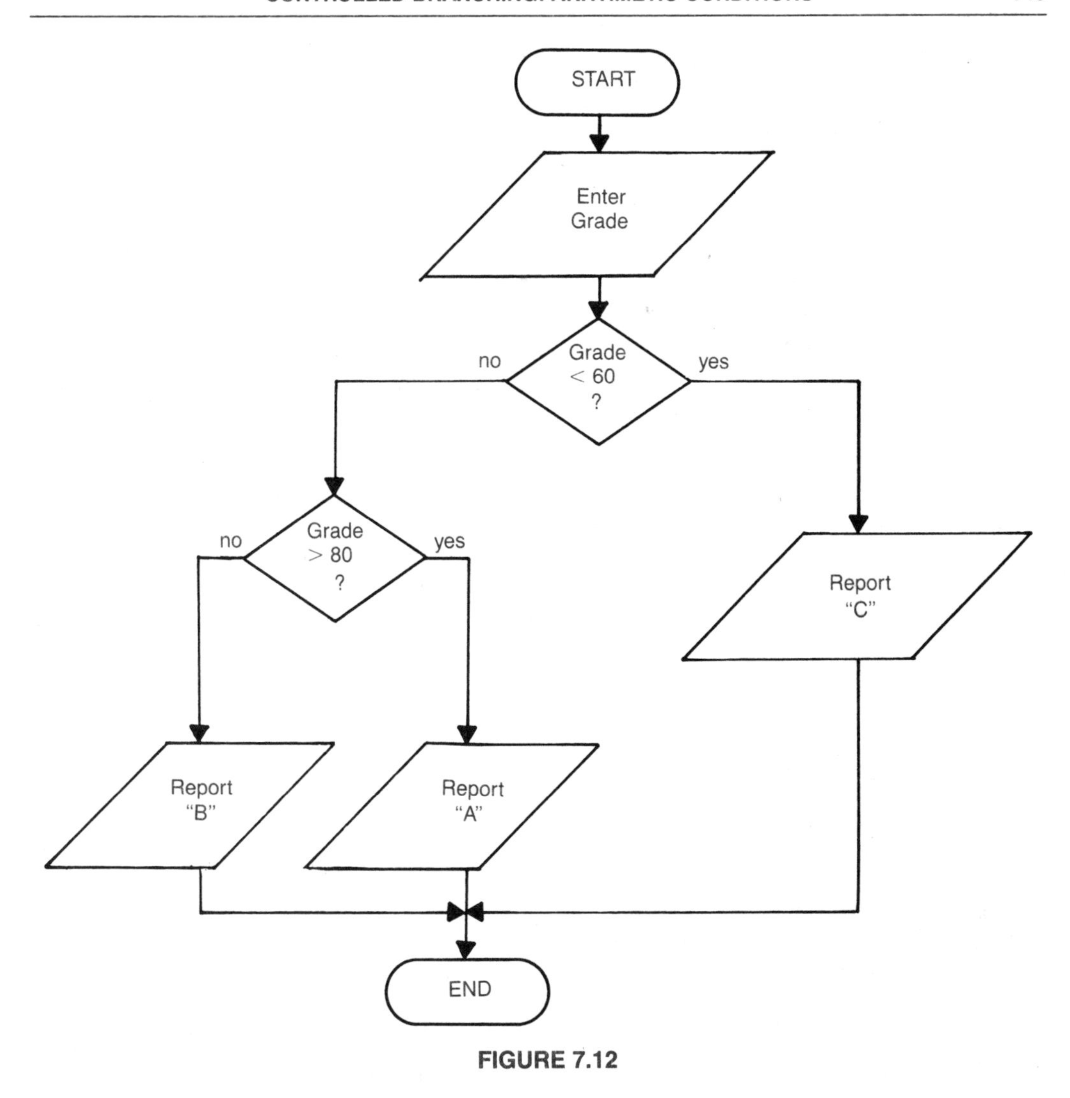

FIGURE 7.12

In any case, whatever the flowchart looks like, it can be transcribed into code accordingly. Usually the criterion separating good coding from bad coding is whether the logic structure is good or bad.

Chapter Exercises Program code structuring, **IF** logic structure (Using **PRINT**, **CLS**, **END**, **LET**, functions, **DEF FN**, **INPUT**, **FOR/NEXT**, **WHILE/WEND**, **IF/THEN/ELSE**)

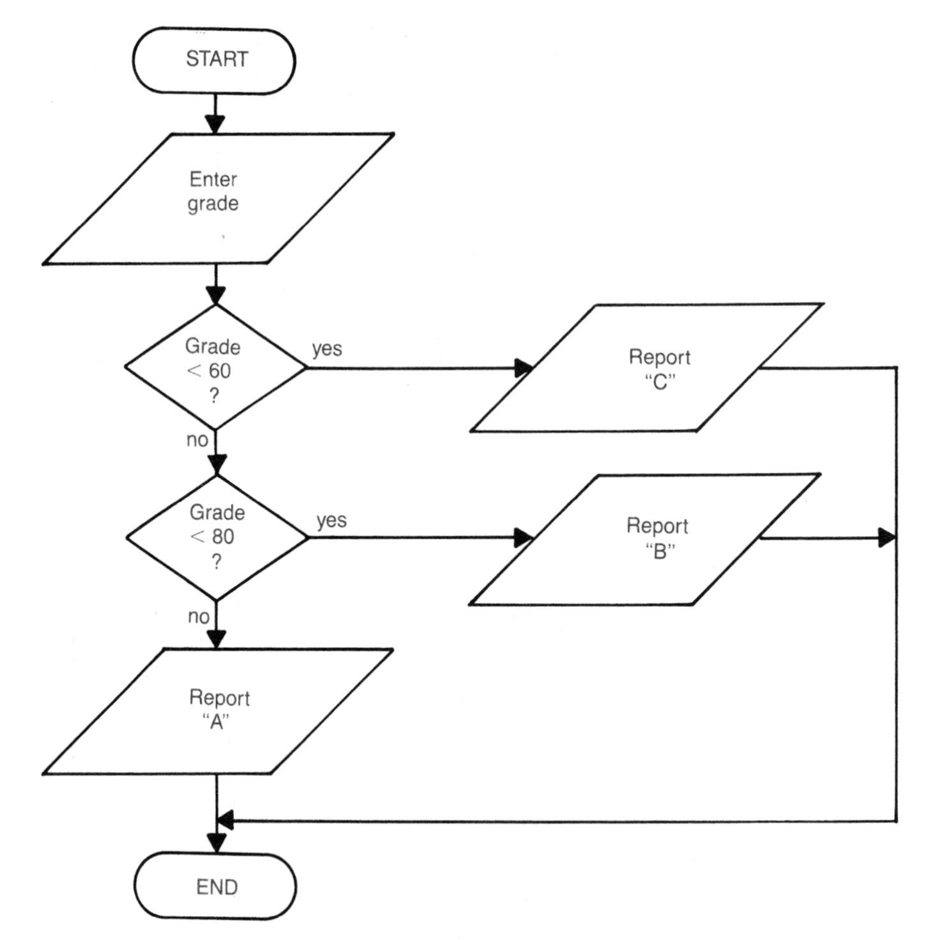

FIGURE 7.13

A. Redesign the following flowcharts to give better logic structures:

1. (See Figure 7.14.)
2. (See Figure 7.15.)

B. Flowcharting and code transcription:

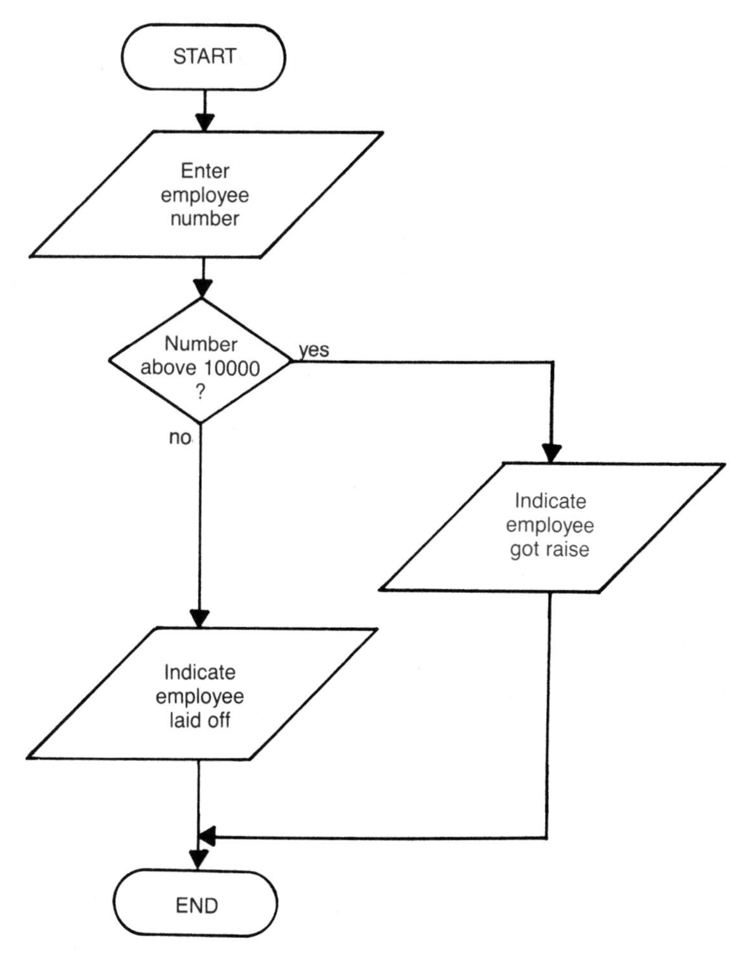

FIGURE 7.14

3. The decibel compensation factors for airport noise measurement are:

Measurement (decibels)	*Adjustment (decibels)*
0–50	−5
>50–60	+0
>60–70	+5
>70	+ 15

Design a program to compute the average noise levels of measurements taken on seven consecutive days.

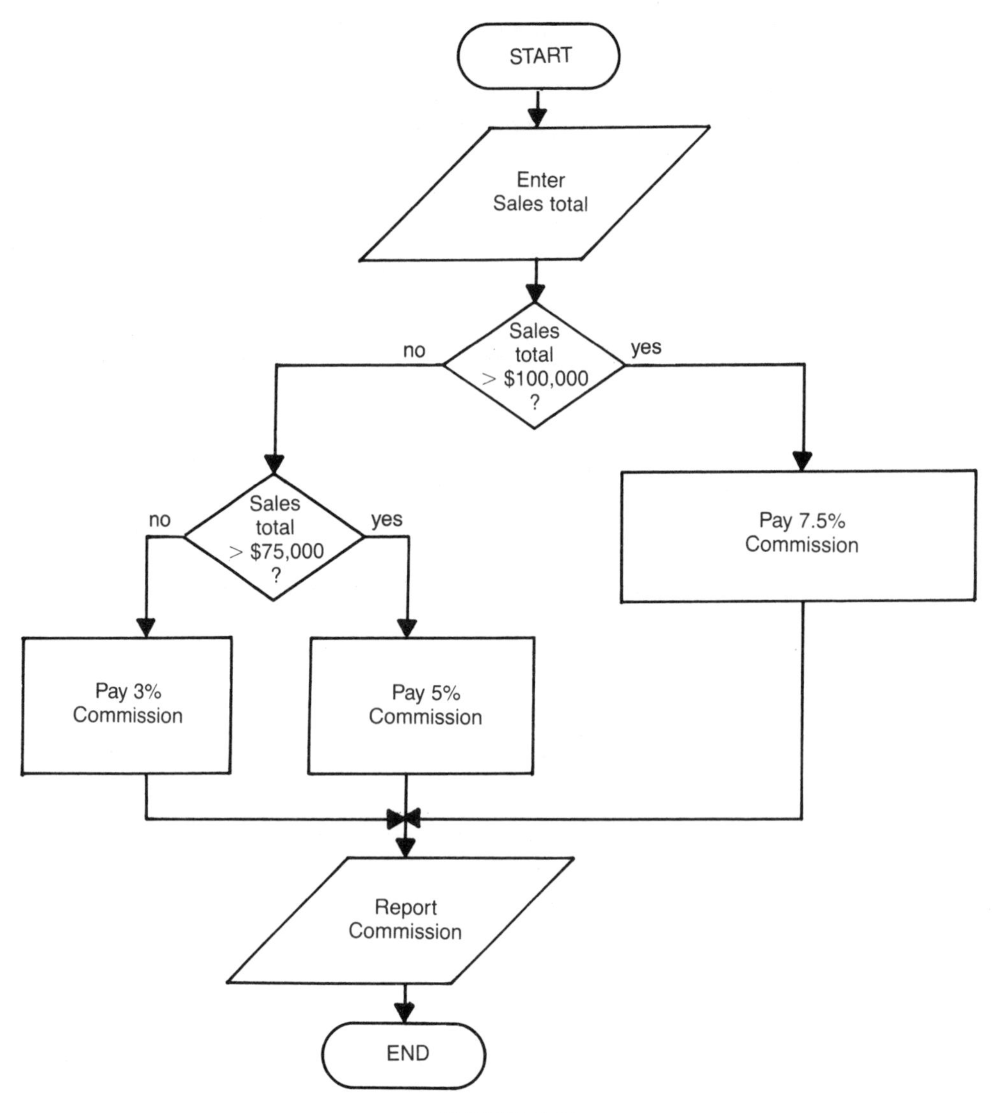
START
Enter
Sales total
no
Sales
total
> $100,000
?
yes
no
Sales
total
> $75,000
?
yes
Pay 7.5%
Commission
Pay 3%
Commission
Pay 5%
Commission
Report
Commission
END

FIGURE 7.15

4. For Hurry-hurry Manufacturing, Inc., the assembly-line workers are paid on a base hourly rate plus performance incentive. The base hourly rate is $5.25, and no one works overtime. Each worker is expected to produce 1,000 widgets per each forty-hour week. But for every 200 widgets produced by each worker over the base quota, the pay is increased 10 percent compounded. The maximum production per worker per week is 1,600 widgets. Design a program that will allow the line manager to compute a worker's wage by keying in pertinent data.

8 / CONTROLLED BRANCHING: LOGICAL OPERATORS

Let us write a program to accept a meaningful grade from the keyboard. A meaningful grade is one between 0 and 100. One way to do it is illustrated in Figure 8.1 and the following code:

```
10 INPUT "Enter grade : ", GRADE
20 IF GRADE < 0 THEN 10
30 IF GRADE > 100 THEN 10
40 END
```

In this effort, two **IF** statements are employed—one to guard against grade entries that are below 0, the other against those above 100.

Dual conditions can be expressed in the same sentence in English. The two conditions above can be worded as: Reject all grades either below 0 or above 100. The same logical expression can be accomplished in programming with the help of the logical operators.

LOGICAL OPERATORS

Let us study the following alternate program (see Figure 8.2).

Example 8.1

```
10 'LOGICAL OPERATORS
20 '
30 CLS
40 INPUT "Enter grade : ", GRADE
```

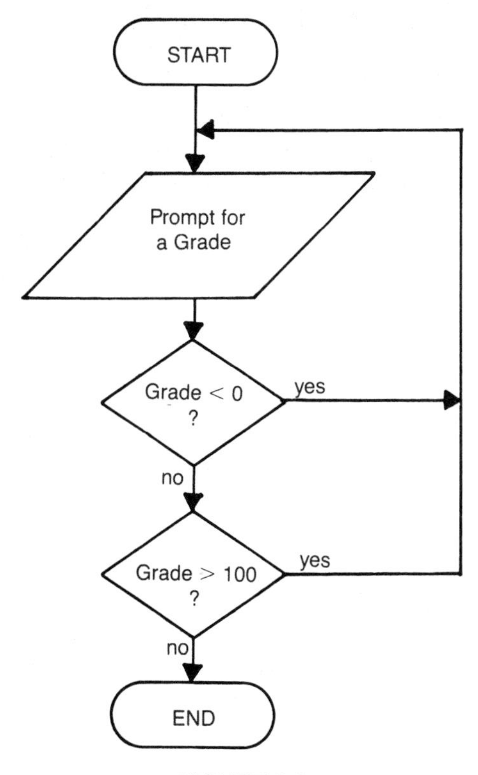

FIGURE 8.1

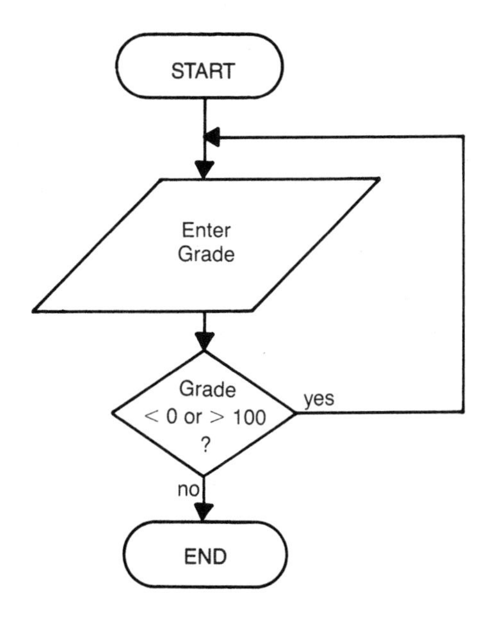

FIGURE 8.2

```
50 IF GRADE < 0 OR GRADE > 100 THEN 40
60 END
```

The **OR** in statement 50 is a *logical operator*. A logical operator combines two component conditions to produce one condition. In Example 8.1, two basic arithmetic conditions **GRADE < 0** and **GRADE > 100** are combined to form one integral condition with the **OR** operator.

BASIC recognizes six logical operators altogether with the first three following the order of executional precedence and operations:

1. **NOT** Condition
   Example: **NOT A > 10**
   The final status of the condition can be ascertained with the help of the following table:

	Condition	Result
NOT	T	F
	F	T

2. Condition 1 **AND** Condition 2
   Example: **G >= 0 AND G <= 100**
   The status of the condition can be assessed with:

	Condition 1	Condition 2	Result
AND	T	T	T
	T	F	F
	F	T	F
	F	F	F

3. Condition 1 **OR** Condition 2
   Example: **G < 0 OR G > 100**
   The truth/fallacy table for **OR** is:

	Condition 1	Condition 2	Result
OR	T	T	T
	T	F	T
	F	T	T
	F	F	F

For the IBM PC BASIC, besides **NOT**, **AND**, and **OR**, there are three more logical operators: **XOR**, **EQV**, and **IMP**. In this book, only the first three will be discussed, as they are the most commonly used ones.

Except for the **NOT** operator, all logical operators take on two component conditions.

NOT, which is followed by one component condition, reverses the true/false status of the component condition.

OR, as illustrated in Example 8.1, combines two true/untrue statuses into one true status by demanding that at least one be true. If both component conditions are untrue, then the resultant status will be untrue as well.

AND requires that both component conditions be true in order to arrive at a combined true status. All other combinations result in the untrue status. For instance, instead of rejecting the grades, the program can accept a meaningful grade with the **AND** operator.

Example 8.2

In this example a grade between 0 and 100 will be displayed. Figure 8.3 shows the flowchart.

```
10 'AND
20 '
30 CLS
40 INPUT "Enter grade : ", GRADE
50 IF GRADE >= 0 AND GRADE <= 100 THEN PRINT GRADE : END
60 GOTO 40
```

The condition in this example is known as the *complement* of the condition in Example 8.1. This can be shown with the number line in Figure 8.4.

The condition **GRADE < 0 OR GRADE > 100** isolates all numbers to the left of 0 and to the right of 100, but not including either number.

On the other hand, the condition **GRADE > = 0 AND GRADE < = 100** isolates all those numbers between 0 and 100 inclusively (see Figure 8.5).

The numbers 0 and 100 are called the **boundary values**. In designing conditional branches, the programmer must ensure that the boundary values are tested as well as one number from each side of the boundary values, or errors are likely to "sneak through." For instance, if only values on either side of the boundary values are tried, then the following erroneous program would have been passed as valid:

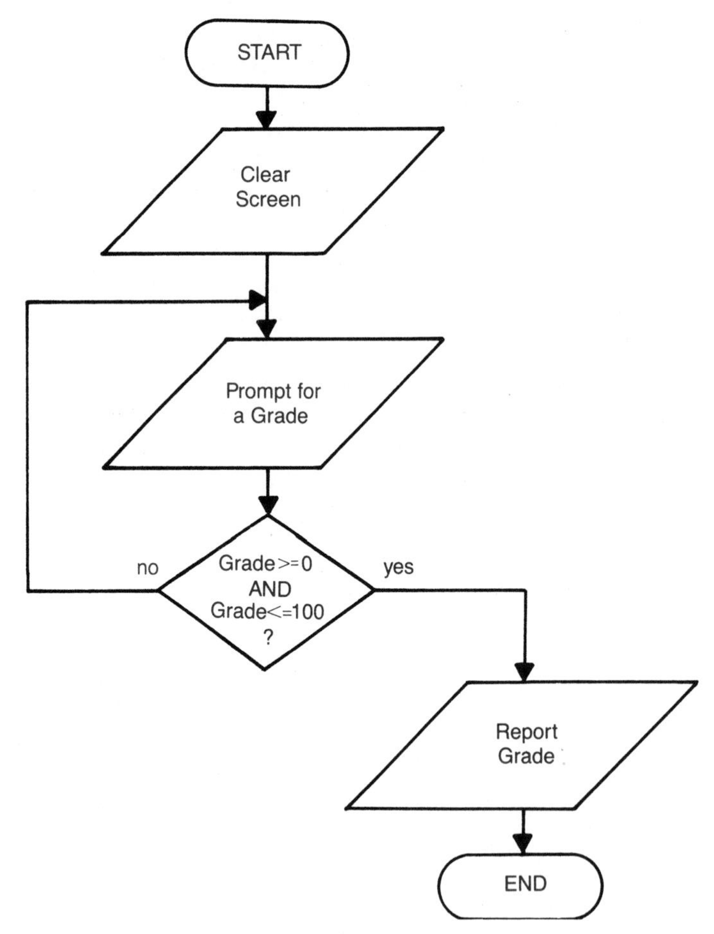

FIGURE 8.3

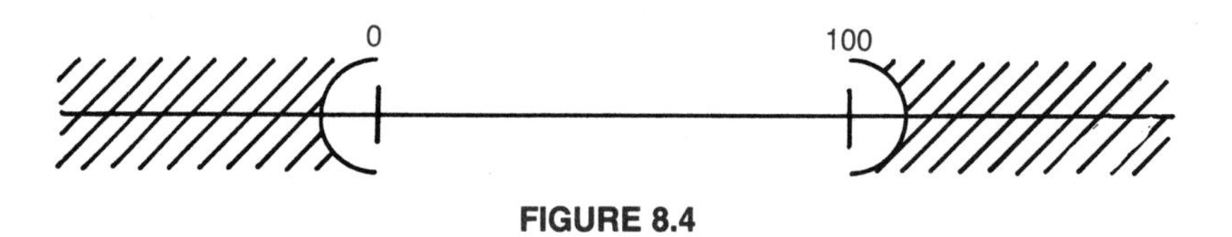

FIGURE 8.4

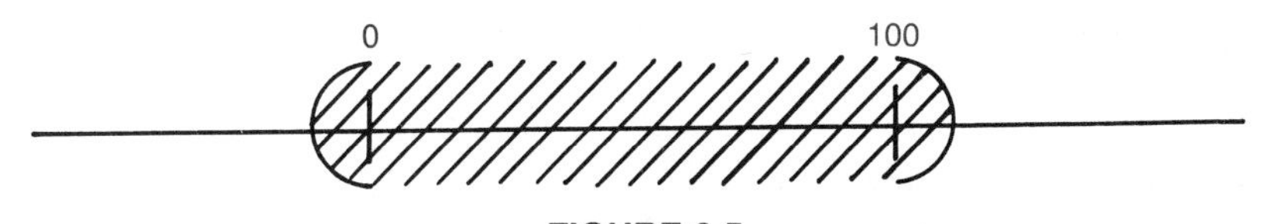

FIGURE 8.5

```
10 'AND
20 '
30 CLS
40 INPUT "Enter grade : ", GRADE
50 IF GRADE > 0 AND GRADE < 100 THEN PRINT GRADE ELSE 40
60 END
```

RUN this example program and enter the numbers 0 and 100.

The logical operator **NOT** takes on one component condition. What **NOT** does is reverse the status of the component condition. Its use is illustrated in Example 8.3.

Example 8.3

In the zeal of programming, the programmer made an error in constructing a condition: The reverse sense of what was sought was actually implemented and discovered during program testing. All numbers that should have been rejected were accepted instead:

```
10 'AND
20 '
30 CLS
40 INPUT "Enter grade : ", GRADE
50 IF GRADE >= 0 AND GRADE <= 100 THEN 40
60 END
```

To reverse the sense of the condition, all that needs to be done is place the **NOT** operator in front of the condition.

Example 8.4

```
10 'NOT
20 '
30 CLS
40 INPUT "Enter grade : ", GRADE
50 IF NOT ( GRADE >= 0 AND GRADE <= 100 ) THEN 40
60 END
```

Notice that, in applying the **NOT** logical operator, the programmer should use parentheses to surround the complex component condition. This is because, according to the order of precedence, BASIC evaluates **NOT** before **AND** and **OR**. Thus, the condition:

```
NOT GRADE >= 0 AND GRADE <= 100
```

will not produce the desired status, because **NOT GRADE >= 0** is evaluated first instead of **GRADE >=0 AND GRADE <= 100.**

If a complex condition becomes too difficult to assess directly, its status can always be ascertained through successive analyses of its components. For example, assuming that:

A = 100
B = 50
C = −50
D = −100

then the condition:

```
NOT ( A > 20 OR ( B > 100 AND NOT C < 50 ) AND D = -50 )
```

can be analyzed as shown in Figure 8.6.

Exercise Set 8.1 Logical operators, number lines, complex logical condition reduction

A. Write conditions for the following darkened areas of the number lines:

1.

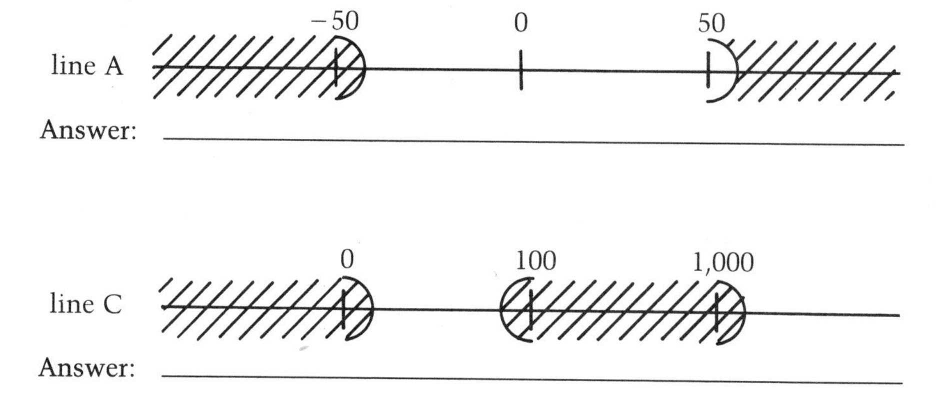

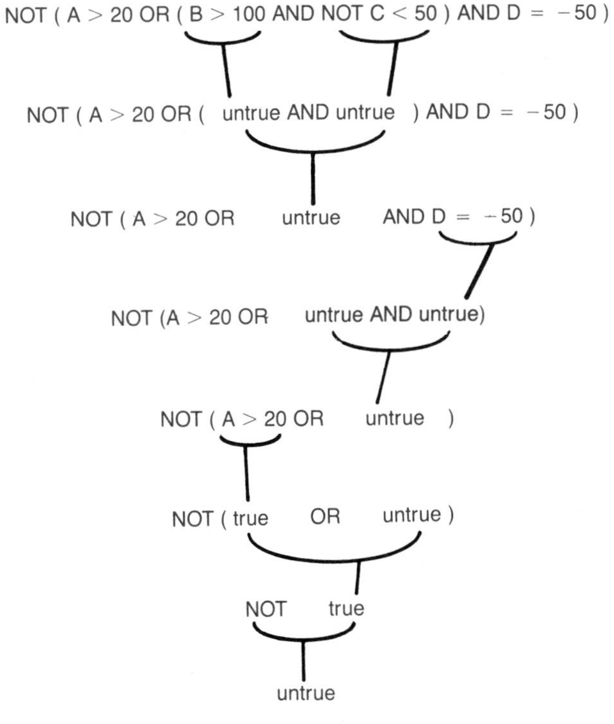

NOT (A > 20 OR (B > 100 AND NOT C < 50) AND D = −50)
NOT (A > 20 OR (untrue AND untrue) AND D = −50)
NOT (A > 20 OR untrue AND D = −50)
NOT (A > 20 OR untrue AND untrue)
NOT (A > 20 OR untrue)
NOT (true OR untrue)
NOT true
untrue

FIGURE 8.6

2.

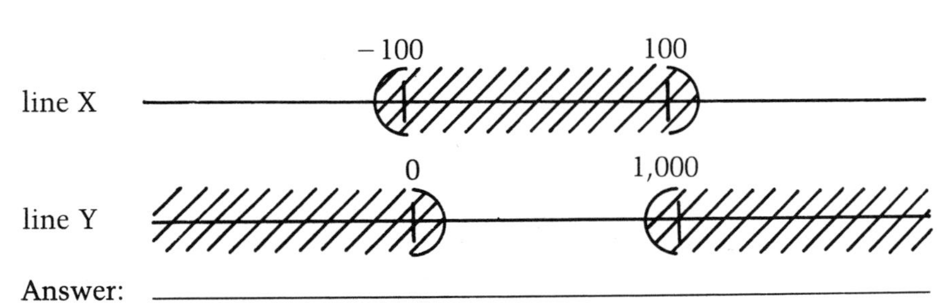

Answer: ____________________

B. Assess the true/false statuses of the following conditions:

3. For A = 50, B = 100, C = 200, D = 300
   a. NOT A < 75 OR B > 75 AND C − D <> 80 OR A * D > 100

Answer: ____________________

b. NOT (B + C >=D OR A − D <= C AND B / A <> 20)

Answer: ______________________________

IF/THEN/ELSE **PROGRAMMING PROCEDURES**

In programming, one does not prepare a program for a preconceived type of coding implementation. When confronted by a problem, a programmer should not ask: Now let me see how I can work an **IF/THEN/ELSE** into this. Program codes are designed to implement problem solution logic; hence the logic (that is, the flowchart) must first exist, and then the appropriate coding constructions are selected to express the logic. The flowchart-to-code transcription process is achieved scientifically; it is not arbitrary. In this section, the techniques of logic branching transcription are explored.

First of all, due to the code structure of **IF/THEN**, all efforts should be made during flowcharting to keep the no arrow pointing downward and to maintain the yes arrow as the branch. (How this can be accomplished is discussed below.) The flowchart and coding relationship for the **IF** statement transcription is shown in Figure 8.7.

For logical choices—because the two consequences of the decision are of equal logical standing—the two outward-pointing arrows should emerge from the diamond horizontally, as shown in Figure 8.8.

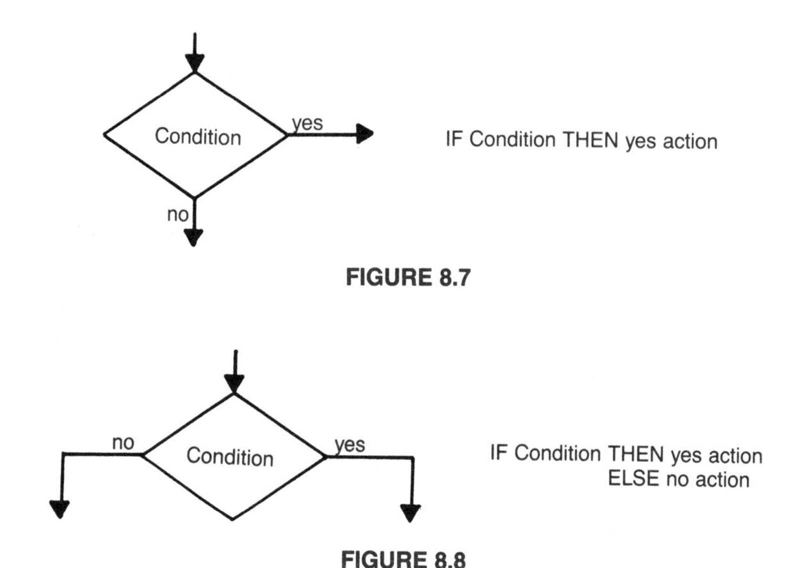

FIGURE 8.7

FIGURE 8.8

In expressing the logic in flowchart form during problem analysis, however, do not worry about the placement of the yes and no arrows initially. Design freely, and if the resulting yes and no branches are misplaced, they can be corrected easily, as demonstrated in Example 8.5.

Example 8.5

Suppose, in guarding against input grades below 0, you have arrived at the flowchart in Figure 8.9. There are two ways to reverse the yes and no designations:

1. Redraw the flowchart arrows.
2. Reverse the yes and no designation by reversing the condition.

For the second option, you may redesign the condition, such as making the condition Grade >=0, or, more simply, by preceding the existing condition with the **NOT** operator, as demonstrated in Example 8.4. The use of the **NOT** operator is straightforward and in general does not introduce secondary errors, as a reconstruction of the primary condition might (for example, by arriving at Grade > 0 instead of Grade >= 0). The **NOT** operator is particularly useful for reversing complex conditions.

The corrected flowchart, then, is shown in Figure 8.10.

In designing flowcharts involving decisions, do not struggle to come up with complex logical conditions involving **AND** and **OR**. Complex logical conditions can be "engineered."

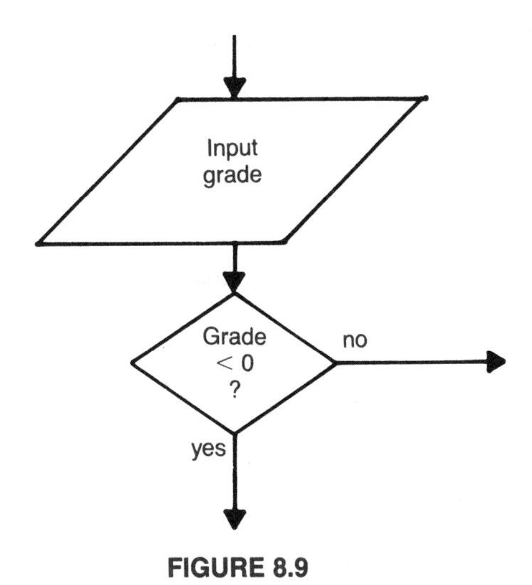

FIGURE 8.9

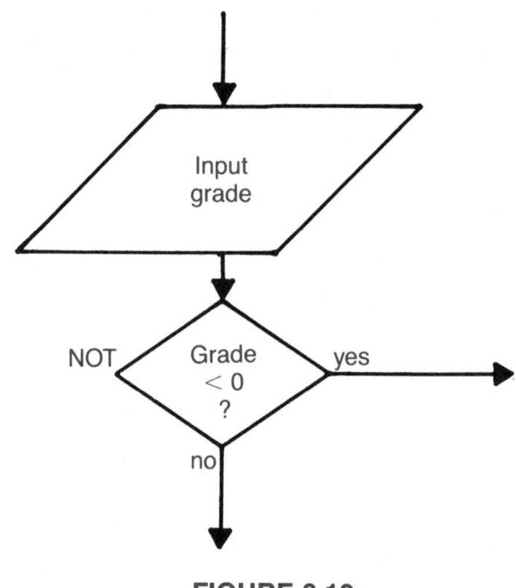

FIGURE 8.10

Again using the grade segregation problem as an example, suppose the flowchart in Figure 8.11 is constructed.

When two diamonds are arranged:

1. In a series vertically (with the no arrows pointing downward) and
2. The two true paths are joined

then the two diamonds are combined to form a logical **OR** diamond (see Figure 8.12), and the code transcription becomes simply:

```
IF G < 0 OR G > 100 THEN
```

When the flowchart shows two diamonds:

1. In a series horizontally (with the no arrows pointing downward) and
2. With joining false paths

then the two diamonds are combined to form a single **AND** diamond (see Figure 8.13).

As long as the basic requirements are met, the flowchart reduction schemes can be applied to more than two diamonds: Every two diamonds are combined to form one resulting diamond, and then the resulting diamond is combined with the neighboring diamond to further reduce the flowchart.

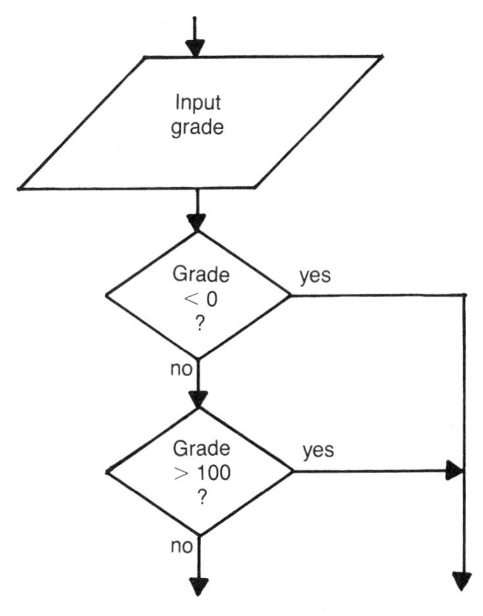

FIGURE 8.11

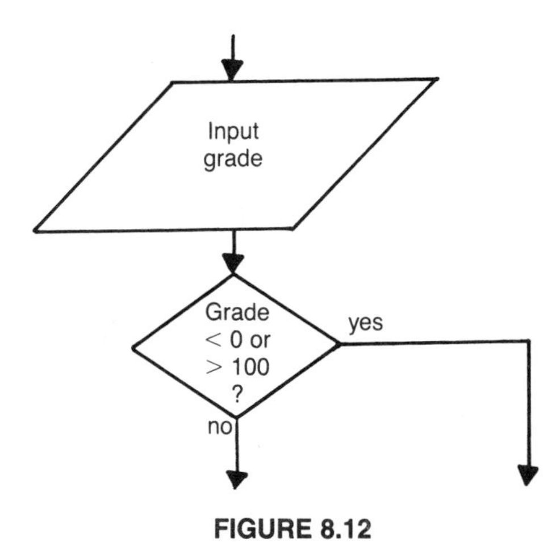

FIGURE 8.12

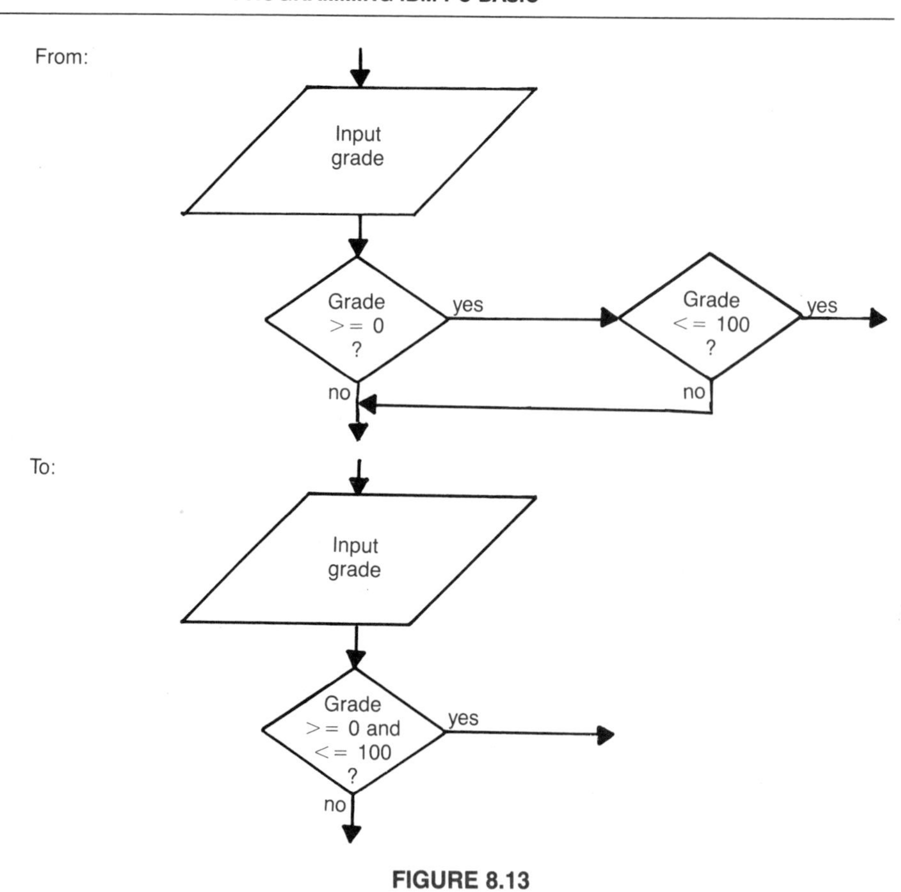

FIGURE 8.13

Exercise Set 8.2 Logical operator reduction

Redesign the following flowcharts so that they become transcribable:

1. (See Figure 8.14.)
2. (See Figure 8.15.)
3. (See Figure 8.16.)

When all of the above flowcharting techniques have been used, then the flowchart is transcribed according to the main flow of the logic. That is to say, each "box" along the main flow of the flowchart will become one BASIC statement, and the resultant coding will have as many statements as there are boxes along the main flow of the flowchart. Stated in

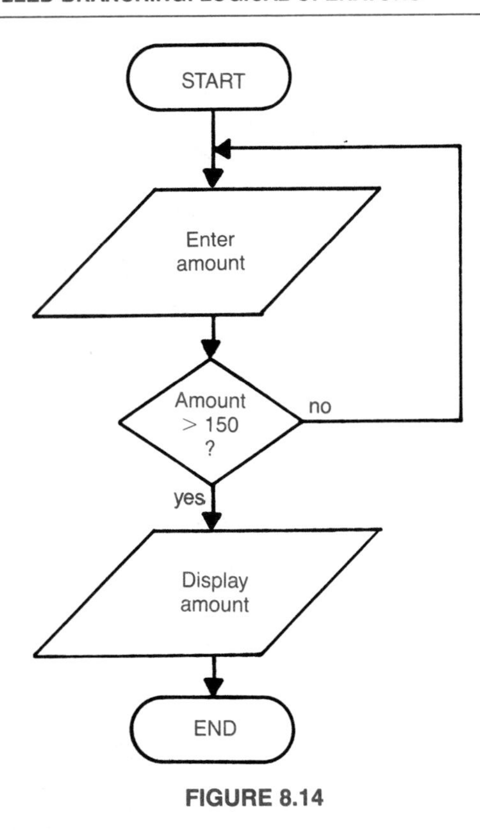

FIGURE 8.14

another way, this means branch boxes will not become distinct program statements. An example of flowchart transcription is illustrated in Figure 8.17.

The following "transcription," on the other hand, is spaghetti code:

```
10 INPUT S
20 IF S < 65 THEN 40
30 GOTO 50
40 LET S = S * 0.95
50 PRINT S
60 END
```

Occasionally flowchart transcription does run into trouble. This is the case either when the branch logic is more complicated than the main logic or when both are equally complex, as in Figure 8.18.

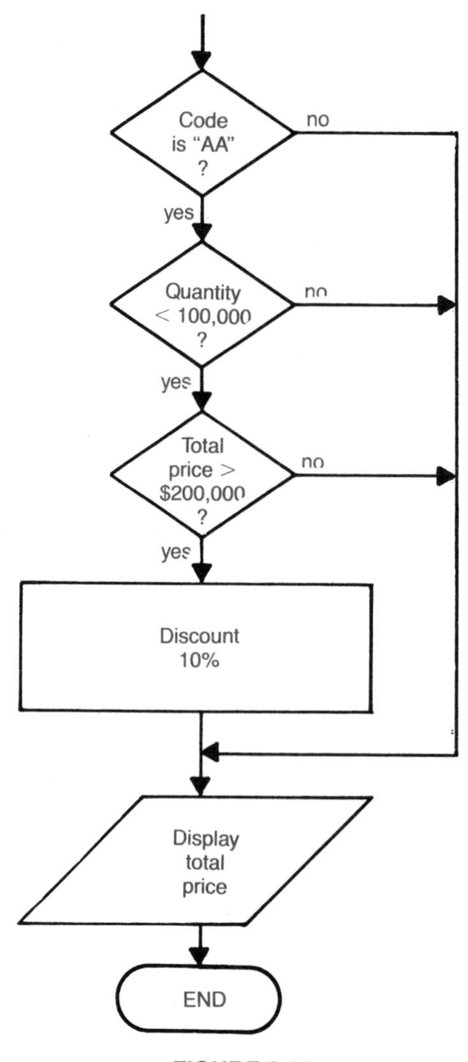

FIGURE 8.15

For the first case, where the branch activities are more complex than the main flow, the flowchart may be redrawn with the branch as the main flow. The result is that the yes and no arrows will have switched places. But this can easily be corrected.

If both logical paths are equally complicated, then the modular programming technique presented in chapter 11 may be used.

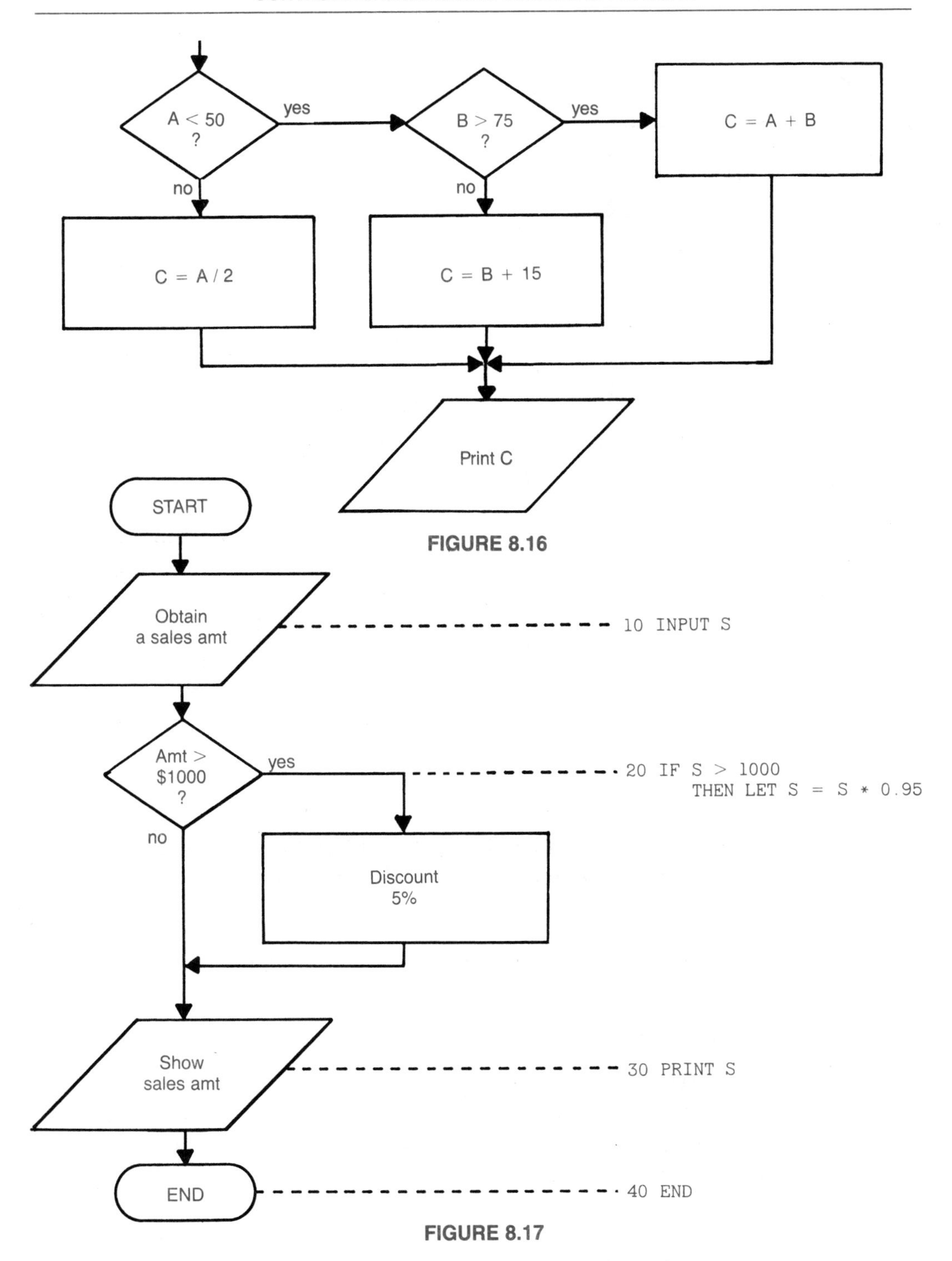

FIGURE 8.16

FIGURE 8.17

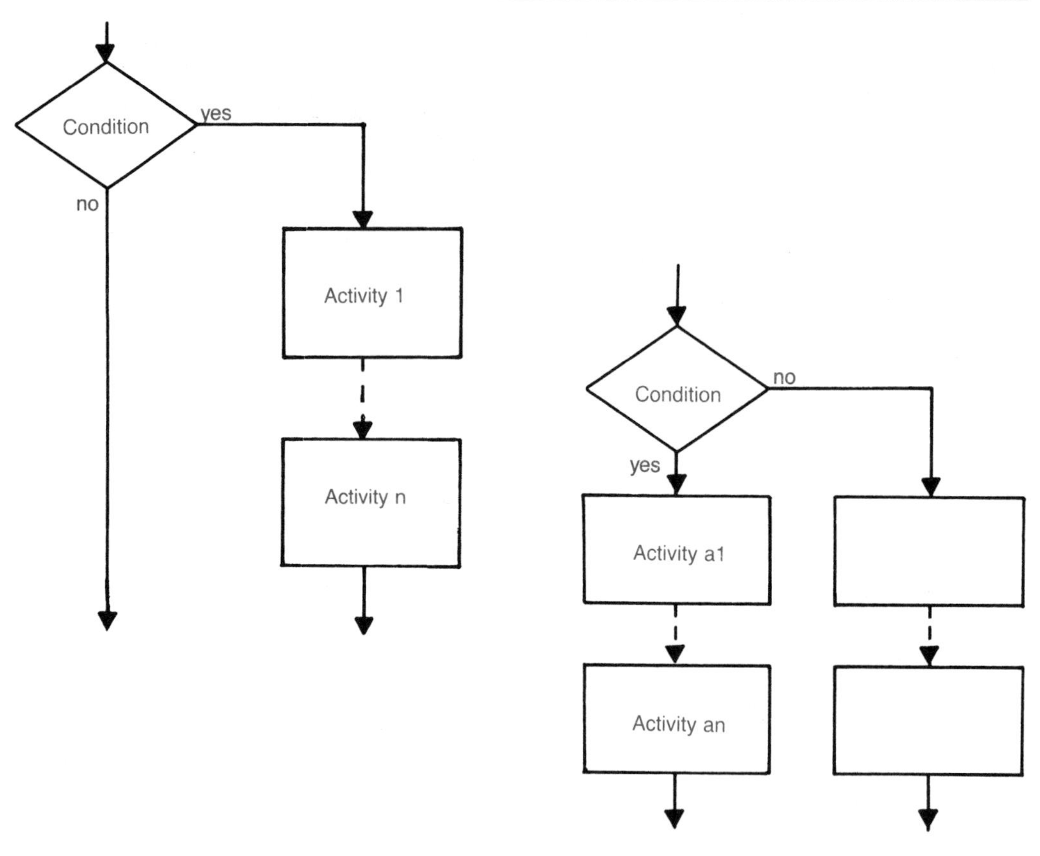

FIGURE 8.18

Chapter Exercises (Using **PRINT**. **CLS**. **END**. **LET**. functions, **DEF FN**. **INPUT**. **FOR/NEXT**. **WHILE/WEND**. **IF/THEN/ELSE**. logical operators)

1. A meat-processing company has the following requirements for the beef it can use:

	Fat	*Gristle*
Type 1	< 15%	< 30%
Type 2	>= 15% to < 30%	>= 15% to <= 25%
Type 3	>= 30% to < 50%	< 15%

2. Design a program to find out what percentages of workers worked up to ten, more than ten up to twenty, more than twenty up to thirty, and more than thirty hours of overtime during a forty-hour week. (Not all workers work overtime.)
3. During a preelection poll, the potential voter parameters tallied are: sex, age, income, and party to vote for. Design a program to project the voter breakdowns and report the results in the following form:

	Democratic	*Republican*
Male	%	%
Female	%	%
50 and below	%	%
Above 50	%	%
Income above $25,000/year	%	%
Income $25,000 and below	%	%
Others	%	%

9 / ASSIGNING QUANTITIES OF DATA

So far we have learned two methods through which data can be assigned to variables: the **LET** statement, designed for the programmer, and the **INPUT** statement, intended for data entry at the keyboard. Multiple data items can be assigned through **INPUT**, but the **LET** statement is restricted to assigning one data item at a time. This restriction is not without reason. **LET** has a dual function: Besides assigning data, it is also employed in arithmetic operations. Arithmetic operations produce single results. For data assignment purposes, **LET** therefore is not the most efficient means. To assign quantities of data, the programmer should resort to the **READ/DATA** statements.

READ/DATA

Let us begin by studying an example.

Example 9.1

```
10 'READ/DATA 1
20 '
30 READ A, B, C, D
40 DATA 10, 200, 35, 87
50 PRINT A, B, C, D
60 END
```

If you **RUN** this program, you will see the display:

```
10              200             35              87
```

as if the results were produced by:

```
10 LET A = 10
20 LET B = 200
30 LET C = 35
40 LET D = 87
50 PRINT A, B, C, D
```

The **READ** statement lists the variables, while the **DATA** statement lists the data to be assigned to the **READ** variables. The **READ/DATA** statements are cooperative statements similar to the **FOR/NEXT** and **WHILE/WEND** statements. In a BASIC program, **READ** statements cannot exist without accompanying **DATA** statements.

In the **READ/DATA** statement pair, as is obvious from the example, the first data item in the **DATA** statement is assigned to the first variable in the **READ** statement, the second data item to the second variable, and so on. As with all other forms of data assignment, the data types of the corresponding variable and data items must agree.

The primary efficiency of the **READ/DATA** statement is gained through the compact form of the statements. As with **INPUT**, multiple variables and data can be listed in the same statements, and the comma is the delimiter used to separate variables and data items.

Unlike **LET**, however, between **READ** and **DATA** there is no direct one-to-one correspondence between the variables and the data, although Example 9.1 seems to give the impression that the variables and the data must always match up perfectly. In processing the **READ** and **DATA** statements, BASIC is concerned only that the variables in the **READ** statement get their data. The fact that there may be more data than needed by the variables is not detrimental to program execution. Example 9.2 illustrates this point.

Example 9.2

```
10 'TOO MANY DATA
20 '
30 READ A, B, C, D
40 DATA 10, 200, 35, 87, -33, 64
50 PRINT A, B, C, D
60 END
```

When this program is **RUN**, the same four numbers as in Example 9.1 are displayed. The extra −33 and 64 are not used by BASIC.

```
 10              200             35              87
```

However, BASIC does object if there are not enough data for the requesting variables, as demonstrated in Example 9.3, where only two data items are provided for four requesting variables.

Example 9.3

```
10 'Out of DATA
20 '
30 READ A, B, C, D
40 DATA 10, 200
50 PRINT A, B, C, D
60 END

RUN

Out of DATA in 30
```

The **Out of DATA in 30** error message will be triggered to indicate that in statement 30 some variables were not assigned data.

Also unlike **LET**, the variables are not tied to the data items rigidly. BASIC will assign data to whatever variable happens to be requesting the data. For instance, the same variable can request data many times. Example 9.4 shows that a variable is made to request data four times as controlled by a loop.

Example 9.4

```
10 'READ BY REQUEST
20 '
30 FOR C% = 1 TO 4
40   READ A
50   PRINT A
60 NEXT C%
70 DATA 10, 200, 35, 87
80 END
```

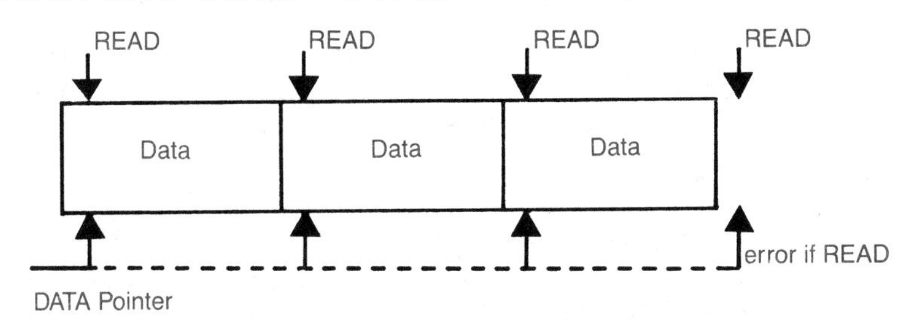

FIGURE 9.1

DATA items are managed by BASIC sequentially. Although there may be more than one **DATA** statement in a program, as far as BASIC is concerned, there is but one **DATA** item list, with the list order dictated by the sequential appearance of the data items presented in the **DATA** statements. The data items in this list are then assigned to the variables according to the sequence of request.

To understand this, you must realize that BASIC maintains an internal **DATA** counter that always points to the next unassigned data item. Each time a data item has been assigned, this pointer is adjusted so that the same data item is not assigned again. Thus, BASIC does not count the number of **READ** variables, nor does it count the number of **DATA** items. It merely resets the data pointer and triggers the **Out of DATA** error message when a **READ** request is encountered with the pointer pointing beyond the **DATA** list (see Figure 9.1).

Example 9.5 shows that two **READ** statements with two variables each will be assigned the four data items held in one **DATA** statement.

Example 9.5

```
10 'READ IN SEQUENCE, NOT MATCHING FORM
20 '
30 READ A, B
40 READ C, D
50 DATA 10, 200, 35, 87
60 PRINT A, B, C, D
70 END
```

The display is again:

```
 10             200            35             87
```

This is because BASIC assigns data according to the sequence of **READ** requests. After 10 and 200 have been assigned to variables **A** and **B**, the internal **DATA** pointer is pointing at 35, the third data item in the **DATA** list. When **READ C** is reached, 35 is assigned.

In Example 9.6, although there are two **DATA** statements, each listing two data items, internally BASIC sees only one **DATA** list: 10, 200, 35, 87. This internal list is based on the order of data appearance in the program text. If statement 50 had been entered in the program text before statement 40, then the internal **DATA** list would have been: 35, 87, 10, 200.

Consequently, Example 9.6 also produces the display:

```
 10              200             35              87
```

Example 9.6

```
10 'READ IN SEQUENCE, NOT MATCHING FORM
20 '
30 READ A, B, C, D
40 DATA 10, 200
50 DATA 35, 87
60 PRINT A, B, C, D
70 END
```

It must be pointed out that **DATA** statements are not executed. A **DATA** statement is a typical nonexecutable BASIC statement. In other words, the **DATA** statement does not do anything, as do **LET**, **PRINT**, and **INPUT**. Consequently, Examples 9.7 and 9.8 express exactly the same logic as in the previous examples. This means that the **DATA** statements can be placed anywhere in the program, as long as the order of appearance of the data items is maintained. Notice in Example 9.8 that the **DATA** statement is actually after the **END** statement. But this does not matter, as **END** only terminates the program logic execution and has no effect on a nonexecutable statement such as **DATA**.

Example 9.7

```
10 'DATA NOT LOGIC
20 '
30 DATA 10, 200, 35, 87
40 READ A, B, C, D
50 PRINT A, B, C, D
60 END
```

Example 9.8

```
10 'DATA NOT LOGIC
20 '
30 READ A, B, C, D
40 PRINT A, B, C, D
50 END
60 DATA 10, 200, 35, 87
```

The fact that **DATA** is not a logic statement also implies that it is not represented as logic in the flowchart, which documents the program logic. The flowchart symbol for **READ** is the same as for **LET**: the rectangle. (In FORTRAN, a high-level language invented before BASIC, the same keyword **READ** is used to denote data inputting and is represented by the input symbol. This habit has often been carried into BASIC, which is erroneous. In BASIC, **READ** does not obtain data from an input device.)

Examples 9.7 and 9.8 (and all the previous quadruple **READ** examples) are thus flowcharted with the data shown as annotations (see Figure 9.2).

Because the **DATA** statements can only hold constants, string data will not be recognized as variables. Therefore, all string data will be treated as literals. In fact, string data should be expressed as literals, as shown in Example 9.9.

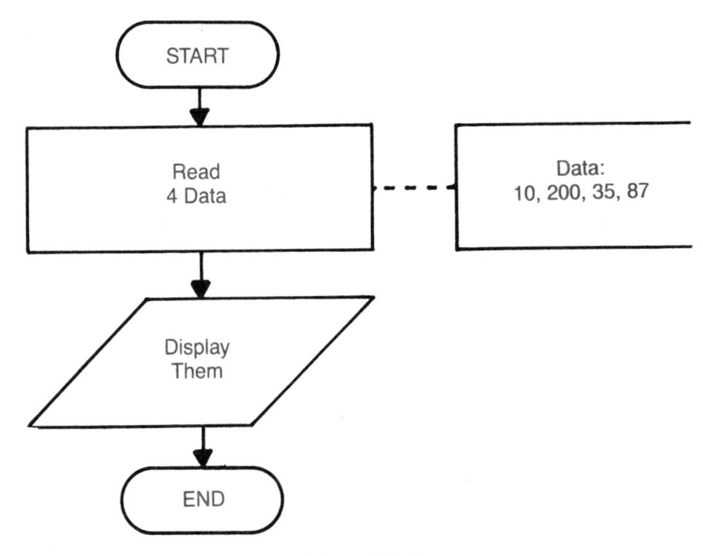

FIGURE 9.2

Example 9.9

```
10 'STRING DATA
20 '
30 READ A$, B$
40 PRINT A$, B$
50 END
60 DATA "JAMES", "BARBARA"
```

which displays:

```
JAMES          BARBARA
```

But since there is no confusion with other variables, Example 9.10 is also acceptable.

Example 9.10

```
10 'STRING DATA
20 '
30 READ A$, B$
40 PRINT A$, B$
50 END
60 DATA JAMES, BARBARA
```

producing on the CRT:

```
JAMES          BARBARA
```

The drawback with not using the double quotation marks is that blank characters will not be included during the data assignment. For such data specifications without the quotation marks, BASIC looks to the first nonblank character of the data item as the start of the data. Example 9.11 will include the blank characters as parts of the data.

Example 9.11

```
10 'STRING DATA
20 '
30 READ A$, B$
40 PRINT A$, B$
50 END
60 DATA "     JAMES", "BARBARA"
```

displaying:

```
    JAMES     BARBARA
```

Example 9.12, on the other hand, displays:

```
JAMES         BARBARA
```

despite the apparent leading blanks in the **DATA** statement.

Example 9.12

```
10 'STRING DATA
20 '
30 READ A$, B$
40 PRINT A$, B$
50 END
60 DATA      JAMES,      BARBARA
```

Variables and data can be mixed in the same **READ** and **DATA** statements, as long as requesting variables and the data to be assigned are of the same data types.

In summary:

READ
Form: READ variable[, variable list]
Function: To request data from the DATA statement(s) to be assigned to the variable(s).

DATA
Form: DATA data[, data list]
Function: To provide data for requesting READ statement variables.

READ APPLICATIONS

The use of the **READ/DATA** statements is at its most efficient when executed in conjunction with the loop. (How the **READ/DATA** structure is best used to assign large amounts of data to lists and tables will be discussed in chapter 10.) In this section, some of the special data processing effects that can be achieved with the **READ/DATA** statements are examined.

Example 9.13

In this example, a loop is employed to display a list of data through one variable, thus saving the extra memory storage that normally would be spent if the **LET** statement were used.

```
10 'READ/DATA DESIGNED FOR LOOPING
20 '
30 CLS
40 FOR C% = 1 TO 5
50 READ A$
60 PRINT A$,
70 NEXT C%
80 END
90 DATA "Adam", "Bill", "Cindy", "David", "Evelyn"
```

As each loop passes, a new name from statement 90 is assigned to variable **A$** and is promptly displayed:

```
Adam          Bill          Cindy          David          Evelyn
```

Be aware, however, that only one data item is stored in the computer memory area at the end of the program—namely, "**Evelyn**", the last item assigned to **A$**. The first four names are not kept as stored data. They are continuously replaced as the program is **RUN**.

Example 9.14

In this example, the names in the DATA statement represent a student roster, established by the programmer teacher in a preset order. The position of the student name in the list is used as the student identification number. A user may therefore use this identification number to determine a student name.

Because there are only five names, only identification numbers from 1 to 5 are acceptable to the program. Statement 50 guards against all inputs other than these five numbers. The accepted input number is then used by the program to control a **FOR/NEXT** loop. The flowchart for this program is shown in Figure 9.3.

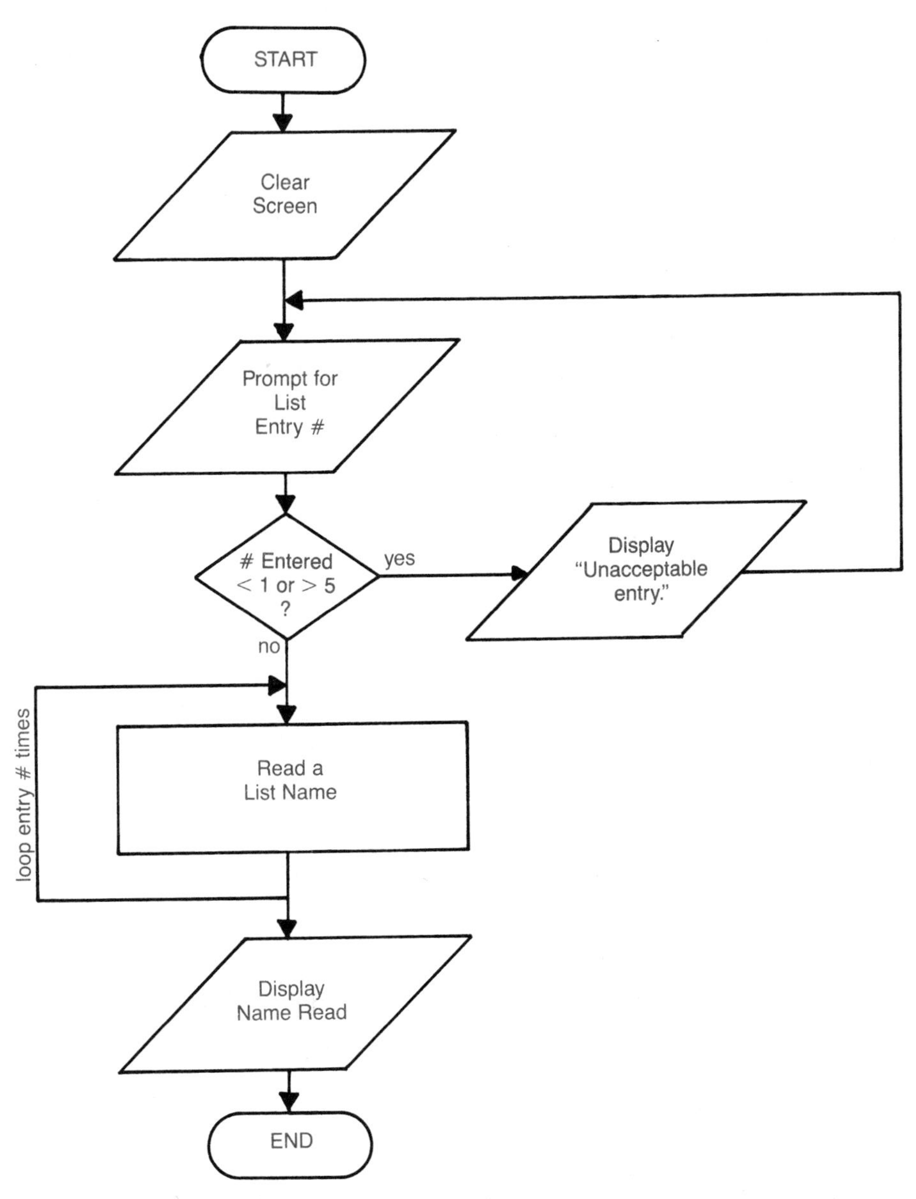

FIGURE 9.3

```
10 'NAME SELECTION
20 '
30 CLS
40 INPUT "Enter student number (1 TO 5): ", N%
50 IF N% < 1 OR N% > 5 THEN PRINT "Unacceptable entry."
   : GOTO 40
60 FOR C% = 1 TO N%
70   READ A$
80 NEXT C%
90 PRINT A$
100 END
110 DATA "Adam", "Bill", "Cindy", "David", "Evelyn"
```

RUN the program to observe the effect.

Example 9.15

In this example, the user inputs a student name and the program responds with the corresponding identification number. The program is set to **READ** all five names through a **FOR/NEXT** loop, but it exits the loop when the roster name matches that of the input. If none of the names **READ** is the same as the input, then the program concludes that the input name is not on the list. Figure 9.4 shows the flowchart.

```
10 'STUDENT IDENTIFICATION
20 '
30 CLS
40 INPUT "Enter student name to be located : ", N$
50 FOR C% = 1 TO 5
60 READ A$
70 IF A$ = N$ THEN PRINT N$; " is I.D. number"; C% :
   GOTO 100
80 NEXT C%
90 PRINT N$; " not found."
100 END
110 DATA "Adam", "Bill", "Cindy", "David", "Evelyn"
```

Exercise Set 9.1 READ/DATA (Using **PRINT, CLS, END, LET,** functions, **DEF FN, INPUT, FOR/NEXT, WHILE/WEND, IF/THEN/ELSE,** logical operators, **READ/DATA**)

A. Correct the errors, if any, in the following programs:

1.

```
10 FOR C% = 1 TO 5
20 READ A$
```

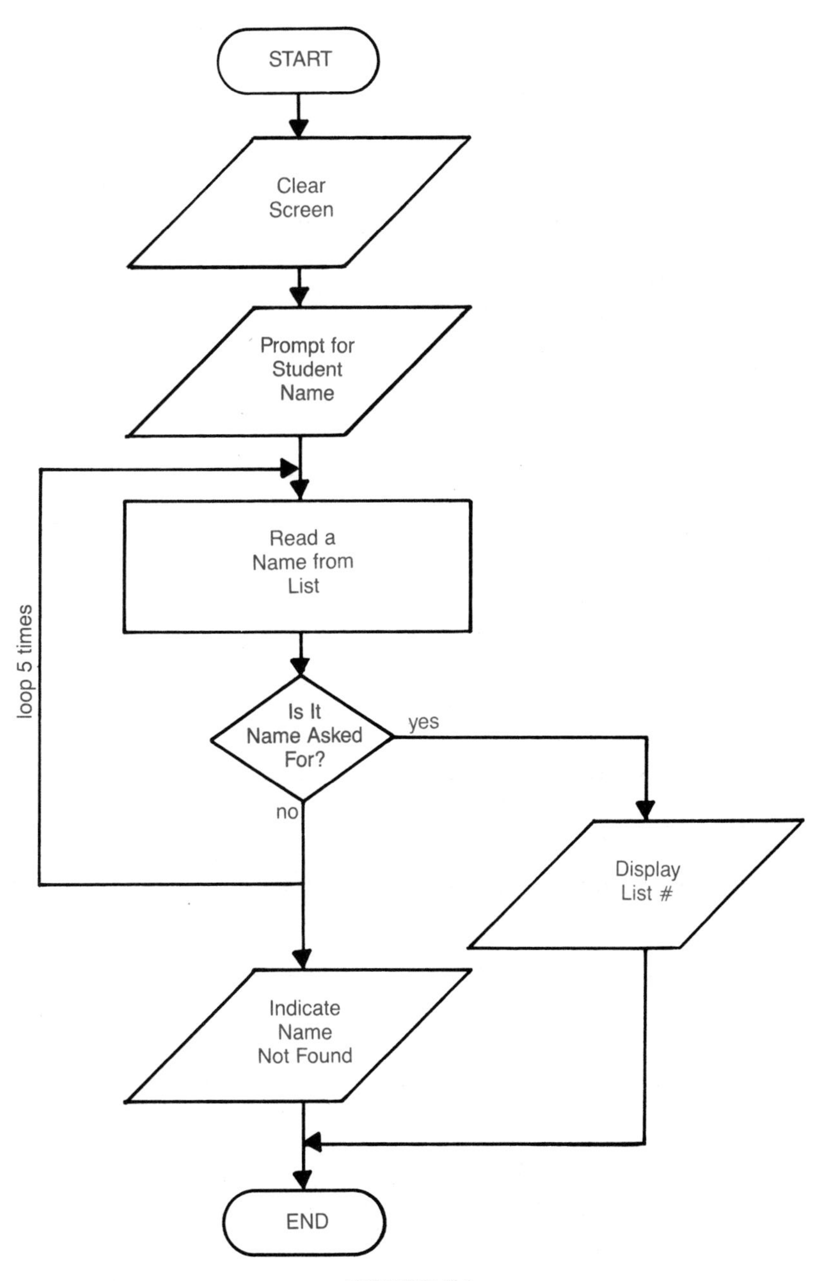
START
Clear
Screen
Prompt for
Student
Name
Read a
Name from
List
loop 5 times
Is It
Name Asked
For?
yes
no
Display
List #
Indicate
Name
Not Found
END

FIGURE 9.4

```
30 PRINT A$
40 NEXT C%
50 END
```

Answer: ______________________________

____

2.

```
30 READ X$, Y$
40 PRINT X$, Y$
50 END
60 DATA "Item 1, Item 2
```

Answer: ______________________________

____

3.

```
10 READ A, B, C
20 PRINT A, B, C
30 END
40 DATA 50, 60, A - B
```

Answer: ______________________________

____

B. What does the following program do?

4.

```
10 INPUT "Enter choice : ", C
20 FOR I = 1 TO C
30   READ A
40 NEXT I
50 PRINT A
60 END
70 DATA 1, 2, 3, 4, 5, 6, 7, 8, 9, 10
```

Also, what is wrong with it? How would you correct it?

Answer: ______________________________

____

____

C. Flowcharting and code transcription:

5. Design a program to assign the data "banana", "apple", and "grape" to appropriate variables and display them in a column.
6. Design a program to assign the data "Length", "Elasticity", "Yield point", and "Break point" to appropriate variables, then use them as prompts to help a user enter associated data.

RESTORE

The internal **DATA** pointer maintained by BASIC normally resets only in the forward direction. However, it can be reset to the beginning of the **DATA** list if required. This is known as ***DATA** pointer reinitialization,* and it is an internal BASIC function accomplished through the **RESTORE** statement.

The **RESTORE** statement, like the **END** statement, is a single-keyword statement. When issued, **RESTORE** restores the internal **DATA** pointer to the beginning of the **DATA** list, and all the data can be assigned anew.

Example 9.16

```
10 'RESTORE
20 '
30 READ A, B, C
40 RESTORE
50 READ D, E, F
60 PRINT A, B, C, D, E, F
70 END
80 DATA 1, 2, 3, 4, 5, 6
```

Statement 30 assigns the first three **DATA** items to the variables **A**, **B**, and **C**. If the data **READ**ing were permitted to continue, then the last three items would have been assigned to variables **D**, **E**, and **F**. But because the **RESTORE** statement is issued, the internal **DATA** pointer is reinitialized to the start of the **DATA** list. Thus, when the variables **D**, **E**, and **F** are **READ**, the first three **DATA** items are reassigned, resulting in the program displaying:

```
1             2             3             1             2
3
```

The last three **DATA** items will not be assigned.

RESTORE does not directly affect the application logic. It invokes a systems function internal to BASIC. What it does is to reset an internal system housekeeping counter. The flowchart symbol for **RESTORE** is therefore the system setup symbol (see Figure 9.5).

Example 9.16 is thus flowcharted as shown in Figure 9.6.

When is **RESTORE** used? Obviously, when there is a need to start the **DATA** list over again. This need usually arises when the program logic involving the **READ**ing of the **DATA** list is repeated, as illustrated in Example 9.17.

Example 9.17

If the program in Example 9.15 is to be executed more than one time, then each time the **DATA** list must begin at the beginning, and **RESTORE** must be used to reset the **DATA** pointer at the start of every new search except the first.

```
10 'STUDENT IDENTIFICATION
20 '
30 CLS
40 INPUT "Enter student name to be located : ", N$
50 FOR C% = 1 TO 5
60   READ A$
70   IF A$ = N$ THEN PRINT N$; " student I.D. is"; C% :
     GOTO 100
80 NEXT C%
90 PRINT N$; " not found."
100 PRINT
110 PRINT
120 INPUT "Retry? (y/n) : ", REPLY$
130 IF REPLY$ = "y" THEN RESTORE : GOTO 30
140 END
150 DATA "Adam", "Bill", "Cindy", "David", "Evelyn"
```

Exercise Set 9.2 RESTORE, find data, nested loop (Using **PRINT**, **CLS**, **END**, **LET**, functions, **DEF FN**, **INPUT**, **FOR/NEXT**, **WHILE/WEND**, **IF/THEN/ELSE**, logical operators, **READ/DATA**, **RESTORE**)

A. Correct the errors, if any, in the following programs:

1.

```
10 FOR X% = 1 TO 3
20   READ A, B, C
```

FIGURE 9.5

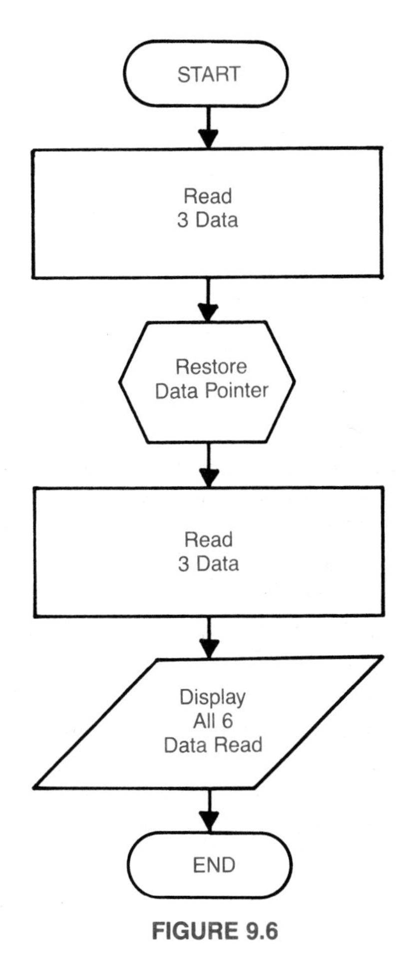

FIGURE 9.6

```
30   PRINT A, B, C
40 NEXT X%
50 END
60 DATA 12.66, 37.5, 8
```

Answer: ________________________________

____

2.

```
10 FOR C% = 1 TO 4
20   RESTORE
30   READ A, B, C
40 NEXT C%
50 READ D
60 END
70 DATA 12.66, 7.53, 8.99, 4
```

Answer: ________________________________

____

B. Flowcharting and code transcription:

3. Design a program to help an engineer log in material properties. The program should show a property on the CRT, and the engineer should enter "Y" to indicate the existence of such a property in the material. The property list is: electrical conductance, heat resistance, vibration dampening, and solubility. The program should be designed to run continuously all day so as to accommodate the logging of new materials tested.
4. Modify the preceding problem so that the engineer can indicate the associated measurements for each item in addition to the existence of the properties. Negative-number entries are not permissible. If an entry is erroneously made, the engineer can redo the particular data item entry by entering the number −999.

DATA STRUCTURE

Data are normally set up for a particular use, so their arrangement not only should facilitate the data assignment process but should also reflect the data structure for good documentation purposes. For instance, a data list can be arranged linearly as one continuous **DATA** statement or structured into multiple **DATA** statements. BASIC's data assignment operation is not affected by either arrangement. However, if the data exist logically as groups, then a linear continuous **DATA** statement does not readily reflect their logical structure. Example 9.18 illustrates this point.

Example 9.18

In this example, three sets of name/address/phone data are to be displayed. A loop is constructed in which three string variables are used to **READ** a data set. The data could be arranged as:

```
110 DATA "ABC Cleaning", "Downtown", "777-2626", "Joe's Food",
"Hillside", "256-8950", "Ava's", "Towers", "Unlisted"
```

or if a screen wraparound is to be avoided:

```
110 DATA "ABC Cleaning", "Downtown", "777-2626", "Joe's Food"
120 DATA "Hillside", "256-8950", "Ava's", "Towers", "Unlisted"
```

In either case, the three data sets each made up of three data items are not clearly represented. It is better to keep the three data sets in individual **DATA** statements:

```
10 'DATA STRUCTURE
20 '
30 CLS
40 PRINT "Name", "Address", "Phone"
50 PRINT
60 FOR C% = 1 TO 3
70     READ A$, B$, C$
80     PRINT A$, B$, C$
90 NEXT C%
100 END
110 DATA "ABC Cleaning", "Downtown", "777-2626"
120 DATA "Joe's Food", "Hillside", "256-8950"
130 DATA "Ava's", "Towers", "Unlisted"
```

As mentioned before, **DATA** statements can be placed anywhere in the program. Obviously, there is no reason to scatter them all over the program unless the purpose is specifically to make the program code difficult to follow. **DATA** statements, therefore, are usually placed at the very beginning of the program text, immediately following the **READ** statement(s), or at the end of the program text. Each placement preference has its logical justifications.

If the data are intimately associated with the **READ** statement variables and are never or very seldom changed, then the **READ** and **DATA** statements should be located as close to each other as possible.

If the data are closely associated with the **READ** variables but are likely to change, then they should be placed at the beginning or end of the program text for easy location purposes.

For example, the following mathematical equation is to be solved through a BASIC program:

$$y = c1(x1)^{e1} + c2(x2)^{e2} + c3(x3)^{e3}$$

where c1, c2, e1, e2, and so on are empirical coefficients that may change from time to time.

The translated program code may be:

```
10 DATA c1, c2, c3
20 DATA e1, e2, e3
  .
  .
  .
100 READ C1, C2, C3
110 READ E1, E2, E3
120 Y = C1 * X1 ^ E1 + C2 * X2 ^ E2 + C3 * X3 ^ E3
```

With this **DATA** arrangement, the coefficients can be easily located in the program and changed.

If the data may not only change but may also grow, then there is no better place to put them than at the very end of the program, where the statement numbers are not bounded on the high end. Suppose the three name/address/phone data sets were placed immediately after the **READ** statements in Example 9.18. As the data sets grow (with the loop adjusted accordingly), the program text would have to be completely renumbered to accommodate the new data—a very impractical undertaking.

In any case, if one **DATA** statement placement philosophy is adopted, then all **DATA** in the same program should adhere to this philosophy, since mixed placement philosophies tend to lead to confused **READ/DATA** sequences. Program annotations should also be provided so that the data are easily identifiable. Example 9.18 is therefore better coded as follows:

```
10 'DATA STRUCTURE
20 '
30 CLS
40 PRINT "Name", "Address", "Phone"
50 PRINT
60 READ N%
70 FOR C% = 1 TO N%
80 READ A$, B$, C$
90 PRINT A$, B$, C$
100 NEXT C%
110 END
1000 '------------------------------------------------------
1010 'NUMBER OF DATA SETS
1020 DATA 3
1030 '------------------------------------------------------
1040 'NAME/ADDRESS/PHONE DATA SETS
1050 DATA "ABC Cleaning", "Downtown", "777-2626"
1060 DATA "Joe's Food", "Hillside", "256-8950"
1070 DATA "Ava's", "Towers", "Unlisted"
```

Exercise Set 9.3 DATA statement structuring (Using **PRINT**, **CLS**, **END**, **LET**, functions, **DEF FN**, **INPUT**, **FOR/NEXT**, **WHILE/WEND**, **IF/THEN/ELSE**, logical operators, **READ/DATA**, **RESTORE**)

A. Modify the following program codes to give the data better structure:

1.

```
10 'TEMPERATURE CONVERSION
20 '
30 DATA 9, 5, 32, 12.88, 86, 93.4, 5, 100, 23,
   77.7, 56.3, 83.6, 22, 78.3, 56.4
40 READ A, B, C
50 FOR C% = 1 TO 12
60   READ C
70   LET F = C * A / B + C
80   PRINT F
90 NEXT C%
100 END
```

2.

```
10 CLS
20 READ A$, B$, C$
30 PRINT A$, B$, C$
```

```
40 PRINT
50 READ N%
60 FOR C% = 1 TO N%
70 READ A$, B$, C$
80 PRINT A$, B$, C$
90 NEXT C%
100 END
110 DATA "Name", "Address", "Phone", 3, "ABC
Cleaning", "Downtown", "777-2626", "Joe's Food",
"Hillside", "256-8950", "Ava's", "Towers",
"Unlisted"
```

B. Flowcharting and code transcription:

3. Design a program to display a group of data sets incorporated in the program as **DATA** statements. Each data set is made up of a person's name and five associated account numbers. As new data sets may be added to the group, the program needs to accommodate an occasional update to handle the increased data.

Chapter Exercises (Using **PRINT**, **CLS**, **END**, **LET**, functions, **DEF FN**, **INPUT**, **FOR/NEXT**, **WHILE/WEND**, **IF/THEN/ELSE**, logical operators, **READ/DATA**, **RESTORE**)

Flowcharting and code transcription:

1. Design a program to display a name list vertically on the CRT. The list contains a total of 100 names. The program should stop when the display has filled one whole CRT screen and await a user input. If the input is "U" or "u", then a previous screenful of names should be displayed again. Otherwise the next screenful of names should be displayed.

10 / ARRAYS

In chapter 9, the method for assigning quantities of data to variables was discussed. When are quantities of data encountered in programming? They are used in processing business records, tabulating mathematical charts, and organizing scientific data, to cite but a few instances. Large quantities of data usually exist in list or table form. Lists and tables are known as *arrays* in programming terminology.

In BASIC, arrays are represented in a special way. To understand arrays, let us begin with an example. Figure 10.1 shows a typical set of scientific experimental temperature data.

```
2.004    3.577    2.613    2.966    3.011    1.996
```

FIGURE 10.1

This is a data list, known as a *one-dimensional array*.

Figure 10.2 shows the same set of experimental results but taken in more detail with three thermometers.

```
2.004    3.577    2.613    2.966    3.011    1.996
2.008    3.573    2.618    2.970    3.005    2.001
2.003    3.575    2.615    2.968    3.009    1.999
```

FIGURE 10.2

This data set, arranged in rows and columns, is known as a *two-dimensional array.*

Arrays therefore hold related data in a structured form. The data may all belong to the same class (such as the temperature data), rank equally (such as all the entries in the same invoice), or possess some common characteristics. Mathematically, such data are in general expressed as:

d1 d2 d3 d4 . . .

or

d11	d12	d13	d14	d15
d21	d22	d23	d24	d25
d31	d32	d33	d34	d35

.
.
.

Identification numbers called *subscripts* are used to represent the element positions of the data relative to each other. A data item in a one-dimensional array therefore has one subscript (to indicate the element position), while a data item in a two-dimensional array has two subscripts (to indicate the row and column position). The number of subscripts is the number of dimensions in the array.

In representing array data, BASIC emulates this mathematical representation. First of all, instead of designating individual names to the array variables, BASIC requires that the array have an array name shared by all the array elements. This array name is exactly the same as a common variable name. Thus, an array may be identified as A, just as a single variable can be called A. Data-type declaration suffixes, such as the dollar sign ($), are likewise used to indicate the array data type. So the array A would hold numeric data, while the array A$ would hold string data.

Immediately following this array name is a pair of parentheses, in which the subscript(s) are held. For example, if A is a one-dimensional array (and therefore has one subscript), then the first element of this array can be expressed as A(1). The second element will then be A(2), the third A(3), and so on. These are the array variables, and they are pronounced A sub one, A sub two, and so on (see Figure 10.3).

For a two-dimensional array, the array elements are similarly expressed as A(1,1) (pronounced A sub one one), A(1,2), A(1,3), and so on for the first row, and A(2,1), A(2,2), A(2,3), and so on for the second row (see Figure 10.4).

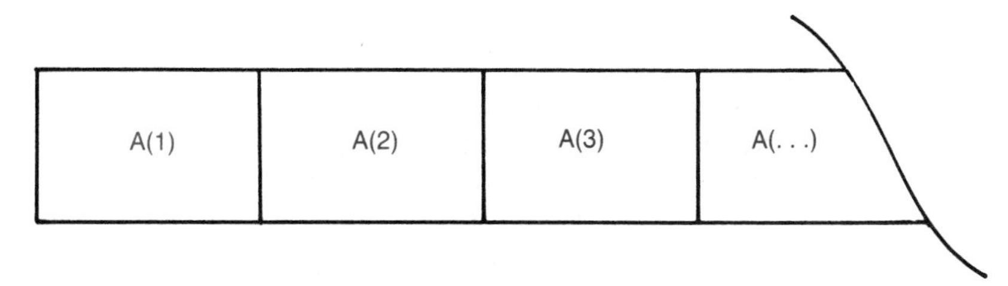

FIGURE 10.3

Except for this particular way in which array and array element names are formed, all array variables can be handled in programming as if they were individually named variables. Example 10.1 shows how array variables can be assigned data exactly as if they were ordinary variables.

ONE-DIMENSIONAL ARRAYS

Example 10.1

```
10 'ASSIGN DATA TO LIST
20 '
30 READ A(1), A(2), A(3)
40 PRINT A(1); A(2); A(3)
50 END
60 DATA 12.4, 3.5, 6.67
```

```
 12.4  3.5  6.67
```

will be displayed.

A(1,1)	A(1,2)	A(1,3)	A(1,4)
A(2,1)	A(2,2)	A(2,3)	A(2,4)
A(3,1)	A(3,2)	A(3,3)	A(3,4)
A(4,1)	A(4,2)	A(4,3)	A(4,4)

FIGURE 10.4

The particular way that array variables are named is not just for organizational purposes, since organization could be equally well expressed if the array variables were named A1, A2, or A3. The reason for putting the subscript within parentheses is that this way BASIC recognizes the general array name, which allows array variables to be handled through general processing schemes, rendering the processing logic highly efficient.

For instance, the subscript does not always have to be an integer numeric constant. It can be another variable as long as this variable has a value corresponding to a subscript. Consequently, this variable subscript can be controlled to identify a particular array element at will.

Example 10.2

This example program shows how a loop can be employed to assign data to an array. The flowchart is shown in Figure 10.5.

```
10 'ARRAY WITH LOOP
20 '
30 FOR L% = 1 TO 3
40 READ A$(L%), B$(L%), C$(L%)
50 NEXT L%
60 END
70 '-----------------------------------------
80 DATA "ABC Cleaning", "Downtown", "777-2626"
90 DATA "Joe's Food", "Hillside", "256-8950"
100 DATA "Ava's", "Towers", "Unlisted"
```

Statement 40 expresses all three elements of the three arrays with the variable subscript **L%**. As the loop iterates, **L%** takes on values of 1, 2, and 3, successively. Thus, the array elements **READ** are **A$(1)**, **B$(1)**, **C$(1)**; **A$(2)**, **B$(2)**, **C$(2)**; and **A$(3)**, **B$(3)**, **C$(3)**, respectively.

The lists established in the computer memory are illustrated in Figure 10.6.

This method of generalizing the array elements is not possible with variable names such as A1 and A2, as the 1 and 2 are innate parts of the variable names and therefore not subject to manipulation.

The efficiency of dealing with quantities of data expressed in array form would easily be appreciated if each list above were to be made up of 1,000 elements.

Similarly, entire arrays can be displayed through the same mechanism.

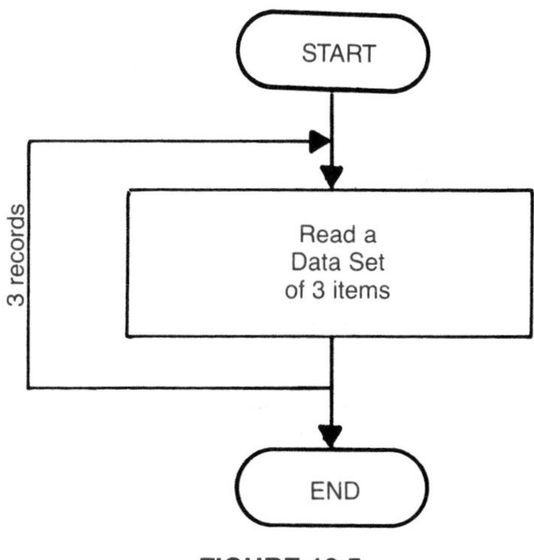

FIGURE 10.5

Example 10.3

Figure 10.7 shows the flowchart for the following program.

```
10 'ARRAY WITH LOOP
20 '
30 FOR L% = 1 TO 3
40      READ A$(L%), B$(L%), C$(L%)
50 NEXT L%
60 CLS
70 FOR L% = 1 TO 3
80      PRINT A$(L%), B$(L%), C$(L%)
90 NEXT L%
100 END
```

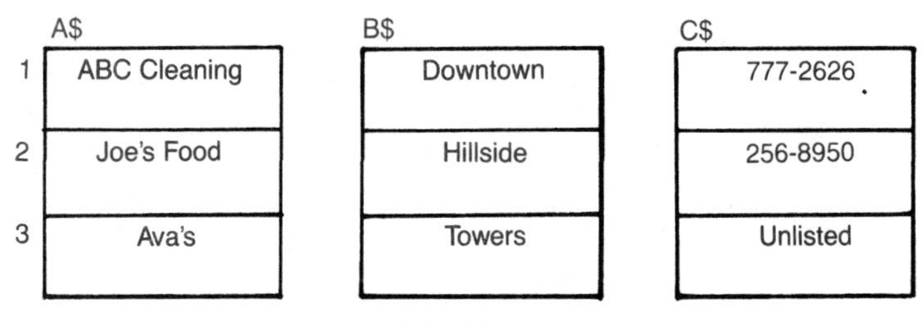

A$
B$
C$
1
ABC Cleaning
Downtown
777-2626
2
Joe's Food
Hillside
256-8950
3
Ava's
Towers
Unlisted

FIGURE 10.6

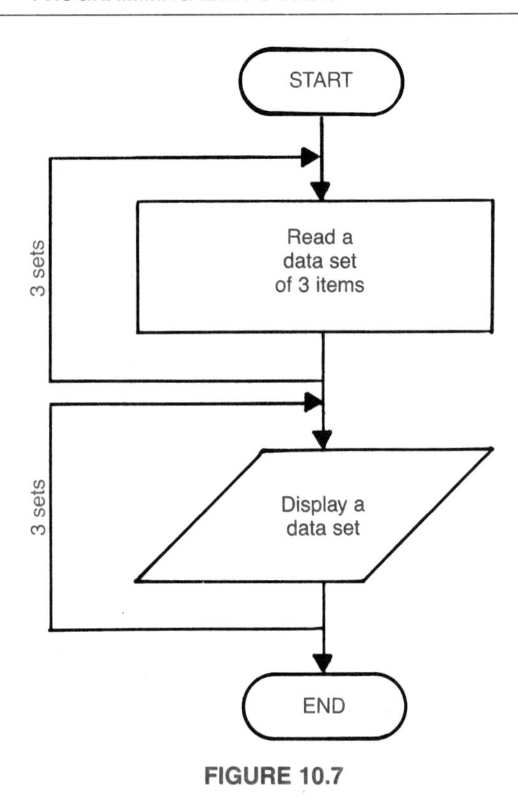

FIGURE 10.7

```
110 '--------------------------------------------------
120 DATA "ABC Cleaning", "Downtown", "777-2626"
130 DATA "Joe's Food", "Hillside", "256-8950"
140 DATA "Ava's", "Towers", "Unlisted"
```

Without arrays, data can be **READ** and promptly displayed by single variables. However, in such cases the data are not retained by the variables and kept in memory. The data remain listed in the **DATA** statements in the program text. With arrays, the data once set up are actually kept in memory and can be processed separately. The above program separated the data input operation from the display, thus showing that all the data are kept under distinct variable names.

Array data do not have to be **READ** from **DATA** statements exclusively. Array data can be supplied through the keyboard as well. Example 10.4 illustrates this.

Example 10.4

```
10 'INPUT TO ARRAY
20 '
30 CLS
40 PRINT "Enter personal data :"
50 PRINT
60 FOR L% = 1 TO 3
70      PRINT "Entry"; L%
80       INPUT "Name : ", A$(L%)
90       INPUT "Address : ", B$(L%)
100      INPUT "Phone no. : ", C$(L%)
110     PRINT
120 NEXT L%
130 CLS
140 FOR L% = 1 TO 3
150      PRINT A$(L%), B$(L%), C$(L%)
160 NEXT L%
170 END
```

When **RUN**, the program will prompt the user for the name, address, and phone data individually. After the arrays are set up, then the array data are displayed. **RUN** the example program and follow the program logic.

Array data are therefore not the same as data listed in the **DATA** statement. Data listed in **DATA** statements are program text and are not actual data that can be processed. Array data are real data kept in the computer memory data area, and they can be processed as often as needed. Also, the facts that data are organized in arrays and that the variables bear common names do not imply that they must always be processed together. Example 10.5 shows that once the arrays exist, the array data can be used an unlimited number of times. Notice, no **RESTORE** is required, or even allowed, which is necessary with **DATA** statements.

Example 10.5

```
10 'INPUT TO ARRAY
20 '
30 '----------------------------------------------
40 'DATA ENTRY
50 CLS
60 PRINT "Enter personal data :"
70 PRINT
80 FOR L% = 1 TO 10
```

```
90      PRINT "Entry"; L%
100      INPUT "Name : ", A$(L%)
110      INPUT "Address : ", B$(L%)
120      INPUT "Phone no. : ", C$(L%)
130      PRINT
140 NEXT L%
150 '----------------------------------------------------------------
160 'DATA LOCATION
170 CLS
180 INPUT "Enter record number to locate : ", N%
190 IF N% < 0 OR N% > 10 THEN 170
200 PRINT A$(N%), B$(N%), C$(N%)
210 PRINT
220 PRINT
230 INPUT "Continue data location? (y/n) : ", REPLY$
240 IF REPLY$ = "y" THEN 170
250 END
```

Exercise Set 10.1 One-dimensional arrays (Using **PRINT**, **CLS**, **END**, **LET**, functions, **DEF FN**, **INPUT**, **FOR/NEXT**, **WHILE/WEND**, **IF/THEN/ELSE**, logical operators, **READ/DATA**, **RESTORE**)

A. Correct the errors, if any, in the following programs:

1.

```
10 FOR L% = 1 TO 4
20   READ A(L%)
30 NEXT L%
40 END
50 DATA "Joe's Cleaner", 12.4, 5.55, 8.45
```

Answer: ____

____

2.

```
10 FOR L% = 1 TO 4
20   INPUT A(L%)
30 NEXT L%
40 PRINT A(7)
50 END
```

Answer: ____

____

B. Flowchart and write a program to:

3. Establish a list for the five coefficients of an equation in the computer memory. The coefficients are to be supplied by the mathematician user.
4. Establish two lists, each five elements long, in the computer memory. One list holds the names of five customers known to the programmer and is used to prompt a user to supply five corresponding billing charges, which are to be stored in the other list.

TWO-DIMENSIONAL ARRAYS

Tables are represented by two-dimensional arrays, which take two subscripts. One subscript marks the array element row position, and the other the column. It does not matter which one goes first; all that matters is how the subscripts relate to people's perceptions of them and whether they are consistent throughout the same application. Take the product sales expectancy table shown in Figure 10.8 as an example. It compares the potential sales outcome between the models of two competing companies.

The first row of data can be expressed as:

```
A(1,1)    A(1,2)    A(1,3)    A(1,4)    A(1,5)
```

if the table is named A.

If this row of data is to be **READ** from a **DATA** statement, then it can be achieved through a loop such as:

```
10 FOR C% = 1 TO 5
20   READ A(1,C%)
30 NEXT C%
```

with the first subscript 1 meaning row 1, and **C%** varied from 1 to 5 to mark the five column positions.

Likewise the second-row data are set up with:

```
40 FOR C% = 1 TO 5
50   READ A(2,C%)
60 NEXT C%
```

Company 1

Company 2: Model \ Company 1: Model	A	B	C	D	E
A	1	3	5	7	9
B	2	4	6	8	10
C	−1	−2	−3	−4	−5
D	9	8	7	6	5

Relative sales expectancy ratio

FIGURE 10.8

If the first three rows were to be set up this way, then the code would be:

```
10 FOR C% = 1 TO 5
20    READ A(1,C%)
30 NEXT C%
40 FOR C% = 1 TO 5
50    READ A(2,C%)
60 NEXT C%
70 FOR C% = 1 TO 5
80    READ A(3,C%)
90 NEXT C%
```

When coded this way, a clear repetitive pattern emerges. It can be seen that the entire array can be set up by surrounding an inner three-statement loop that controls the column-subscript variation with an outer loop that controls the row-subscript variation.

Example 10.6

Figure 10.9 shows the flowchart for the following program.

```
10 'TABLE DATA SETUP
20 '
30 FOR R% = 1 TO 4
40      FOR C% = 1 TO 5
50              READ A( R%,C% )
60      NEXT C%
70 NEXT R%
80 END
```

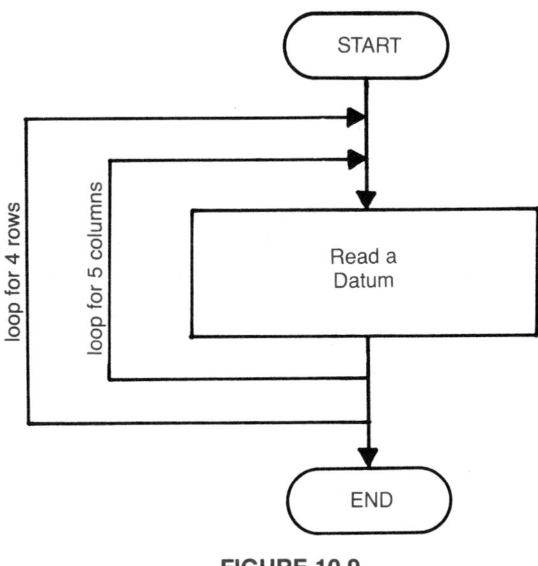

FIGURE 10.9

```
90 DATA 1, 3, 5, 7, 9
100 DATA 2, 4, 6, 8, 10
110 DATA -1, -2, -3, -4, -5
120 DATA 90, 80, 70, 60, 50
```

The array can then be displayed by the code in the next example.

Example 10.7

```
10 'TABLE DISPLAY
20 '
30 FOR R% = 1 TO 4
40       FOR C% = 1 TO 5
50               READ A( R%,C% )
60       NEXT C%
70 NEXT R%
80 CLS
90 FOR R% = 1 TO 4
100      FOR C% = 1 TO 5
110              PRINT A( R%,C% ),
120      NEXT C%
130      PRINT
140 NEXT R%
```

```
150 END
160 DATA 1, 3, 5, 7, 9
170 DATA 2, 4, 6, 8, 10
180 DATA -1, -2, -3, -4, -5
190 DATA 90, 80, 70, 60, 50
```

In these two examples, the variable **R%** has been used to represent the row subscript, and **C%** the column subscript. They were chosen because of the letters *r* and *c* in row and column. It does not really matter what variable names are used for these subscripts. Naturally, the more meaningful they are the better.

String arrays are handled exactly as are numeric arrays. The previous name/address/phone programs can be redesigned as Example 10.8. The key differences here are not only in the looping structure in the coding but also in the flowcharting. Previously, when three lists were used to keep the name, address, and phone data separately, the flowcharts indicated their distinct logical separations. In Example 10.8, the whole name/address/phone record is thought of as one data unit.

Example 10.8

Figure 10.10 shows the flowchart for the following code.

```
10 '2-DIMENSIONAL STRING ARRAY
20 '
30 '---------------------------------------------------
40 'DATA ENTRY
50 CLS
60 PRINT "Enter personal data (Name/Address/Phone) :"
70 PRINT
80 FOR R% = 1 TO 10
90       PRINT "Record"; R%
100      PRINT
110      FOR C% = 1 TO 3
120               INPUT; "      ", A$( R%,C% )
130      NEXT C%
140      PRINT
150      PRINT
160 NEXT R%
```

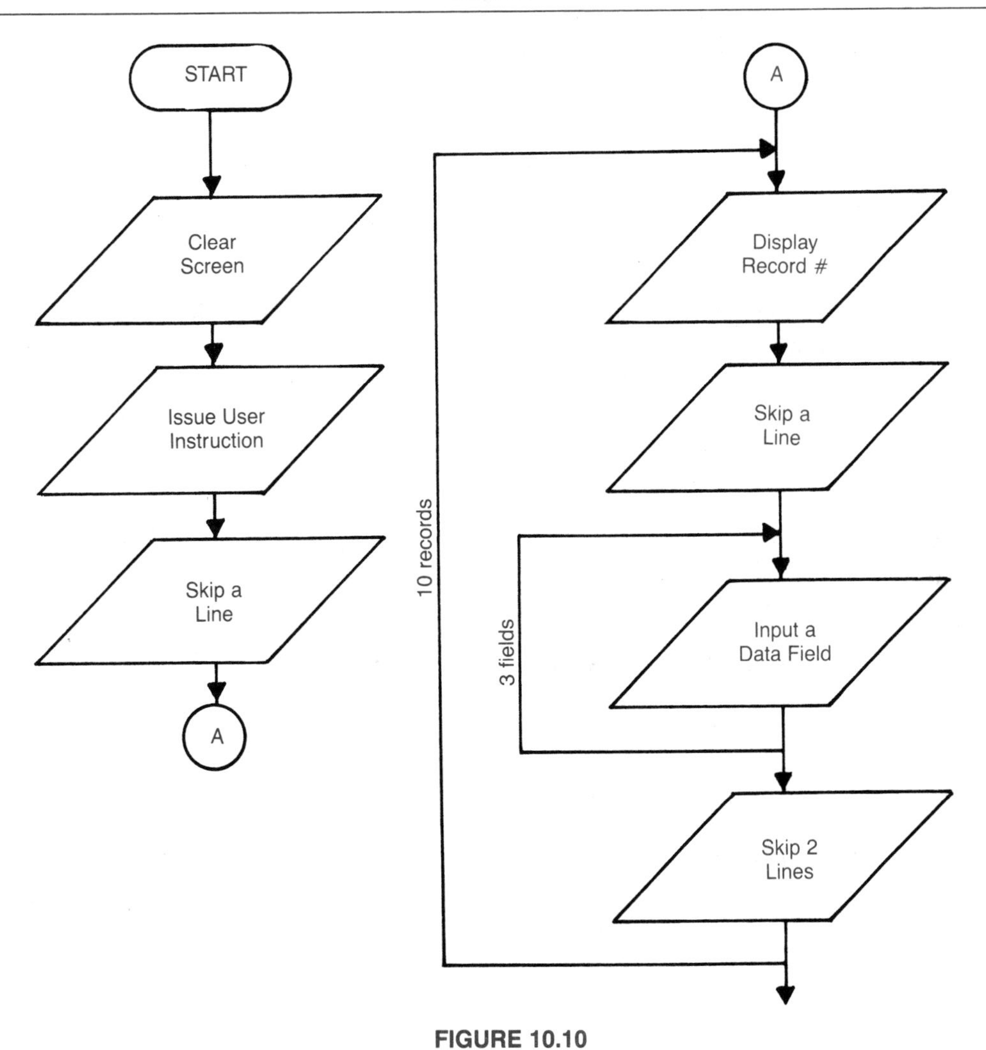

FIGURE 10.10

```
170 '---------------------------------------------------
180 'ARRAY DISPLAY
190 '
200 CLS
210 PRINT "Name", "Address", "Phone"
```

```
220 PRINT
230 FOR R% = 1 TO 10
240      FOR C% = 1 TO 3
250                PRINT A$( R%,C% ),
260      NEXT C%
270      PRINT
280 NEXT R%
```

The program logic for locating the data set up in this program would have been:

```
300 INPUT "ENTER RECORD NUMBER TO LOCATE : ", R%
310 IF R% < 0 OR R% > 10 THEN 300
320 FOR C% = 1 TO 3
330      PRINT A$( R%,C% ),
340 NEXT C%
350 PRINT
360 PRINT
370 INPUT "CONTINUE RECORD LOCATION? (Y/N) : ", REPLY$
380 IF REPLY$ = "Y" THEN 300
390 END
```

For further illustration, the display headings in Example 10.8 can be made into an array as well.

Example 10.9

```
10 'MIXED-ARRAY PROCESSING
20 '
30 '-----------------------------------------------
40 'SET HEADING
50 '
60 FOR C% = 1 TO 3
70       READ H$( C% )
80 NEXT C%
90 DATA "Name", "Address", "Phone"
100 '----------------------------------------------
110 'DATA ENTRY
120 CLS
```

```
130 PRINT "Enter personal data (Name/Address/Phone) :"
140 PRINT
150 FOR R% = 1 TO 10
160     PRINT "Record"; R%
170     PRINT
180     FOR C% = 1 TO 3
190             INPUT; "      ", A$( R%,C% )
200     NEXT C%
210     PRINT
220     PRINT
230 NEXT R%
240 '-------------------------------------------------------
250 'ARRAY DISPLAY
260 '
270 CLS
280 FOR C% = 1 TO 3
290     PRINT H$( C% ),
300 NEXT C%
310 PRINT
320 PRINT
330 FOR R% = 1 TO 10
340     FOR C% = 1 TO 3
350             PRINT A$( R%,C% ),
360     NEXT C%
370     PRINT
380 NEXT R%
390 END
```

In this example, the number of statements has actually grown as compared to Example 10.8. However, the arrays are now generalized; that is, not only can array **A$** take on various working data but the headings can be reset as well. Such generalized arrays can therefore be used for diverse purposes.

Exercise Set 10.2 Two-dimensional arrays (Using **PRINT**, **CLS**, **END**, **LET**, functions, **DEF FN**, **INPUT**, **FOR/NEXT**, **WHILE/WEND**, **IF/THEN/ELSE**, logical operators, **READ/DATA**, **RESTORE**)

A. Flowchart transcription:

1.

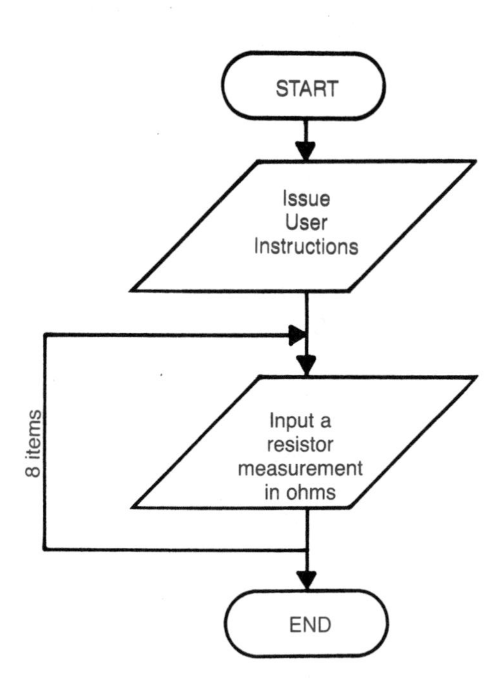

2.

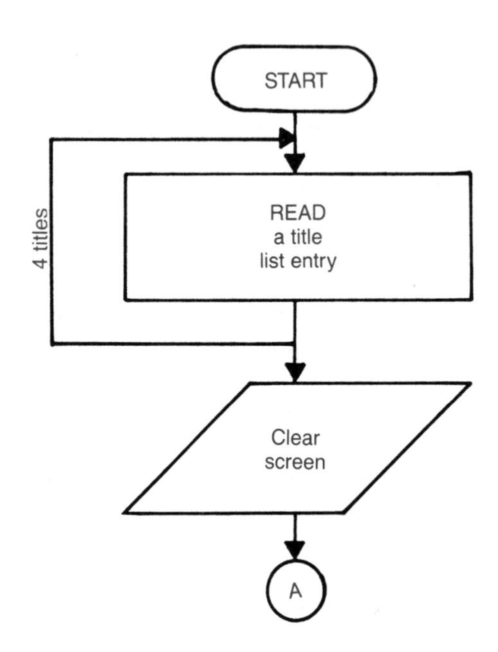

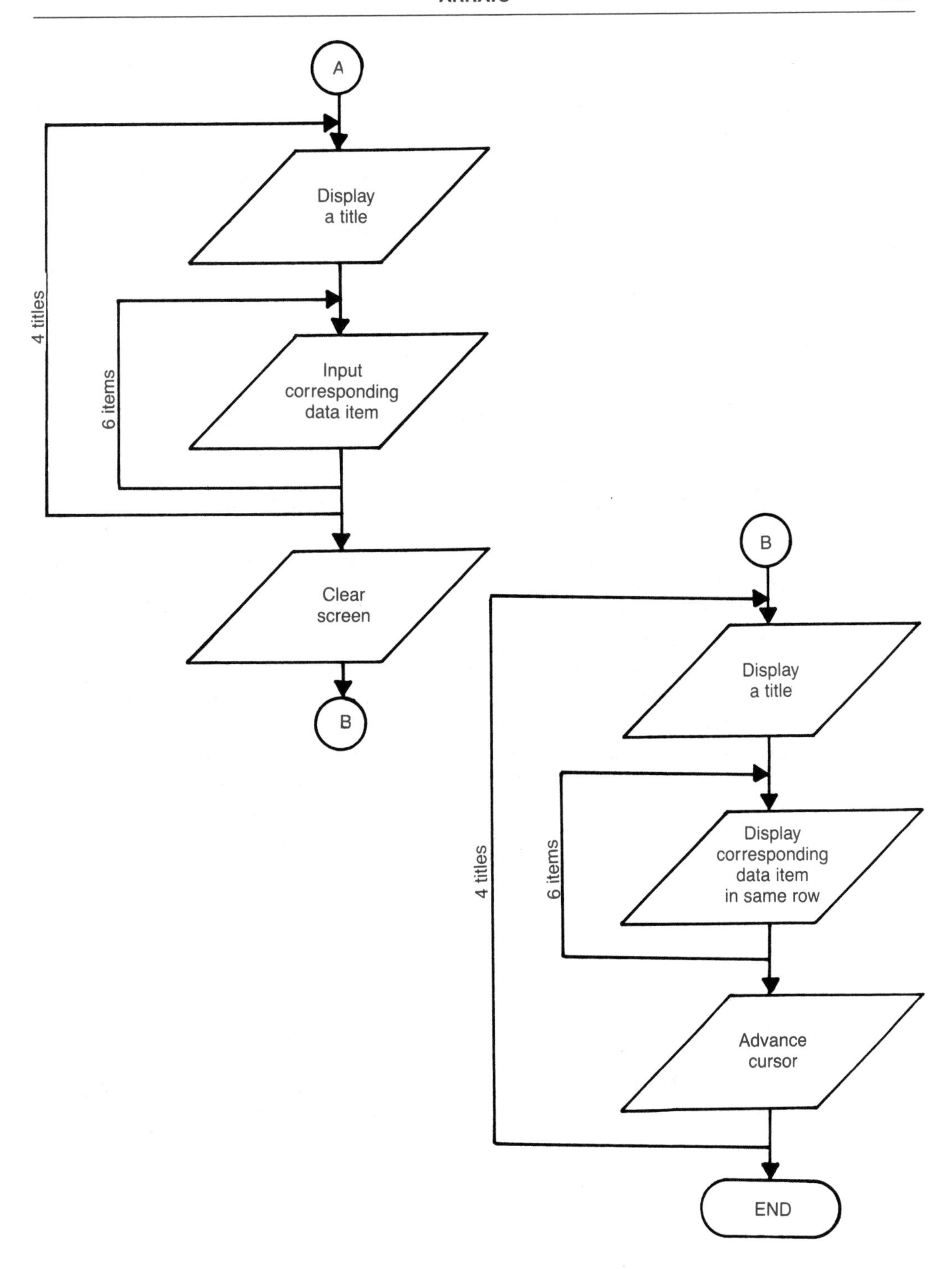
A
Display
a title
4 titles
6 items
Input
corresponding
data item
Clear
screen
B
B
Display
a title
4 titles
6 items
Display
corresponding
data item
in same row
Advance
cursor
END

B. Programming:

3. Complete problem 2 by permitting the user to see any row of data desired.
4. Suppose the data in problem 2 pertain to the four voltmeter readings for a series of laboratory meters. Add headings in the form of a list for the display so that the data displayed are meaningful.

THE DIM STATEMENT

Other than the form, array data differ from other data in another respect: Array data are not kept in the same general memory area as the other data. For organizational reasons, BASIC keeps array data in a special section of the memory. This section must be specially prepared, and BASIC looks to the programmer for information needed to help it perform this internal managerial task. Specifically, BASIC needs to know what the highest array subscript values are prior to the arrays being set up. To inform BASIC of the anticipated array subscript values, the program declares them through the **DIM**ension statement.

The **DIM**ension statement begins with the keyword **DIM**, which is followed by the array name with the highest subscript(s) specified. If there is more than one array, then all the array specifications may be listed in the same **DIM** statement, separated by the comma delimiter, or they may be listed in separate **DIM** statements. For example, in a program, two arrays (A and C) are to be used; A is one dimensional with a highest anticipated subscript of 100, while C is two dimensional with the two highest subscripts being 50 and 60. The program must issue the following **DIM** statement before the arrays can be used by the program:

```
10 DIM A(100), C(50,60)
```

or

```
10 DIM A(100)
20 DIM C(50,60)
```

The **DIM** statement does not specify the actual size of the arrays; it informs BASIC of the highest subscripts that may be used—that is, how many *possible* elements the arrays may have. Thus, even if only three data items are to be assigned to an array, as long as the third data item is stored under subscript 50, the **DIM** statement must specify 50, and not 3.

If no **DIM** statement is issued in a program, then BASIC assumes that no array will have a subscript beyond 10. (Most BASIC dialects automatically allow subscripts up to 10, which is why in the previous example programs no **DIM** statement was necessary.) But for two-dimensional arrays, even if one subscript does not exceed the limit of 10, as long as the other subscript is larger than 10, a **DIM** statement must be issued.

In general, it is therefore best always to use **DIM** statements, even if the arrays do not carry subscripts beyond 10. Not only does a **DIM** statement clearly inform how many arrays a program uses but it also facilitates array size changes.

The **DIM** statement is not program logic. Like the **RESTORE** statement, it deals with an internal systems parameter. The flowchart symbol for **DIM** is thus the system setup symbol (see Figure 10.11). The **DIM** statement is often not even documented in the flowchart.

DIM
Form: DIM array(highest subscripts)[, arrays(highest subscripts)]
Function: To allocate memory storage space for arrays.

In BASIC, array subscripts generally begin at 0 and not 1, as is customary in mathematics. Sometimes the 0 subscript variables can be used to hold special array data if the data are of the same type as the working

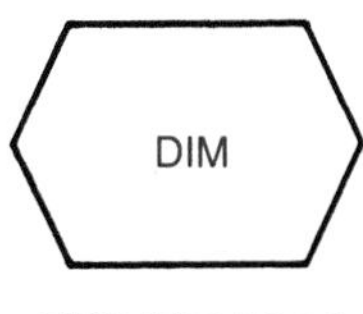

FIGURE 10.11

data. For example, the heading data in Example 10.8 can thus be absorbed into the data array as:

Example 10.10

```
10 'USING THE 0 SUBSCRIPT
20 '
30 '---------------------------------------------
40 'HEADING SETUP
50 FOR C% = 1 TO 3
60      READ A$( 0,C% )
70 NEXT C%
80 '---------------------------------------------
90 'DATA ENTRY
100 CLS
110 PRINT "Enter personal data (Name/Address/Phone) :"
120 PRINT
130 FOR R% = 1 TO 10
140      PRINT "Record"; R%
150      PRINT
160      FOR C% = 1 TO 3
170             PRINT A$( 0,C% );
180             INPUT " : ", A$( R%,C% )
190      NEXT C%
200     PRINT
210     PRINT
220 NEXT R%
230 '---------------------------------------------
240 'ARRAY DISPLAY
250 '
260 CLS
270 FOR C% = 1 TO 3
280     PRINT A$( 0,C% ),
290 NEXT C%
300 PRINT
310 PRINT
320 FOR R% = 1 TO 10
330     FOR C% = 1 TO 3
340             PRINT A$( R%,C% ),
350     NEXT C%
360     PRINT
370 NEXT R%
380 END
```

```
390 '-----------------------------------------------
400 'HEADING DATA
410 DATA "Name", "Address", "Phone"
```

By starting arrays at subscript 1, the use of those variables with subscripts 0 is sacrificed, and sometimes that means some memory space is wasted. But fortunately such waste is not significant, and BASIC does not really care if you never assign any data to the variables with subscript 0. However, if you wish, the 0 subscripts can be eliminated by setting the starting subscripts to be 1 through the **OPTION BASE** statement.

The **OPTION BASE** statement has the form of:

```
OPTION BASE n
```

where n is either 1 or 0.

By setting n to 1, all subsequent arrays in a program will begin their subscripts at 1, and vice versa. Because **OPTION BASE** sets an internal system data item, as with **RESTORE**, the flowchart symbol (if flowcharted) is as shown in Figure 10.12.

For example,

```
10 OPTION BASE 1
20 DIM A(50), B(20)
30 FOR C% = 1 TO 50
40    INPUT A(C%)
50 NEXT C%
  .
  .
  .
```

will begin the array subscripts from 1.

Once the **OPTION BASE** statement is issued, it cannot be used again in the same program, and it cannot be issued after an array has already entered into processing.

FIGURE 10.12

Exercise Set 10.3 DIM (Using **PRINT**, **CLS**, **END**, **LET**, functions, **DEF FN**, **INPUT**, **FOR/NEXT**, **WHILE/WEND**, **IF/THEN/ELSE**, logical operators, **READ/DATA, RESTORE,** arrays, **DIM**)

Flowcharting and code transcription:

1. Modify problem 2 in Exercise Set 10.2 to accommodate data for up to fifty different stocks and twelve possible associated transaction figures. As data are entered by the stockbroker user, utilize the entries at subscript 0 to hold the actual number of data items entered.
2. Design a program permitting the user to resume entering data continuing from the last data entry operation in problem 1.

APPLICATIONS WITH ARRAYS

In this section, two common applications of arrays are illustrated through examples.

Example 10.11

In this example, a set of student grade data is to be averaged. For these data, a two-dimensional array called **GRADES** is first set up to hold six grades per record. The first five are used to hold the actual data, while the sixth is reserved to hold the averages to be computed. After the computations, the averages are displayed. A partial flowchart is shown in Figure 10.13.

```
10 'COMPUTING AVERAGES
20 '
30 '--------------------------------------------
40 'TABLE SETUP
50 DIM GRADES(100,6), NAME$(100)
60 READ N%
70 FOR R% = 1 TO N%
80      READ NAME$( R% )
90      FOR C% = 1 TO 5
100              READ GRADES( R%,C% )
110      NEXT C%
120 NEXT R%
```

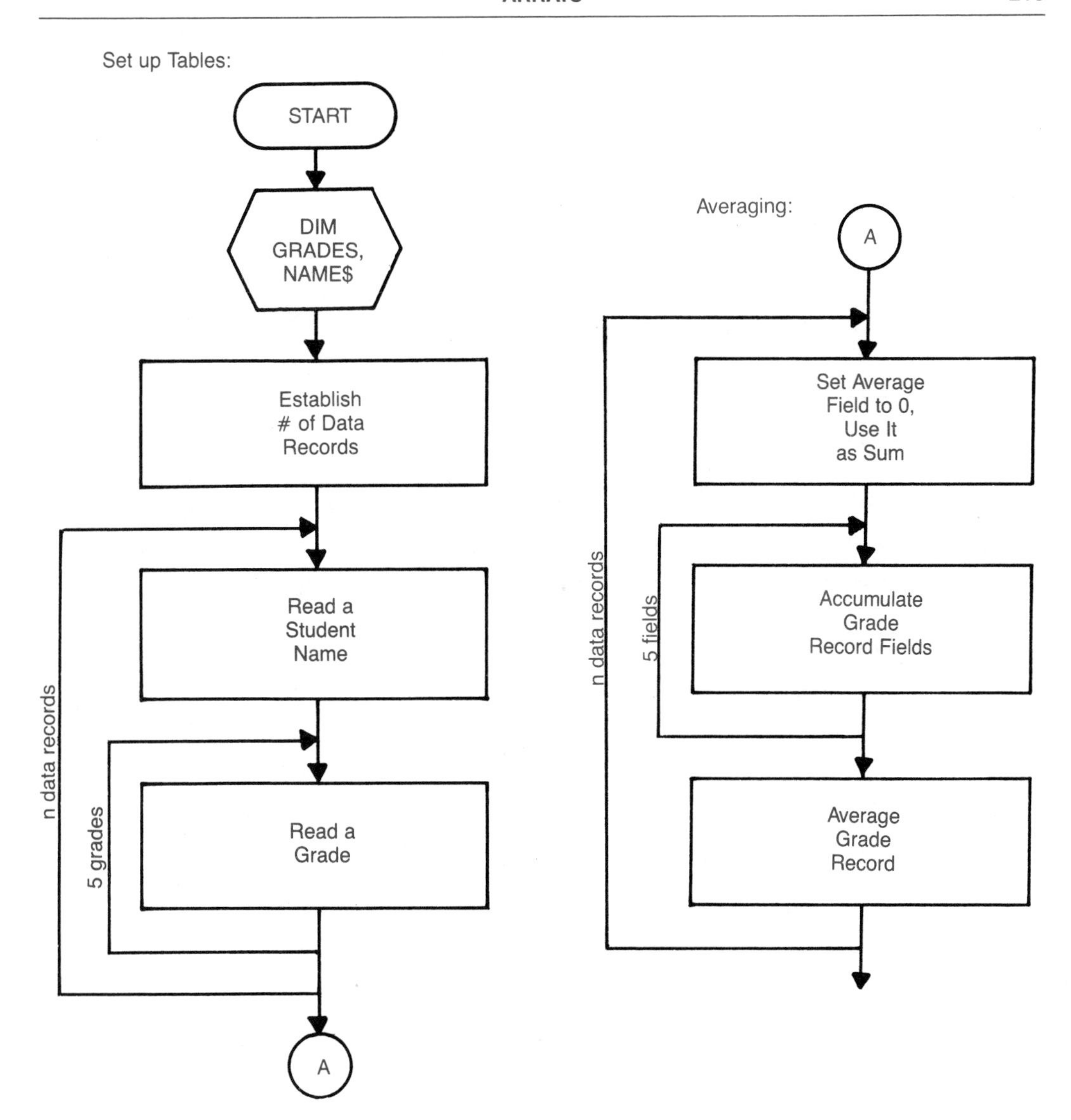
Set up Tables:
START
DIM GRADES, NAME$
Establish # of Data Records
Read a Student Name
Read a Grade
n data records
5 grades
A
Averaging:
A
Set Average Field to 0, Use It as Sum
Accumulate Grade Record Fields
Average Grade Record
n data records
5 fields

FIGURE 10.13

```
130 '--------------------------------------------------
140 'AVERAGING
150 FOR R% = 1 TO N%
160 LET GRADES( R%,6 ) = 0
170     FOR C% = 1 TO 5
180             LET GRADES( R%,6 ) =
                GRADES( R%,6 ) + GRADES( R%,C% )
190     NEXT C%
200     LET GRADES( R%,6 ) = GRADES( R%,6 ) / 5
210 NEXT R%
220 '--------------------------------------------------
230 'DISPLAY SUMMARY
240 CLS
250 FOR R% = 1 TO N%
260     PRINT NAME$( R% ),
270 NEXT R%
280 PRINT
290 PRINT
300 FOR R% = 1 TO N%
310     PRINT GRADES( R%,6 ),
320 NEXT R%
330 PRINT
340 PRINT
350 END
360 '--------------------------------------------------
370 'DATA RECORDS
380 DATA 3
390 DATA "Jane", 85, 80, 87, 90, 75
400 DATA "Larry", 65, 70, 65, 75, 75
410 DATA "Fred", 85, 90, 85, 90, 90
```

As another example, let us see how the data-location problem from the last chapter would come out if arrays were used.

Example 10.12

In this example, the existence of a product inventory record is to be ascertained.

```
10 'INFORMATION RETRIEVAL
20 '
```

```
30 '---------------------------------------------
40 'TABLE SETUP
50 DIM INV(100,6), PROD$(100)
60 READ N%
70 FOR R% = 1 TO N%
80      READ PROD$( R% )
90      FOR C% = 1 TO 5
100              READ INV( R%,C% )
110      NEXT C%
120 NEXT R%
130 '---------------------------------------------
140 'AVERAGING
150 FOR R% = 1 TO N%
160 LET INV( R%,6 ) = 0
170     FOR C% = 1 TO 5
180             LET INV( R%,6 ) = INV( R%,6 ) + INV( R%,C%
190     NEXT C%
200     LET INV( R%,6 ) = INV( R%,6 ) / 5
210 NEXT R%
220 '---------------------------------------------
230 'INFORMATION RETRIEVAL
240 CLS
250 INPUT "Enter product number : ", SEARCH.KEY$
260 PRINT
270 FOR R% = 1 TO N%
280     IF PROD$( R% ) = SEARCH.KEY$ THEN 320
290 NEXT R%
300 PRINT "Product number not found."
310 GOTO 400
320 PRINT PROD$( R% ); " : "
330 PRINT
340 FOR C% = 1 TO 5
350     PRINT INV( R%, C% ),
360 NEXT C%
370 PRINT
380 PRINT "AVERAGE : "; INV( R%,6 )
390 PRINT
400 INPUT "CONTINUE . . . (Y/N)? ", REPLY$
410 IF REPLY$ = "Y" THEN 240
420 END
```

```
430 '--------------------------------------------------
440 'DATA RECORDS
450 DATA 10
460 DATA "D4AE66", 3.4, 5.5, 6.2, 2.8, 4.8
470 DATA "D5BB13", 8.7, 9.2, 7.8, 6.4, 9.1
480 DATA "F1BD82", 1.3, 1.4, 2.0, 1.7, 1.6
490 DATA "F2CD17", 2.3, 2.5, 3.4, 2.8, 2.6
500 DATA "F2CD19", 7.4, 7.6, 7.1, 7.8, 8.1
510 DATA "F4AD22", 0.3, 0.4, 0.5, 0.7, 0.6
520 DATA "G1AE16", 4.5, 4.4, 4.0, 4.7, 4.3
530 DATA "G2BC31", 9.8, 9.4, 9.5, 9.2, 9.9
540 DATA "H3DE04", 5.0, 4.8, 5.3, 5.5, 5.2
550 DATA "H4AF06", 6.6, 6.6, 6.5, 6.7, 6.4
```

Exercise Set 10.4 Averaging, data location (Using **PRINT**, **CLS**, **END**, **LET**, functions, **DEF FN**, **INPUT**, **FOR/NEXT**, **WHILE/WEND**, **IF/THEN/ELSE**, logical operators, **READ/DATA**, **RESTORE**, arrays, **DIM**)

Flowcharting and code transcription:

1. Design a program to input the actual hours worked per day by twenty assembly-line workers for one week, to compute the total and average hours worked per week for each worker, and to store all data in the same array.
2. Design a program to help a lab technician locate a particular test result based on an experiment number input into the computer.

Chapter Exercises (Using **PRINT**, **CLS**, **END**, **LET**, functions, **DEF FN**, **INPUT**, **FOR/NEXT**, **WHILE/WEND**, **IF/THEN/ELSE**, logical operators, **READ/DATA**, **RESTORE**, arrays, **DIM**)

Flowcharting and code transcription:

1. Design a data entry program for Kingman Gallery to log in new art acquisitions. For each title and artist, Kingman Gallery assigns an internal inventory number.
2. Design a program based on the array(s) in problem 1 allowing Kingman Gallery's manager to track down the inventory number provided the title of the art piece is known.

3. The following represents the breakdown of surveys on attendants conducted at three junior colleges:

	Male	*Female*	*Under 21*
College 1	527	504	844
College 2	379	618	799
College 3	622	473	913

Design a program to compute for each college the average attendance and the average percentages of male, female, and students twenty-one years old and older.

11 / MODULAR PROGRAMMING

SUBROUTINES: GOSUB/RETURN

Programming solutions to problems are rarely single-functioned. Complex programs usually contain so many distinct logical parts that the programs almost look as if they were many separate programs combined into one. Chapter 10 showed you that, to locate a data item, you must set up an array holding the master data set before you can proceed to use the data. Setting up the array and the subsequent use of it are conceptually quite distinct activities. Program logic segments that serve these distinct functions often are independent of each other. These logically self-contained program segments within a program are called *program modules*. A module is a part of a larger system: A program module thus does not exist by itself; it must function in coordination with the other modules in the same program to achieve a desired end result. A program code segment that expresses such a module is known as a *subroutine*. In BASIC, a subroutine is functionally complete and exists apart from the rest of the same program.

A BASIC subroutine is accessed (reached) through the **GOSUB** statement. After the logic in a subroutine has been executed, the main flow of the program logic is rejoined when the **RETURN** statement (which is the last statement to be executed in the subroutine) is encountered. The structure of a subroutine and the actions of **GOSUB** and **RETURN** are illustrated in Example 11.1.

Example 11.1

```
10 'GOSUB
20 '
30 CLS
40 GOSUB 100
50 GOSUB 200
60 GOSUB 100
70 END
100 FOR I% = 1 TO 80
110     PRINT "_";
120 NEXT I%
130 PRINT
140 RETURN
200 PRINT ,,"Report"
210 RETURN
```

In this example program, there are two subroutines. One begins with statement 100 and ends at statement 140; the other has statement numbers 200 to 210. When the program is executed and statement 40, **GOSUB 100**, is reached, BASIC will break from the sequential program execution mode and temporarily jump to statement 100 and continue program execution. When statement 140 is reached, **RETURN** sends BASIC back to statement 50 (which is the statement in sequence after **GOSUB 100** at statement 40), and BASIC resumes its sequential program execution. This subroutine draws a horizontal line across the screen.

But because statement 50 is again a **GOSUB** statement, BASIC will jump to statement 200 as directed. This subroutine displays the literal **Report** and returns when statement 210 is reached.

Statement 60 is another **GOSUB**. This time BASIC is told to jump to statement 100 again; thus, the same subroutine as the previous one is executed a second time, producing another horizontal line.

The action of **GOSUB** and **RETURN** thus resembles the pulling apart of a BASIC program and inserting an entire subroutine code segment in between the separated parts, as illustrated in Figure 11.1.

In effect, the program in Example 11.1 is the same logically as:

```
10 FOR I% = 1 TO 80
20     PRINT "_";
30 NEXT I%
40 PRINT
50 PRINT ,,"Report"
60 FOR I% = 1 TO 80
```

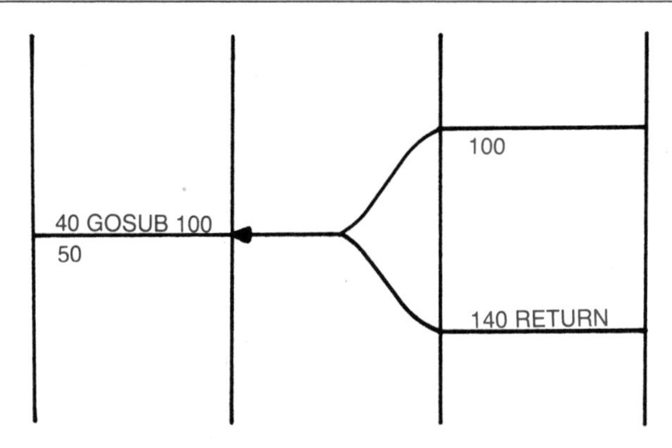

FIGURE 11.1

```
70      PRINT "_";
80 NEXT I%
90 PRINT
100 END
```

Thus, you can see that subroutines eliminate the repetition of program code segments that serve the same function, producing program code that is much more compact.

Each **GOSUB** in a program thus invokes a major program function. In designing programs, the programmer should therefore first formulate the thoughts in terms of major ideas, express them as **GOSUB**s, and then implement the logic in the subroutines independently. The result is a more logical approach to programming and better organization in the thought process.

If the program was thought out originally as:

1. First draw a top line.
2. Display a heading.
3. Then draw a line again.

then the logic can be expressed by the flowchart in Figure 11.2. Notice the new flowchart symbol used to express the two subroutines.

GOSUB is essentially a special form of branching. A program segment branched to through **GOSUB** can thus also **GOSUB** to another subroutine. For instance, the program code above performs a specific function: It produces a heading sandwiched between two lines. This function may be

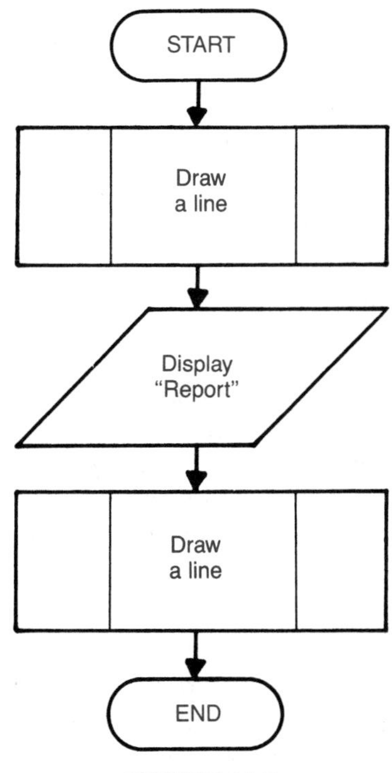

FIGURE 11.2

used repeatedly in the same program. The programming code will thus appear as:

```
100 LET TITLE$ = "Title 1"
110 GOSUB 1000
  .
  .
  .
200 LET TITLE$ = "Title 2"
210 GOSUB 1000
  .
  .
  .
1000 GOSUB 2000
1010 PRINT ,,TITLE$
```

```
1020 GOSUB 2000
1030 RETURN
  .
  .
  .
2000 FOR I% = 1 TO 80
2010      PRINT "_";
2020 NEXT I%
2030 PRINT
2040 RETURN
```

If the subroutines are themselves complex, then they may also be separately flowcharted. This process is illustrated in Example 11.2.

As pointed out, the examples in chapter 10 were really made up of major functions. Let us redesign the program code of Example 10.4 in terms of subroutines for illustration purposes.

Example 11.2

The purpose of this program is to permit the user to enter data into an array and then display the array thus established.

First the logic for the data entry operation is worked out (see Figure 11.3). Then the array display logic is ascertained (see Figure 11.4). The main logic of the program is then constructed (see Figure 11.5).

Figures 11.3 and 11.4 are called the *modular flowcharts,* and Figure 11.5 is called the *master flowchart* or *main flowchart.* A master flowchart ends with **END**, while modular flowcharts end with **RETURN**. The modular flowcharts support the master flowchart, and the master flowchart coordinates the modular flowcharts. The modular flowcharts document only a logic component of the entire program, but the master flowchart is considered logically complete.

Notice that a different kind of symbol is used to express the program modules in the master flowchart. This is in principle the same symbol as the one used in Figure 11.2. However, with the horizontal bar, a numbering system can be set up to refer from the master flowchart to the various modular flowcharts.

When the flowcharts are translated, the following code is produced.

```
10 'EXAMPLE 10.4 MODULAR
20 '
30 DIM A$(100,3)
40 GOSUB 100 'DATA ENTRY
50 GOSUB 300 'TABLE DISPLAY
```

Example 11.2–Data Entry (Subroutine 1):

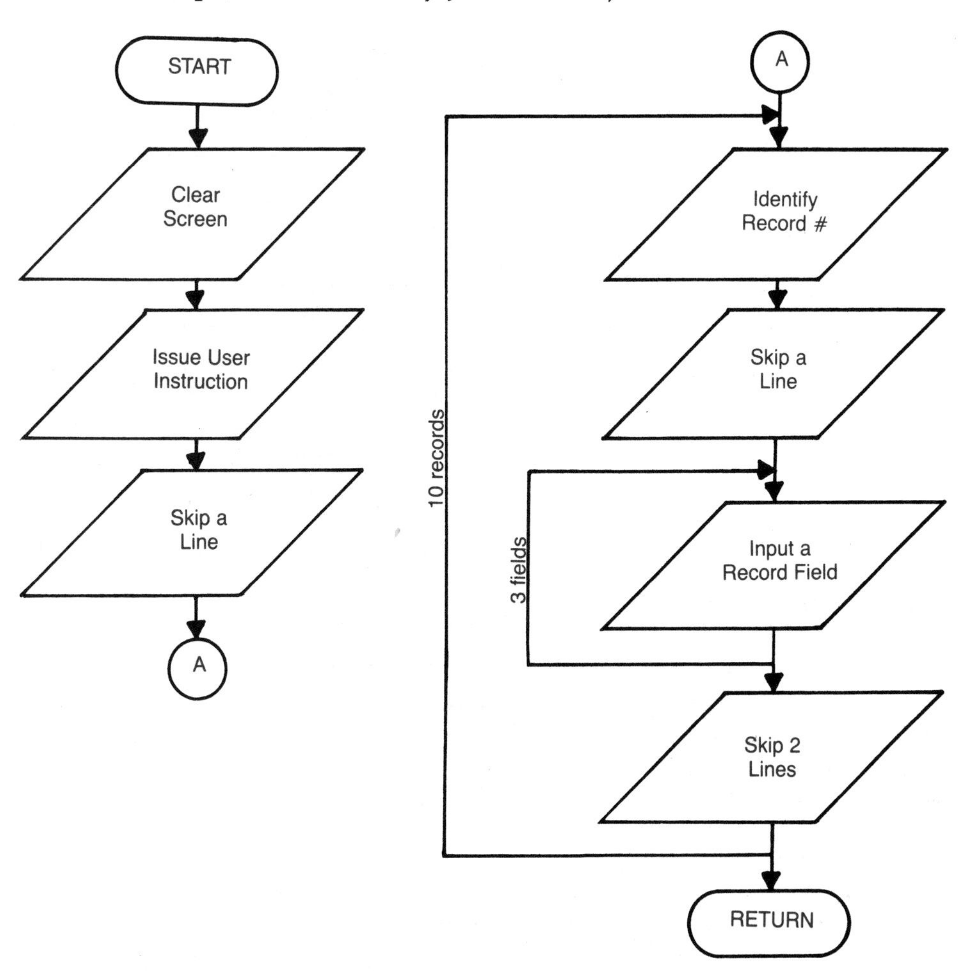

FIGURE 11.3

```
60 END
100 '--------------------------------------------------------
110 'DATA ENTRY
120 CLS
130 PRINT "Enter personal data (Name/Address/Phone) :"
140 PRINT
150 FOR R% = 1 TO 10
160      PRINT "Record"; R%
170      PRINT
180      FOR C% = 1 TO 3
```

Example 11.2–Array Display (Subroutine 2):

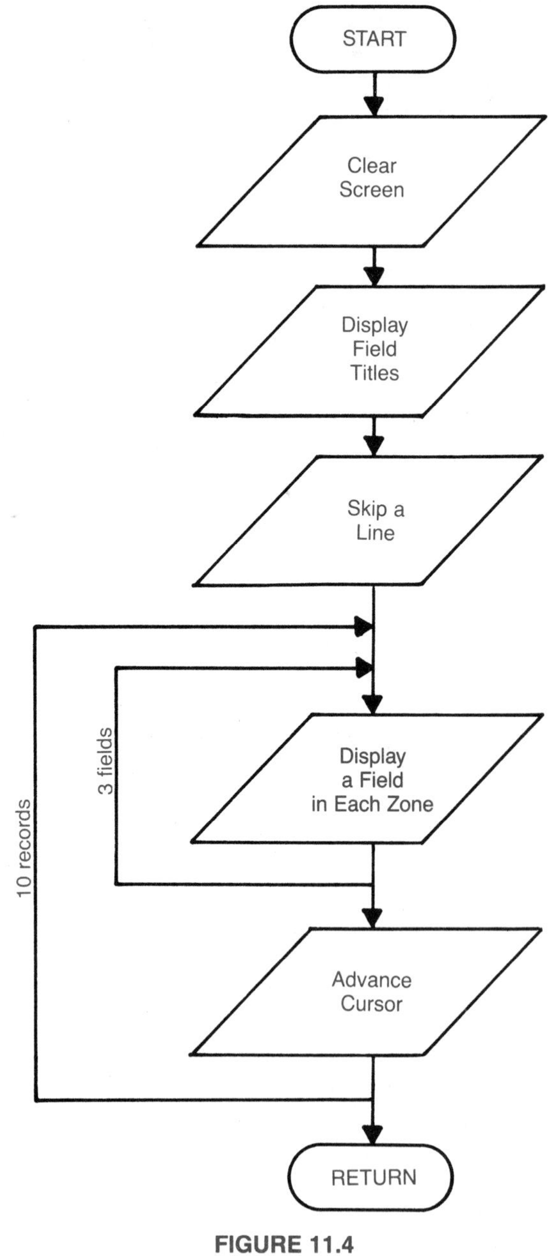

FIGURE 11.4

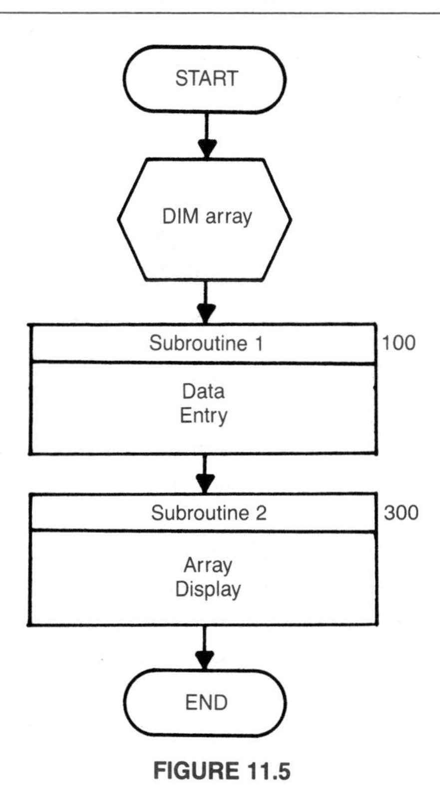

FIGURE 11.5

```
190              INPUT; "      ", A$( R%,C% )
200       NEXT C%
210      PRINT
220      PRINT
230 NEXT R%
240 RETURN
300 '---------------------------------------------------
310 'ARRAY DISPLAY
320 '
330 CLS
340 PRINT "Name", "Address", "Phone"
350 PRINT
360 FOR R% = 1 TO 10
370     FOR C% = 1 TO 3
380              PRINT A$( R%,C% ),
```

```
390       NEXT C%
400       PRINT
410 NEXT R%
420 RETURN
```

Exercise Set 11.1 GOSUB (Using **PRINT**, **CLS**, **END**, **LET**, functions, **DEF FN**, **INPUT**, **FOR/NEXT**, **WHILE/WEND**, **IF/THEN/ELSE**, logical operators, **READ/DATA**, **RESTORE**, arrays, **DIM**, **GOSUB**)

Flowcharting and code transcription:

1. Design a subroutine for entering data into the array A(R%,C%) through the keyboard, permitting the user to terminate the session at will. The maximum size of the array is 10,000 by 5.
2. Design a program permitting a user to enter data into a list, display the list on the CRT, allow the user to selectively reenter data into the list (editing), and display the list again.
3. Design a set of detailed user's instructions to accompany the last data entry operation. Allow these instructions to be displayed on the CRT on demand during the data entry operation.

MODULAR PROGRAMMING TECHNIQUES AND APPLICATIONS

Not only is programming in modular form more efficient than programming in a linear manner but modular programming also offers two other advantages:

1. The program code is usually more compact, due to the repeated code segments being consolidated into subroutines, as demonstrated earlier in this chapter.
2. Frequently used data processing functions, called *standard modules*, can be designed once and reused.

For instance, if displaying a line clear across the screen is used frequently in your program, then the code segment:

```
10 FOR I% = 1 TO 80
20   PRINT "_";
30 NEXT I%
40 PRINT
```

may be saved and combined with the new programs when it is needed, thus saving its redesign each time the same function is called for.

Besides major processing functions, subprogram logic can also be expressed as modules. Subprogram functions are often found in loops and branchings.

For instance, let us reexamine Example 7.9, whose flowchart is reproduced in Figure 11.6.

The no path of the first decision is itself a complex logic that cannot be expressed as one BASIC statement. Conceptually, the handdrawn circle part of the flowchart can be thought of as a subprogram logic, handling the activities that are to be implemented when the input grade is not below 60. This group of activities can be made into a module. The flowchart will then become that shown in Figure 11.7. Notice how the original portion of the flowchart outside of the handdrawn circle is unchanged.

The transcribed coding then becomes:

```
10 INPUT "ENTER GRADE : ", GRADE
20 IF GRADE < 60 THEN PRINT "C"
                  ELSE GOSUB 100     'HANDLE GRADES >= 60
30 END
100 IF GRADE < 80 THEN PRINT "B"
                  ELSE PRINT "A"
110 RETURN
```

Likewise, a looping logic may be made into a subroutine, and the **FOR/NEXT** or **WHILE/WEND** statements will then enclose only a **GOSUB** statement. The general representation of this is:

FOR statement

loop logic

NEXT statement

becoming:

FOR statement
GOSUB statement 'annotation
NEXT statement
loop logic
RETURN

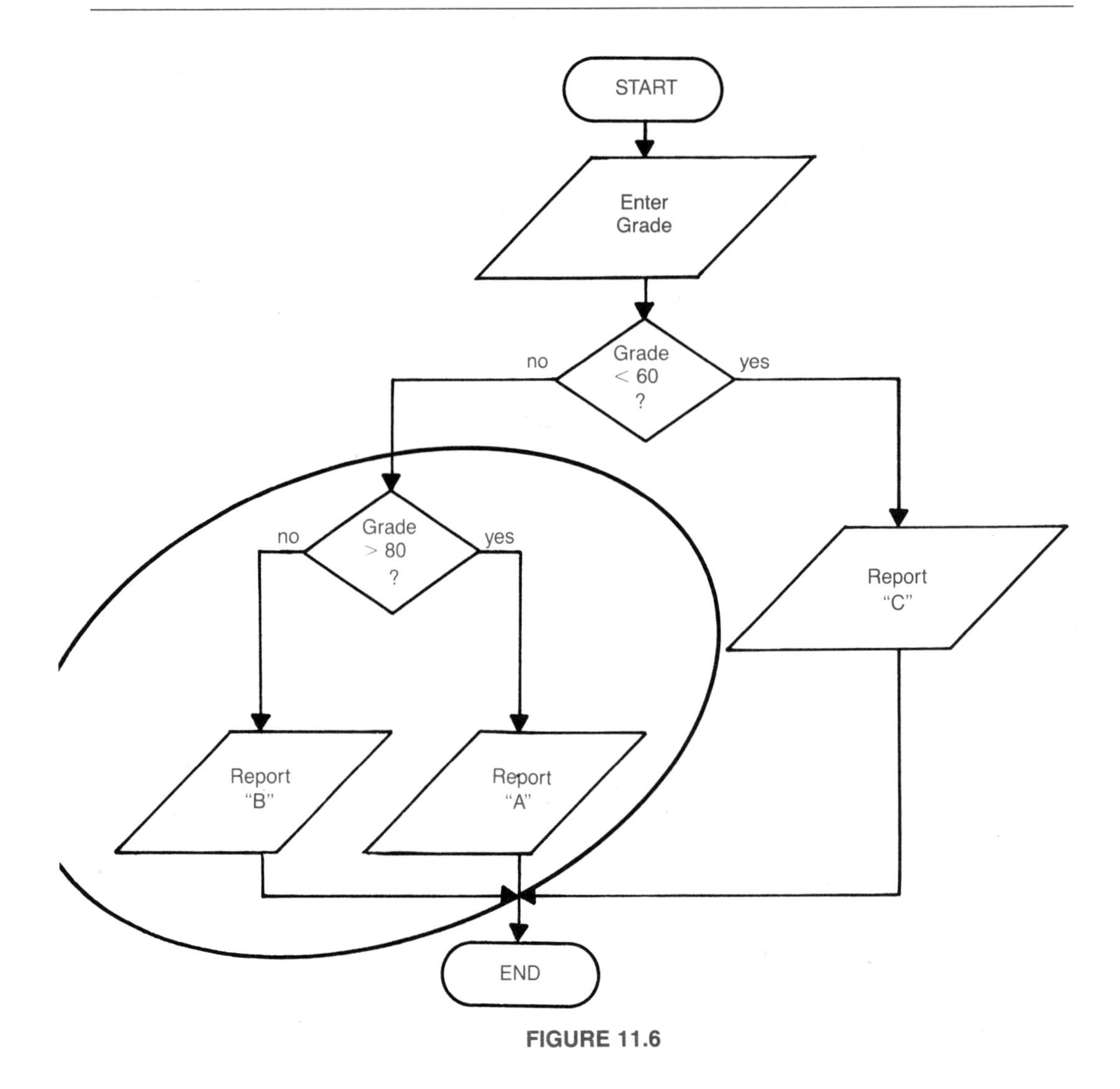

FIGURE 11.6

In general, any portion of a flowchart that has a single entry arrow and a single exit arrow can be transformed into a subroutine. In other words, as long as you can draw a circle enclosing a flowchart portion and the circle intersects only one inward arrow and one outward arrow, then the enclosed flowchart portion can be made into a subroutine, simplifying the program code. The following exercises are provided for you to practice these techniques.

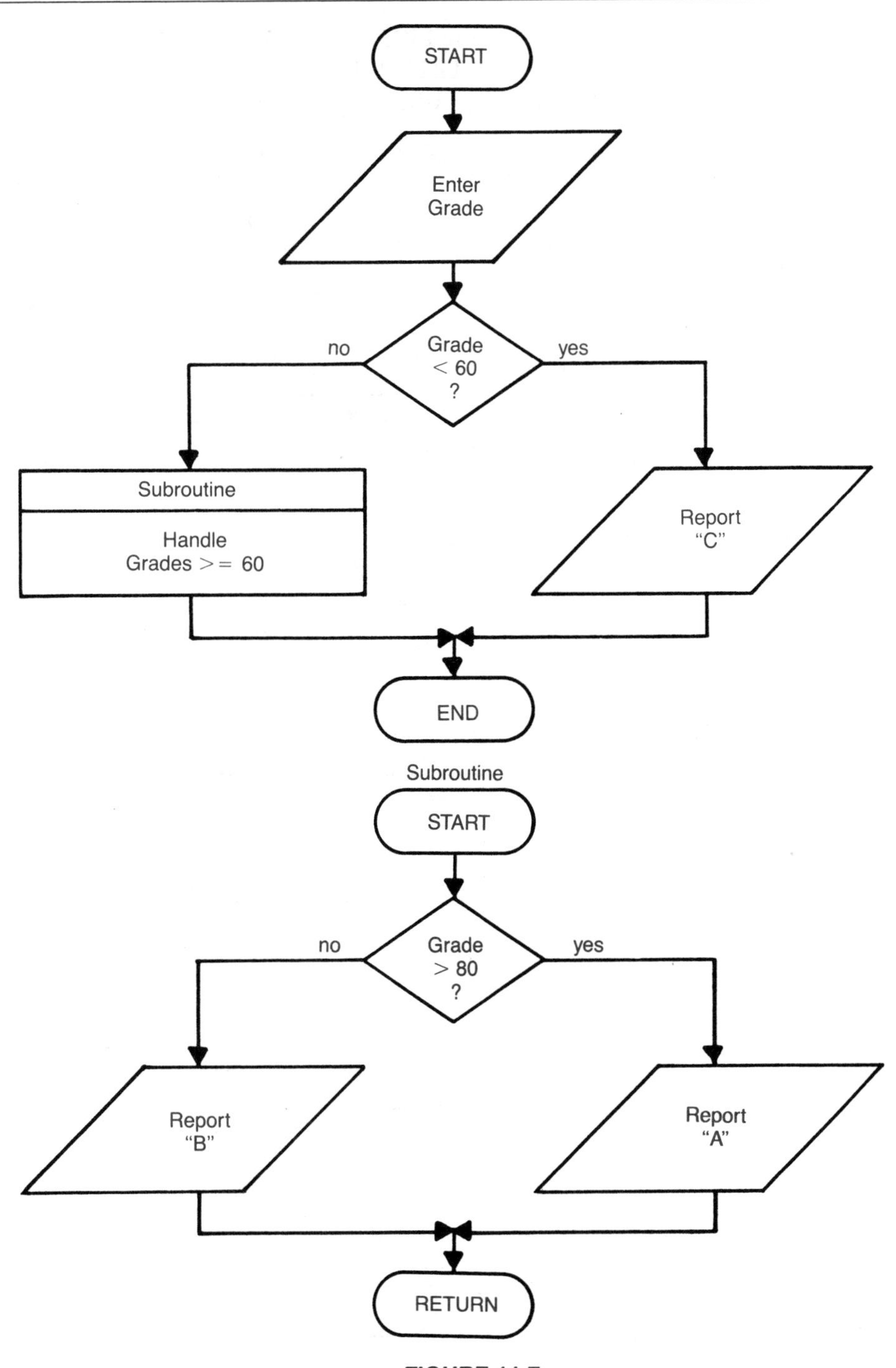
START
Enter
Grade
Grade
< 60
?
no
yes
Subroutine
Handle
Grades >= 60
Report
"C"
END
Subroutine
START
Grade
> 80
?
no
yes
Report
"B"
Report
"A"
RETURN

FIGURE 11.7

Exercise Set 11.2 (Using **PRINT**, **CLS**, **END**, **LET**, functions, **DEF FN**, **INPUT**, **FOR/NEXT**, **WHILE/WEND**, **IF/THEN/ELSE**, logical operators, **READ/DATA**, **RESTORE**, arrays, **DIM**, **GOSUB**)

A. Transcribe the following flowcharts into code by first redoing the flowcharts in modular form:

1. (See Figure 11.8.)

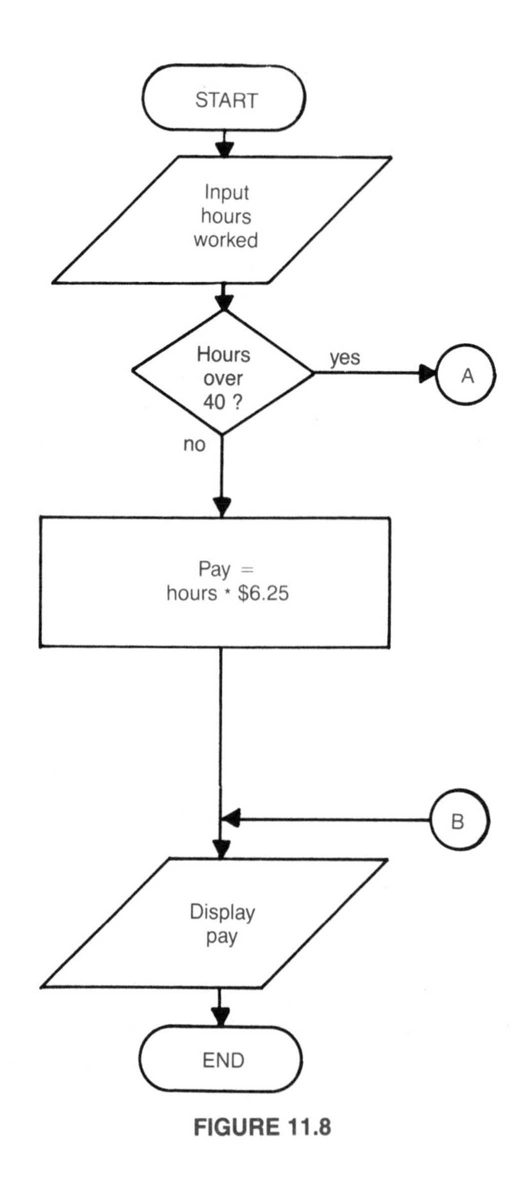

FIGURE 11.8

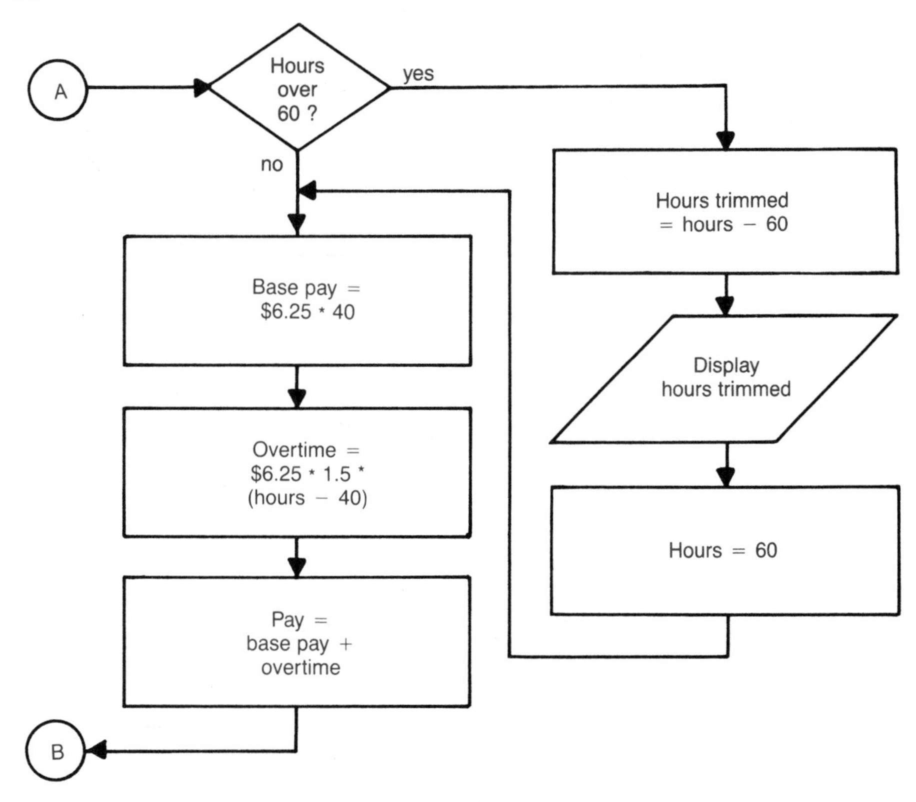

FIGURE 11.8 (continued)

2. (See Figure 11.9.)

B. Flowcharting and code transcriptions:

3. Design a program to total separately the withdrawal and deposit data for a bank checking account. All withdrawals and deposits are entered through the keyboard as positive numbers. There are no zero amounts. The program should ask what kind of data item it is before each data input operation. At the end of the program, the totals and number of transactions for each category are reported in a meaningful manner.

Chapter Exercises (Using **PRINT**, **CLS**, **END**, **LET**, functions, **DEF FN**, **INPUT**, **FOR/NEXT**, **WHILE/WEND**, **IF/THEN/ELSE**, logical operators, **READ/DATA**, **RESTORE**, arrays, **DIM**, **GOSUB**)

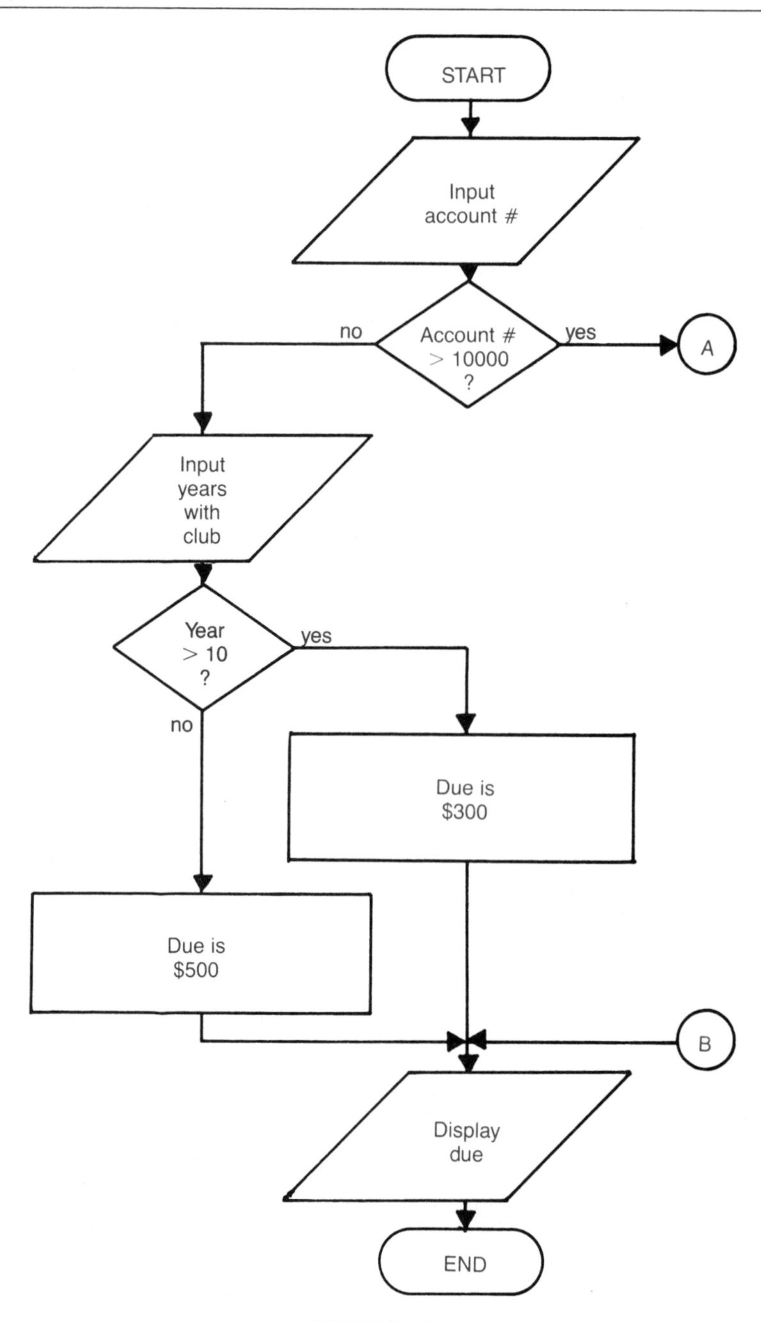
START
Input
account #
Account #
> 10000
?
no
yes
A
Input
years
with
club
Year
> 10
?
yes
no
Due is
$300
Due is
$500
B
Display
due
END

FIGURE 11.9

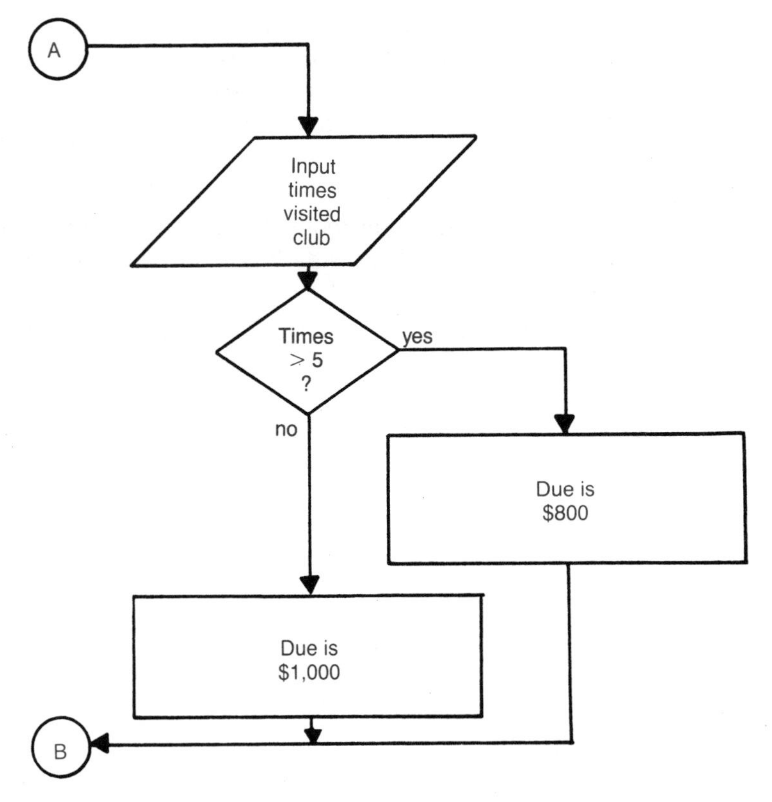

FIGURE 11.9 (continued)

Flowcharting and code transcription:

1. A laboratory maintains a computer inventory list of all equipment. For control purposes, each time a piece of equipment is checked out the word *out* is stored next to the equipment entry in the computer data array. At the end of each day, a report is produced listing all the equipment borrowed, and a separate report is also produced listing all the equipment that is still on the shelf. Design a program to support these operations.
2. Peelnot Paint Co. carries four kinds of paints: latex, water based, enamel, and gloss. Each kind comes in colors of red, orange, yellow, green, indigo, blue, and purple. Design a program to keep track of the

up-to-date inventories of each kind of paint for Peelnot. This program is to be used for daily sales operations. For each order filled, the appropriate inventories must be adjusted to reflect the true inventory levels. If the inventory is zero, a message shall be displayed indicating "out of stock."

3. Doctor Goodskill works ten hours a day. Patient appointments are made at half-hour intervals. Design a program for daily use to keep track of Dr. Goodskill's daily appointments. (Obviously, time slots that are taken cannot be used again, and a time slot will become available again when a patient cancels an appointment.)

12 / INTRODUCTION TO GRAPHICS

GRAPHICS FUNDAMENTALS

Besides string and numeric data processing, IBM PC BASIC also provides extensive graphics capabilities. Through special commands and keywords and with the proper hardware support, a great variety of shapes and colors can be displayed on the CRT. They can be used for personal programming or to enhance output operations by providing pictorial renditions of output data. Pie charts, bar charts, and line charts are all possible with these graphics features. This chapter is devoted to explaining some of the most useful graphics commands and the fundamental techniques associated with producing graphics displays.

For systems with color capabilities, the IBM PC functions in three display modes. They are **Text mode**, **Medium-Resolution Graphics mode,** and **High-Resolution Graphics mode**. For monochromatic (black and white) systems, only Text mode is possible. Therefore, except for the extended ASCII characters, graphics are limited to color systems, although not limited to a color monitor. The material presented in this chapter is hence primarily for the color system.

Normally, BASIC is configured in the Text mode, which works with 25 rows and 80 columns of screen text material. In the Medium-Resolution Graphics mode, the screen is viewed as being made up of 320 horizontal and 200 vertical (320 × 200) points, called *pixels* (see Figure 12.1). In High-Resolution Graphics mode, the screen is composed of 640 × 200 pixels (see Figure 12.2).

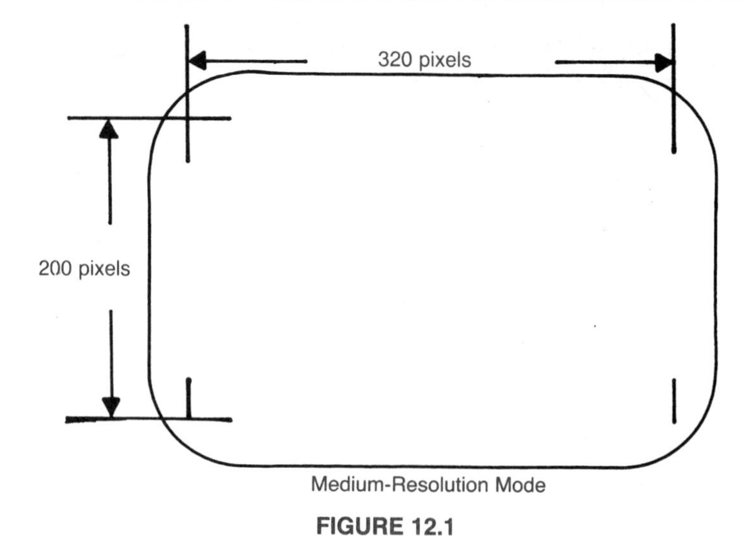

Medium-Resolution Mode

FIGURE 12.1

To begin a programming session for graphics, the proper mode must be selected. The statement to select display modes is the **SCREEN** statement.

For the **SCREEN** statement, the three modes are numbered 0, 1, and 2, respectively. Normally, the **SCREEN** mode is therefore set to 0, and the screen width is eighty characters.

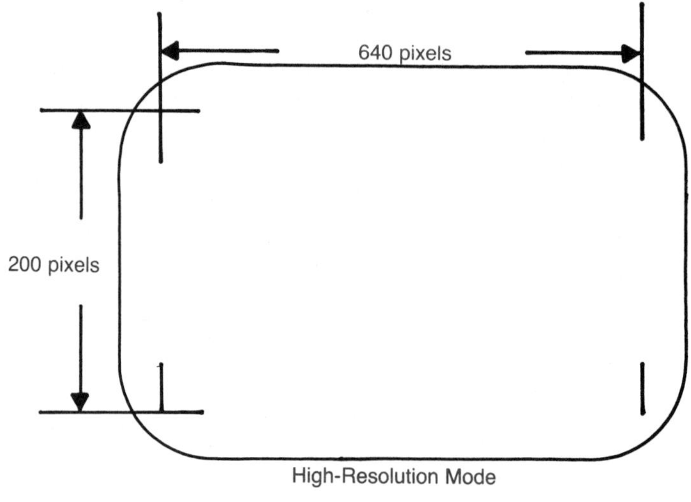

High-Resolution Mode

FIGURE 12.2

If mode 1 is selected, then Medium-Resolution Graphics mode will be invoked, and many graphics statements will become functional.

In High-Resolution mode (selected through **SCREEN** as mode 2), however, no color is available.

The mode selection is hence made possible by one of the following three statements:

```
SCREEN 0
SCREEN 1
SCREEN 2
```

Example 12.1 invokes the Medium-Resolution mode.

Example 12.1

After this program is **RUN**, the screen will become forty columns wide, and all the characters will be double their normal width.

```
10 'Medium-Resolution Graphics
20 '
30 SCREEN 1
40 END
```

To return to Text mode, the following statements must be issued:

```
SCREEN 0
WIDTH 80
```

The **WIDTH** statement sets the column width of the CRT.

Example 12.2 selects the High-Resolution mode. After the program is **RUN**, everything will look more or less normal until graphics statements are issued. However, all displays appear brighter under High-Resolution mode.

Example 12.2

```
10 'High-Resolution Graphics
20 '
30 SCREEN 2
40 END
```

SCREEN
Form: SCREEN [mode][, [burst][, [active page][, visual page]]]
Function: To set the display screen mode.

WIDTH
Form: WIDTH 40 or WIDTH 80
Function: To set the screen width.

For color displays, when the display mode has been selected, then the color specifications must be set. This is performed through the **COLOR** statement.

In Text mode, three color parameters govern the screen displays:

1. The border—This consists of the four edges of the screen, where no display is possible.
2. The background—This is the general screen color, which is normally the same as the border.
3. The foreground—This is the color of the text characters or the graphics shapes.

COLOR (for texts)
Form: COLOR [foreground][, [background][, border]]
Function: To set the color and display attributes for textual displays.

The color settings are selected through a series of sixteen integer codes, which are listed here:

0	Black	8	Gray
1	Blue	9	Light Blue
2	Green	10	Light Green
3	Cyan	11	Light Cyan
4	Red	12	Light Red
5	Magenta	13	Light Magenta
6	Brown	14	Yellow
7	White	15	High-intensity White

Control of many screen properties is exercised through **COLOR**. We shall begin with the simplest, illustrated through the following example.

Example 12.3

This program sets the foreground color to light red and the background and border color to dark red. Remember, the Text mode can work in color as well.

```
10 'COLOR
20 '
30 COLOR 12, 4, 4
40 END
```

light red   dark red

If the twenty-fifth screen row is needed for display purposes, then the keys showing at the bottom of the screen can be turned off with the **KEY** statement.

Example 12.4

```
10 'KEY
20 '
30 KEY OFF
40 END
```

To bring the bottom keys back, issue the command:

```
KEY ON
```

With the setup activities completed, BASIC is ready to execute graphics statements.

Exercise Set 12.1 SCREEN, WIDTH, COLOR for text

A. What do the following programs do?

1.

```
10 SCREEN 0
20 WIDTH 40
30 END
```

Answer: ______________________________

____

2.

```
10 SCREEN 1
20 LET K$ = INKEY$
30 IF K$ = "" THEN 20
40 SCREEN 0
50 WIDTH 80
60 END
```

Answer: ______________________________

____

B. Practice on syntax:

3. Write a program to select the Medium-Resolution Graphics mode with green border and background and yellow foreground.
4. Write a program to permit a user to select the foreground and background colors for a High-Resolution mode CRT display.

DRAWING CIRCLES: CIRCLE

The first graphics statement to be discussed is the **CIRCLE** statement, which draws line circles on the CRT. The **CIRCLE** statement takes on several parameters that describe the circular shape to be drawn and the color settings. The simplest form of its use is to draw a perfect line circle, as illustrated in Example 12.5 in the Medium-Resolution mode.

Example 12.5

Figure 12.3 shows the CRT display that results from the following program.

```
10 'CIRCLE
20 '
30 KEY OFF
40 SCREEN 1
50 CIRCLE( 160, 100 ), 75
60 END
```

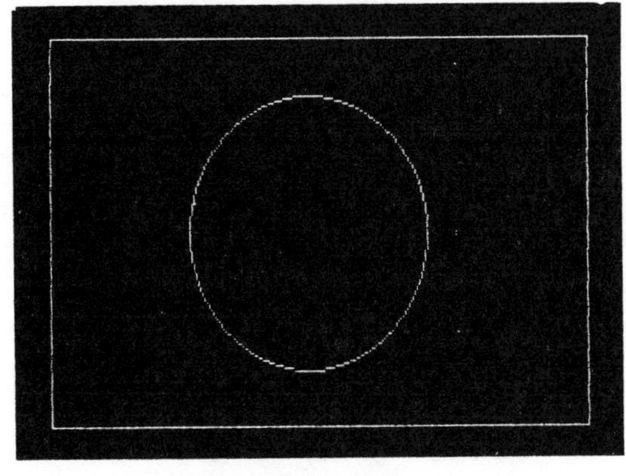

FIGURE 12.3

The various parameters that can be used with **CIRCLE** will be discussed shortly. In this example, a circle with its center at pixel column 160 and row 100 and a radius seventy-five pixels long is drawn.

For systems with color monitors, Example 12.6 draws the same circle with a dark red background.

Example 12.6

```
10 'CIRCLE
20 '
30 KEY OFF
40 SCREEN 1, 0
50 COLOR 0, 4, 4
60 CIRCLE( 160, 100 ), 75
70 END
```

The color of the circle itself can also be set. This is achieved through the fourth parameter (color) in the **CIRCLE** statement. Example 12.7 draws a white circle.

The color parameter can be one of four integers from 0 through 3. In coordination with the **COLOR** statement, it selects a color from the current palette defined by **COLOR**. For graphics, the **COLOR** statement takes the following form:

```
COLOR (for graphics)

Form:
COLOR [background][, palette]

Function: To set the color attributes for graphics.
```

If palette is an even integer, then a set of colors listed under palette A will be invoked. If palette is odd, then the colors of palette B will be activated.

Color	*Palette A*	*Palette B*
1	Green	Cyan
2	Red	Magenta
3	Brown	White

If the color specification in the **CIRCLE** statement is omitted, then BASIC will assume the default colors, which are:

Medium-Resolution mode:	3
High-Resolution mode:	1

The fundamental workings of **COLOR** and **CIRCLE** with colors are demonstrated in Example 12.7.

Example 12.7

In this example, first **COLOR 4, 1** sets the background color to red, with palette B selected. The ensuing **CIRCLE** statement selects the color code 3, which corresponds to white in palette B.

```
10 'Red background, white palette
20 '
30 KEY OFF
40 SCREEN 1, 0
50 COLOR 4, 1
60 CIRCLE( 160, 100 ), 75, 3
70 END
```

A circle drawn in the High-Resolution mode, of course, will have no color.

Example 12.8

```
10 'High Resolution
20 '
30 KEY OFF
40 SCREEN 2
50 CIRCLE( 160, 100 ), 75
60 END
```

Circular arcs can be drawn with the **CIRCLE** statement as well. Two more parameters are available for the **CIRCLE** statement to specify the starting and ending angles of a circular arc to be drawn. A full circle is drawn when these parameters are omitted.

If the starting and ending angles are specified, they must be expressed in radian and not degree; the angular reference is illustrated in Figure 12.4.

Example 12.9 shows how the lower half of a circle is drawn—starting from the left, tracing around the bottom, and ending on the right.

Example 12.9

```
10 'Arc
20 '
30 LET PI = 3.14159
40 SCREEN 1
50 CIRCLE( 160, 100 ), 50,, PI, PI*2
60 END
```

When the starting and ending angles are specified as positive numbers, then open arcs are drawn. However, if they are expressed as negative numbers, then the ends of the arc will be linked to the center of the circle, forming a slice of a pie, as demonstrated in Example 12.10. This form of circle drawing and solid circular figures are used to form pie charts.

Example 12.10

Figure 12.5 shows the CRT display that results from the following code.

```
10 'Pie Chart
20 '
30 SCREEN 2
40 LET PI = 3.141593
50 CIRCLE( 320, 100 ), 150,, -PI/2, -PI*2
60 CIRCLE STEP ( 20, -10 ), 150,, -PI*2, -PI/2
70 END
```

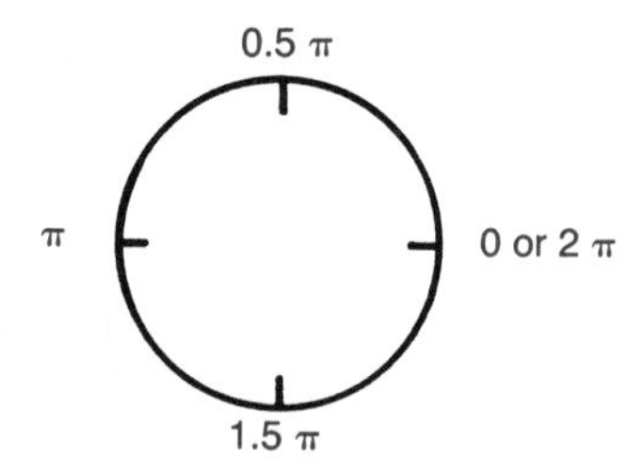

FIGURE 12.4

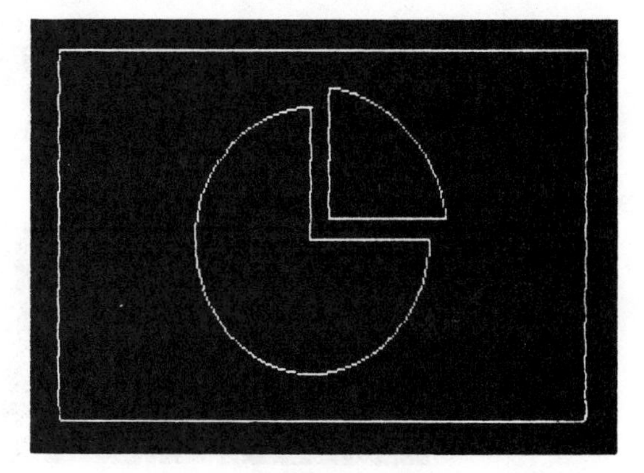

FIGURE 12.5

When titles and annotations are added, then pie charts are formed. **RUN** Example 12.11 and study the program code to understand how graphics and textual material are displayed in High-Resolution mode. Notice that the circle center is defined by a ***STEP*** *coordinate.* This means that the circle center coordinate is not an absolute position but a relative distance from the last circle center defined. This is called *relative coordinate addressing.*

The cursor position can also be discretely defined. This is achieved with the **LOCATE** statement, which specifies the cursor's screen coordinate.

It is important for you to distinguish between a graphics screen coordinate and a test cursor coordinate. A graphics coordinate is a pixel, while a text cursor coordinate is a row-and-column position.

Example 12.11

Figure 12.6 shows the result of this program.

```
10 'Pie Chart with Annotation
20 '
30 KEY OFF
40 CLS
50 SCREEN 2
60 LET PI = 3.141593
70 CIRCLE( 320, 100 ), 150,, -PI/2, -PI*2
80 CIRCLE STEP ( 20, -10 ), 150,, -PI*2, -PI/2
90 LOCATE 15, 30
100 PRINT "FOOD";
```

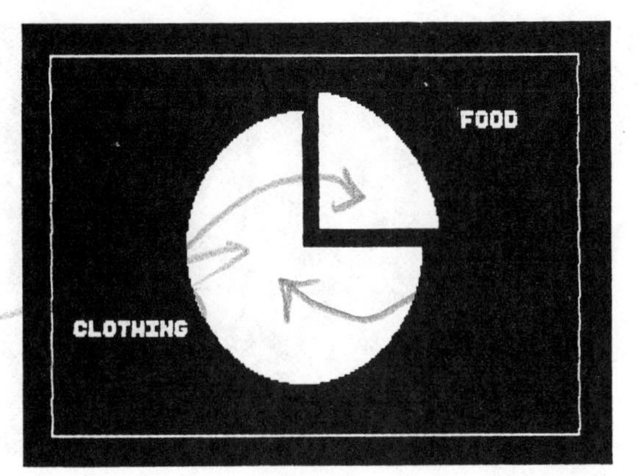

FIGURE 12.6

```
110 LOCATE 9, 47
120 PRINT "CLOTHING";
130 LOCATE 20
140 END
```

CIRCLE
Form: CIRCLE [STEP] (x, y), radius[, color[, start angle, end angle[, aspect]]]
Function: To draw a circular arc on the screen.

Exercise Set 12.2 KEY, CIRCLE, COLOR

A. What do the following programs do?

1.

```
10 LET PI = 3.14159
20 SCREEN 1
30 CIRCLE( 160, 100 ), 50,, PI/3, PI*2/3
40 END
```

Answer: ____

____

2.

```
10 LET PI = 3.14159
20 KEY OFF
30 CLS
40 SCREEN 1
50 FOR I% = 0 TO 50
60      CIRCLE( 160, 100 ), I%,, PI, PI*2
70 NEXT I%
80 END
```

Answer: ______________________________

____

B. Write a program to produce the following displays:

3.

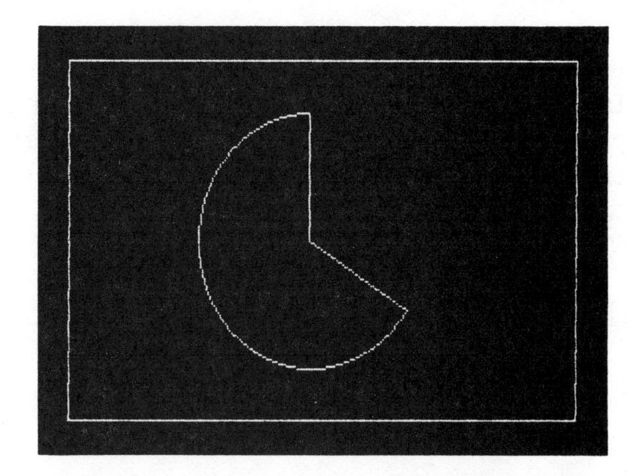

4.

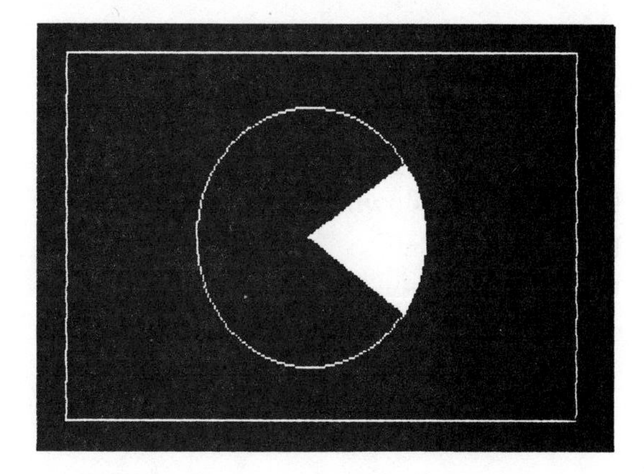

5.

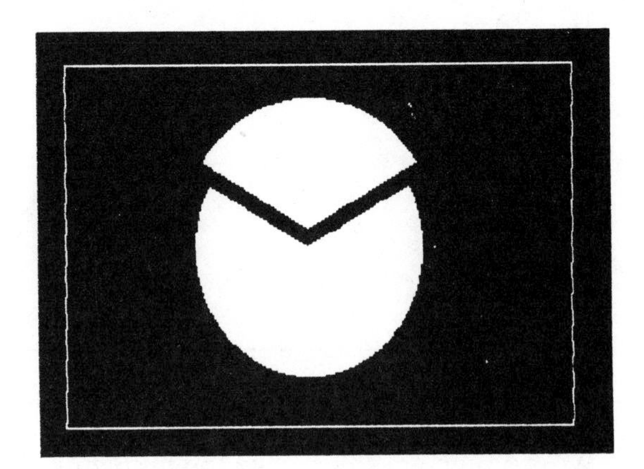

DRAWING FIGURES: DRAW

Figures or noncircular shapes are drawn with the **DRAW** statement. The **DRAW** statement works with a set of subcommands and their associated parameters, all made into string data. The form for **DRAW** and the associated subcommands is listed below:

DRAW
Form: DRAW specification string
Function: To draw a figure as specified.

Specification string subcommands.

U n	Move up.
D n	Move down.
L n	Move left.
R n	Move right.

E n Move diagonally up and right.
F n Move diagonally down and right.
G n Move diagonally down and left.
H n Move diagonally up and left.

The following examples show the use of the **DRAW** subcommands and demonstrate how **DRAW** specification strings are formed.

Example 12.12

Figure 12.7 shows the result of this code.

```
10 'Vertical line
20 '
30 SCREEN 2
40 CLS
50 DRAW "BM100,100"
60 DRAW "D80"
```

In this program, statement 50 defines a beginning point for the **DRAW**ing. In the string **"BM100,100"**, the **B** initiates a point on the screen by telling BASIC to move to that point but not produce an image. **M** moves to the coordinates as specified—the point at x = 100, y = 100. Statement 60 then says: Draw downward 80 points from the initial point.

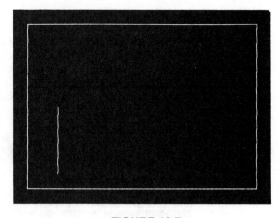

FIGURE 12.7

Example 12.13

This program draws a straight line to the right 80 points (**R80** in statement 60). Figure 12.8 shows the result.

```
10 'Horizontal line
20 '
30 SCREEN 2
40 CLS
50 DRAW "BM100,100"
60 DRAW "R80"
```

With combinations of subcommands, you can achieve complete shapes.

Example 12.14

This program draws a rectangle by telling BASIC to move to a point on the screen in four consecutive directions: down, right, up, and left. Figure 12.9 shows the result.

```
10 'Box
20 '
30 SCREEN 2
40 CLS
50 DRAW "BM100,100"
60 DRAW "D80"
70 DRAW "R80"
```

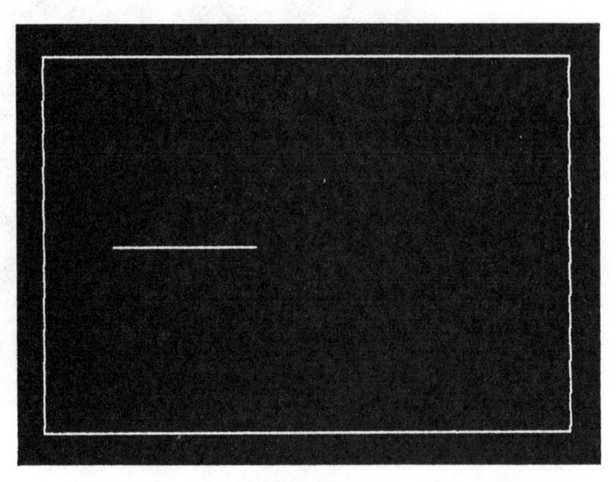

FIGURE 12.8

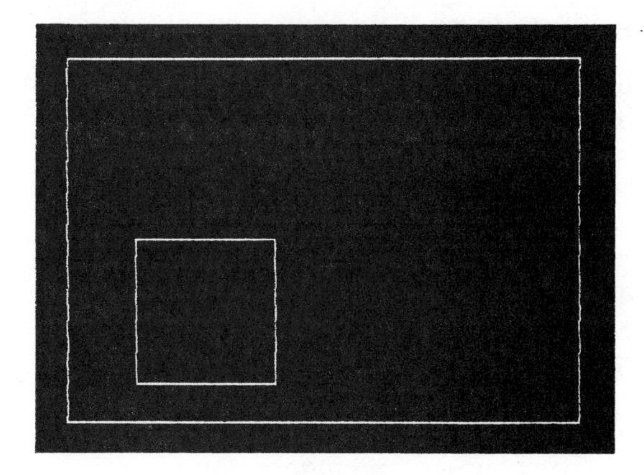

FIGURE 12.9

```
80 DRAW "U80"
90 DRAW "L80"
100 END
```

Individual subcommands can be grouped together and all placed under one string, as shown in the next example, which draws the same rectangle as the one in Example 12.14.

Example 12.15

```
10 'Box
20 '
30 SCREEN 2
40 CLS
50 DRAW "BM100,100"
60 DRAW "D80 R80 U80 L80"
70 END
```

This feature is provided so that once a shape is achieved, it can be "remembered" and used in the future. The string describing the shape essentially becomes a single data item.

Example 12.16

In this example, a prescribed-shape data item is used to display a figure on the screen.

```
10 'Stock Figure
20 '
30 READ BOX$
40 SCREEN 2
50 CLS
60 DRAW "BM100,100"
70 DRAW BOX$
80 END
90 DATA "D80 R80 U80 L80"
```

With the diagonal movement subcommands, nonrectangular shapes can be drawn.

Example 12.17

In this example, the **H** subcommand, which causes a line to move in the northwest direction, is used to produce a triangle (see Figure 12.10).

```
10 'Triangle
20 '
30 READ TRIANGLE$
40 SCREEN 2
50 CLS
60 DRAW "BM100,100"
70 DRAW TRIANGLE$
80 END
90 DATA "D80 R80 H80"
```

If different shape sizes are desired, then a scale factor can be included in the string specification.

Example 12.18

For this program, a triangle five times the size of the previous one is drawn.

```
10 'Triangle
20 '
30 READ TRIANGLE$
40 SCREEN 2
```

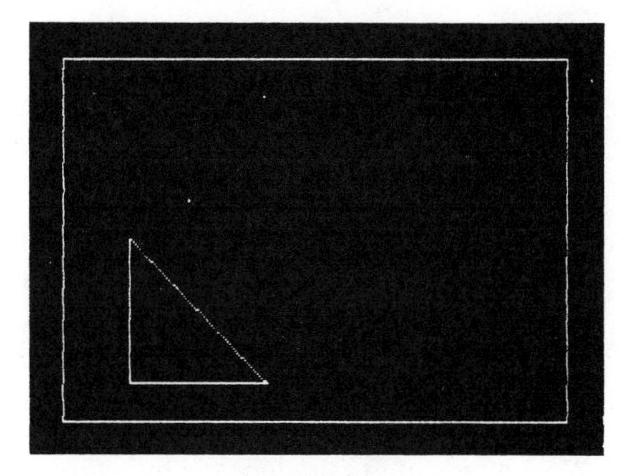

FIGURE 12.10

```
50 CLS
60 DRAW "BM100, 50"
70 DRAW TRIANGLE$
80 END
90 DATA "S5 D80 R80 H80"
```

Exercise Set 12.3 DRAW, subcommands

A. What do the following programs do?

1.

```
10 SCREEN 2
20 CLS
30 DRAW "BM50,50"
40 DRAW "R100"
50 DRAW "D100"
60 DRAW "L100"
70 DRAW "U100"
80 END
```

Answer: ____

____

2.

```
30 READ SHAPE$
40 SCREEN 2
50 CLS
60 DRAW "BM200,100"
70 DRAW SHAPE$
80 END
90 DATA "G80 R80 H80"
```

Answer: ______________________________

____

B. Write a program to produce the following shapes:

3.

4.

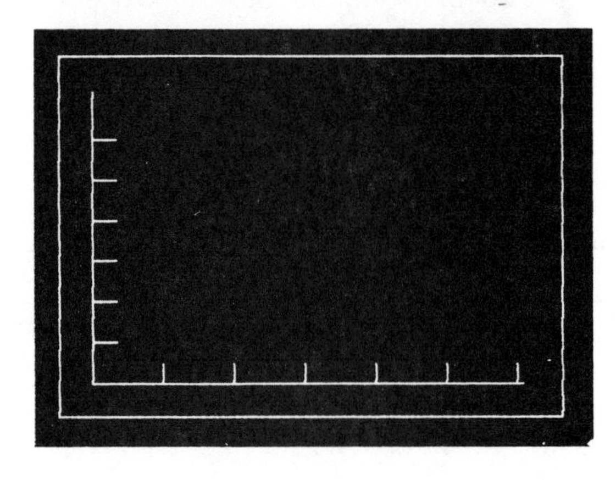

5.

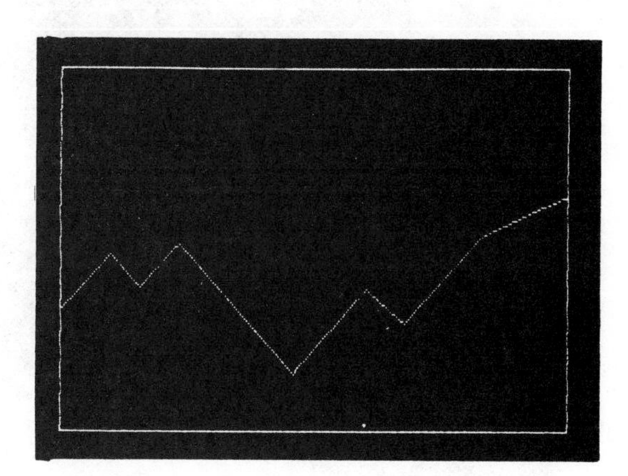

DRAWING STRAIGHT LINES: LINE

The **LINE** statement is used to draw straight lines on the screen. The **LINE** statement essentially works with the x and y coordinate parameters. With the starting and ending point on the screen specified, **LINE** connects the two points by drawing a straight line from one to the other.

LINE
Form: LINE [(start coordinate)] - (end coordinate) [, [color][, B[F]]]
Function: To draw a straight line or a rectangle.

Example 12.19

In this example, a straight line is drawn from the upper left-hand corner of the CRT to the lower right-hand corner (see Figure 12.11).

```
10 'LINE
20 '
30 SCREEN 1
```

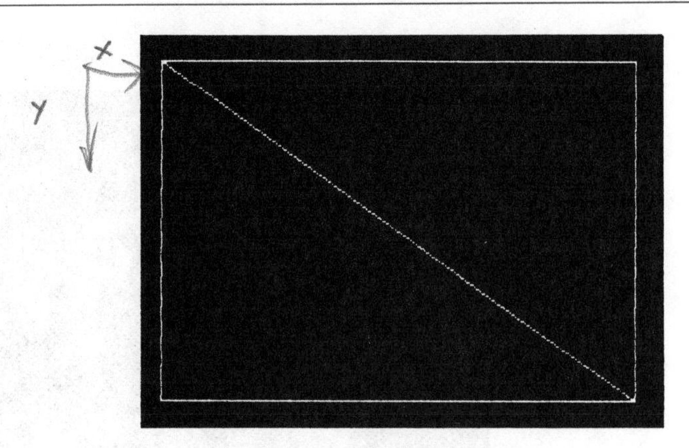

FIGURE 12.11

```
40 KEY OFF
50 CLS
60 LINE (0,0) - (320, 100)
70 END
```

In Example 12.20, a triangle is drawn with three straight lines. Pay attention to statements 70 and 80, where the starting coordinates are omitted. This means the lines will be drawn from the point at which the previous line stopped (see Figure 12.12).

Example 12.20

```
10 'LINE
20 '
30 SCREEN 1
40 KEY OFF
50 CLS
60 LINE (0,100) - (319, 100)
70 LINE  - (319, 1)
80 LINE  - (0, 100)
90 END
```

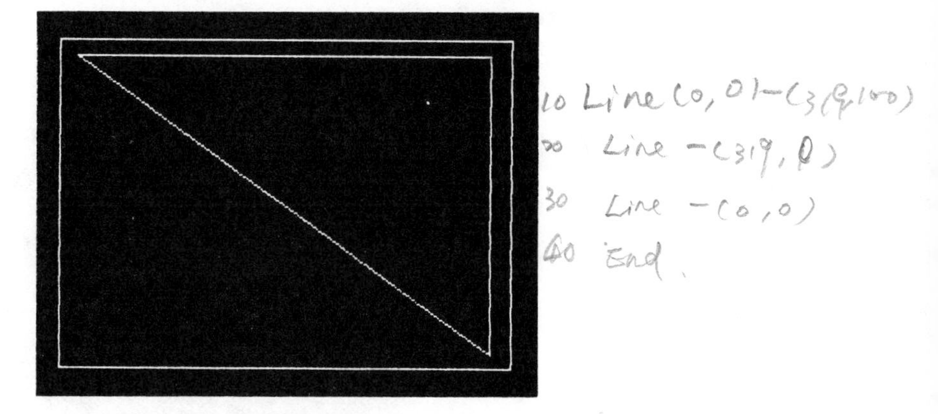

FIGURE 12.12

Three more parameters can be used with **LINE**. The first is for color setting, which works exactly as explained in **CIRCLE** and will not be repeated here. The two remaining parameters **B** and **F** cause a line box and a solid box to be displayed. In such cases, the two coordinate specifications are used to denote the two opposite corners of the box. Thus:

```
LINE (0,0) - (100,100),,B
```

will generate a line box with the upper left-hand corner at (0,0) and the lower right-hand corner at (100,100).

```
LINE (0,0) - (100,100),,BF
```

will generate the same box but solid.

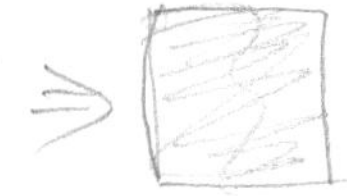

Exercise Set 13.4 LINE

Write programs to produce the following CRT displays:

1.

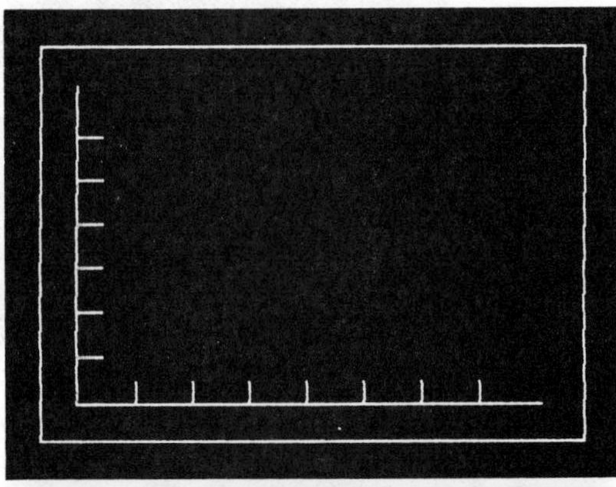

2.

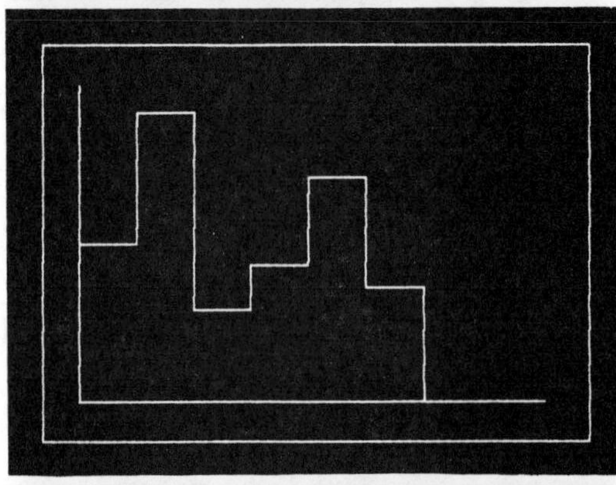

3.

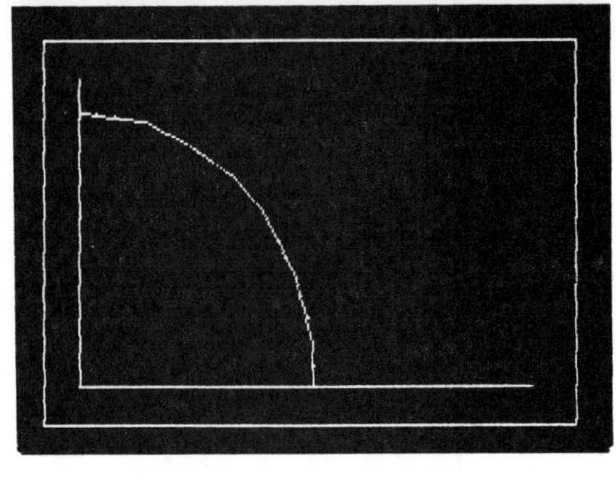

4.

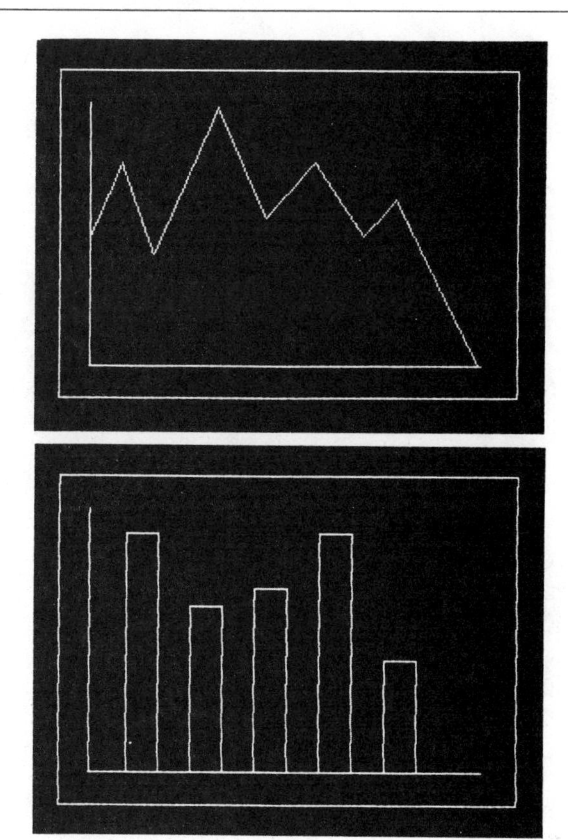

5.

FILLING IN THE FIGURES: PAINT

If solid-colored figures are desired, then the **PAINT** statement can be used. **PAINT** is quite simple. As a parameter, it takes on a coordinate point that is internal to a figure drawn with the foreground color. Once this coordinate parameter is specified, the entire enclosure of the figure will be filled in with the color specified. Its use is illustrated in Example 12.21.

Example 12.21

This example first draws a figure (a triangle) with **LINEs**, then **PAINTs** the interior of the figure. Point (200, 50) in statement 90 is a point inside the triangle drawn. See Figure 12.13 for the result.

FIGURE 12.13

```
10 'PAINT
20 '
30 SCREEN 1
40 KEY OFF
50 CLS
60 LINE (0,100) - (319, 100)
70 LINE  - (319, 1)
80 LINE  - (0, 100)
90 PAINT (200, 50)
100 END
```

The next example **PAINT**s with colors. The color is not set by **PAINT**. **PAINT** works only with the basic color set by **COLOR**, which also governs the color used by **LINE**.

Example 12.22

```
10 'PAINT Color
20 '
30 SCREEN 1, 0
40 COLOR 4, 0
50 KEY OFF
60 CLS
70 LINE (0,100) - (319, 100)
80 LINE  - (319, 1)
```

```
90 LINE  - (0, 100)
100 PAINT (200, 50)
110 END
```

Example 12.23

In this example, because a point outside the figure is selected for **PAINT**, the outside of the figure is **PAINT**ed (see Figure 12.14).

```
10 'PAINT Color
20 '
30 SCREEN 1, 0
40 COLOR 4, 0
50 KEY OFF
60 CLS
70 LINE (5,100) - (315, 100)
80 LINE  - (315, 1)
90 LINE  - (5, 100)
100 PAINT (1, 1)
110 END
```

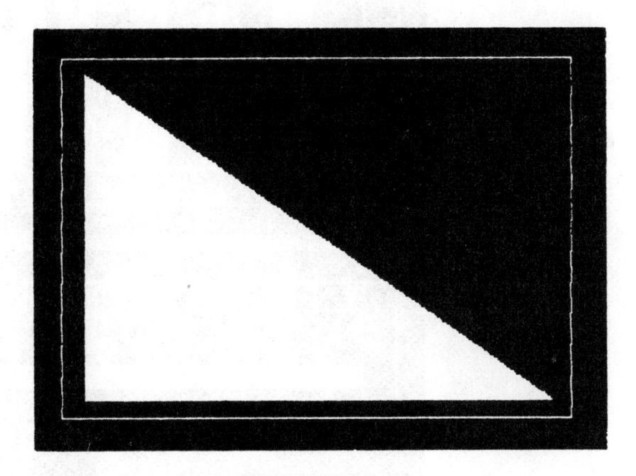

FIGURE 12.14

Exercise Set 12.5 PAINT

Write programs to produce the following CRT displays:

1.

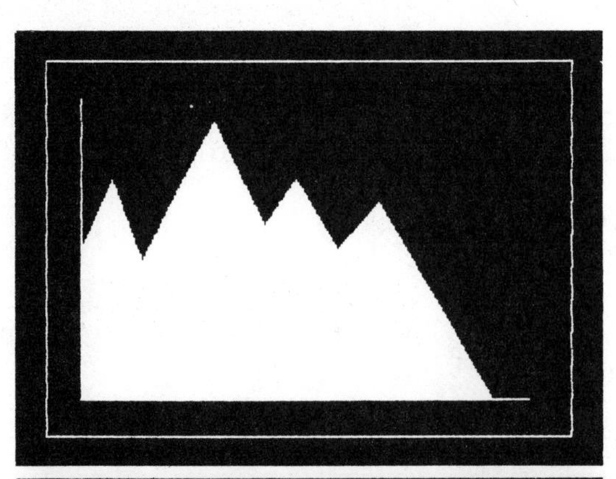

2.

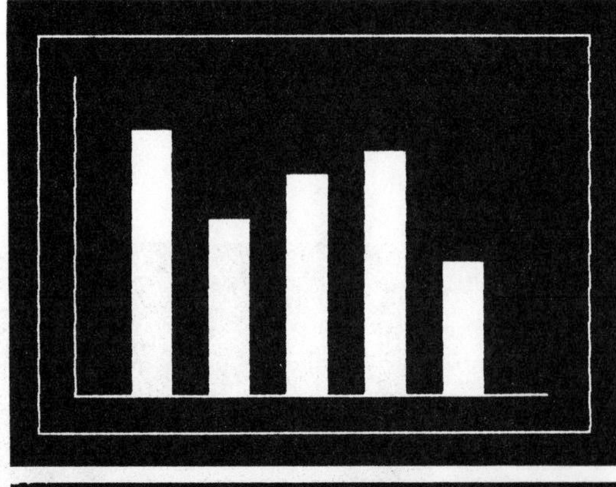

3.

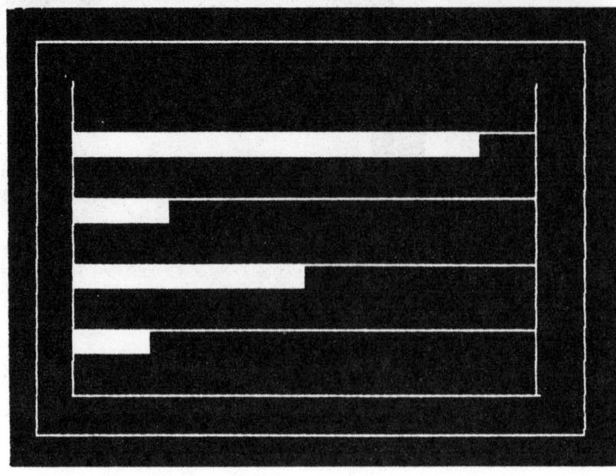

4.

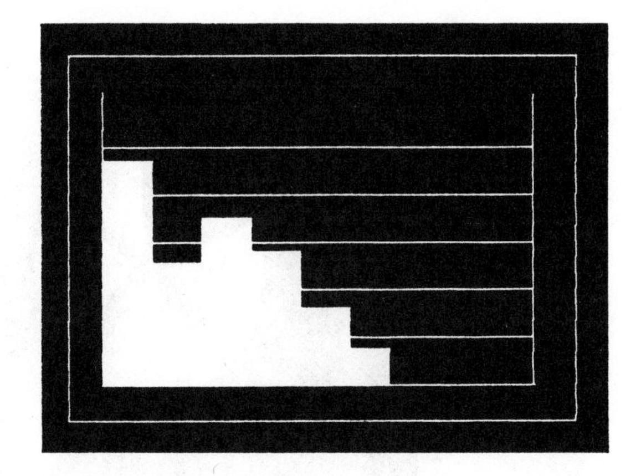

Chapter Exercises (Using **PRINT**, **CLS**, **END**, **LET**, functions, **DEF FN**, **INPUT**, **FOR/NEXT**, **WHILE/WEND**, **IF/THEN/ELSE**, logical operators, **READ/DATA**, **RESTORE**, arrays, **DIM**, **GOSUB**, **SCREEN**, **WIDTH**, **COLOR**, **KEY**, **CIRCLE**, **DRAW**, **LINE**, **PAINT**)

Flowcharting and code transcription:

1. Fastsell Sales has five salespersons. Design a program to display their sales performance, the highest of which is $20,000, as follows:

   a.

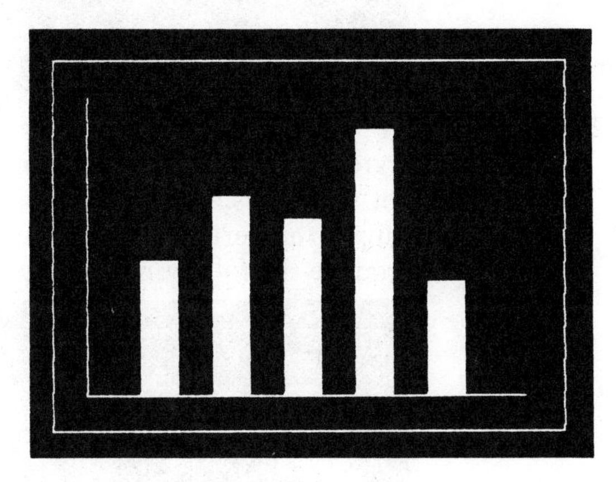

b.

c.

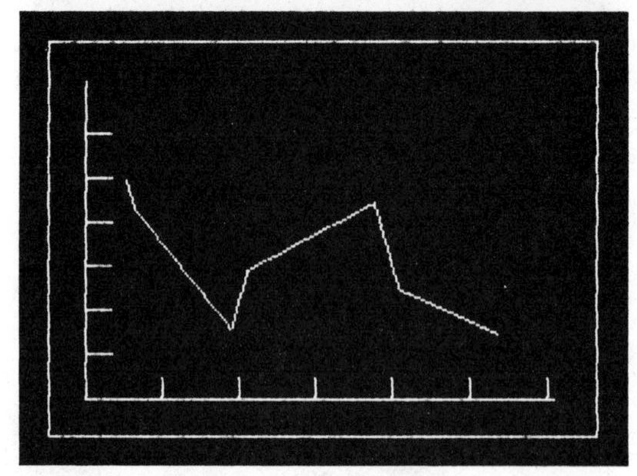

2. Design a program for the research director of NewGene Products, Inc., to study the growth rate of the new genetic engineering product x over a span of five years. The program should permit the research director to supply the pertinent data via the keyboard and then use the data to produce the following display (horizontal bar chart):

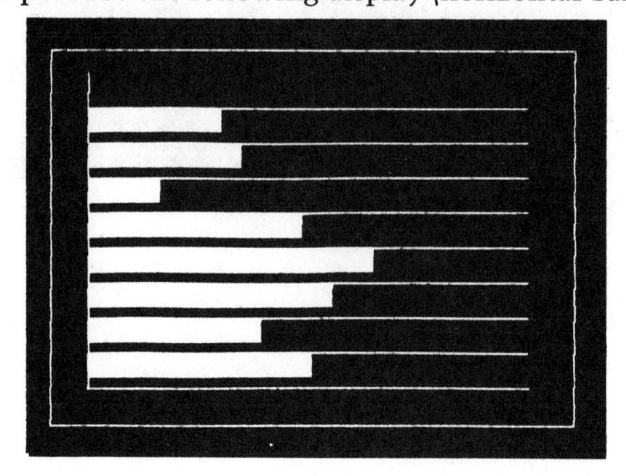

3. Design a graphics display program for Davidson Polls Company to display its 1986 election survey data. The data of potential voters are made up of the following categories: male, female, age 35 and above, age below 35, income above $30,000, income $30,000 and below, white, nonwhite, Republican, or Democrat.
   a. Design a pie chart to show the distribution of male versus female Republican endorsers.
   b. Design a bar chart to show the proportions of white versus nonwhite Democratic endorsers.

A / A SHORT COURSE ON FLOWCHARTING

INTRODUCTION

A flowchart is both a guide for the program logic used during program development and a reference during program review or maintenance. The flowchart is a pictorial rendition of a computer problem solution based on which the ultimate program code will be constructed (see Chapters 3 and 8). The sequence of events for a problem solving session is thus:

Problem → thoughts → flowchart → coding

Because the thoughts (analysis) come before the coding, the flowchart is normally developed in one's mother tongue, preferably with the thoughts not directly expressed in terms of the computer language, thinking in the language (which is unnatural) usually results in inefficiency in logic development. Thus the thought of needing a sales price to be obtained from the keyboard should probably be expressed as:

1. Get sales price.
2. Input sales price.

or

3. **INPUT** sales price.

but not

4. **INPUT S**

Case 3 is known as *pseudo-code,* meaning the thought is expressed in English while pointing to the mechanism to be used ultimately in coding.

Case 4 would be the result of thinking directly in code, and is most difficult to read during reviewing. It also makes flowcharting superfluous.

The thoughts thus formulated are then expressed in sequence and linked up by arrows which indicate the flow of the logic.

SYMBOLS

To aid the eventual coding transcription and the selection of language features, these analytical thoughts are enclosed in flowchart *symbols,* or *boxes.* The flowchart symbols are categorized and standardized to a great extent, with minimal variations mostly due to styles. The symbols pertinent to this text are delineated below.

THE PROCESS SYMBOL

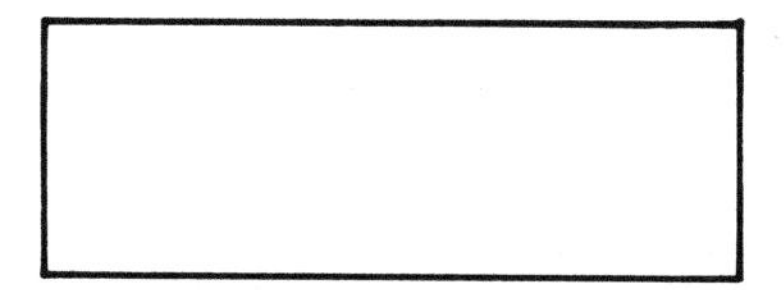

This symbol is used to represent all activities that pertain to the manipulation of data in memory. This applies to data storage, composition, decomposition, and arithmetic operations (which are in reality data storage). Examples of the usage of the process symbol are:

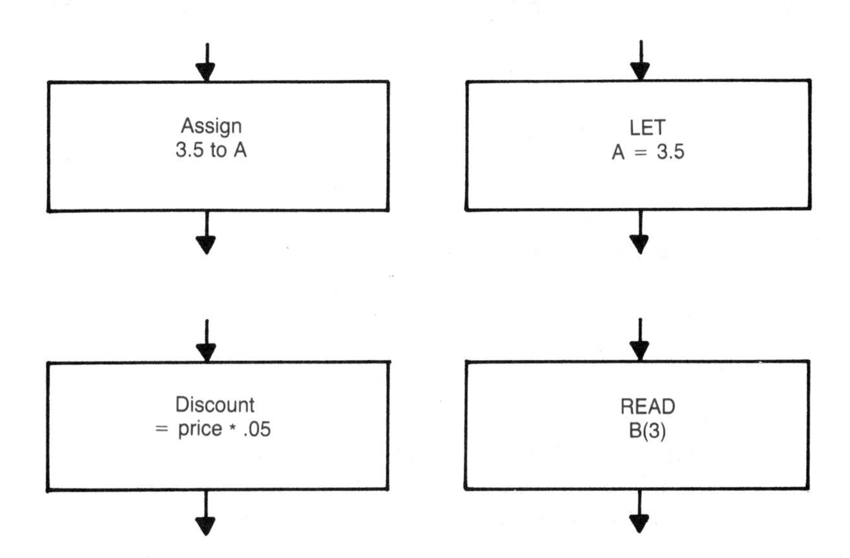

THE INPUT/OUTPUT SYMBOL

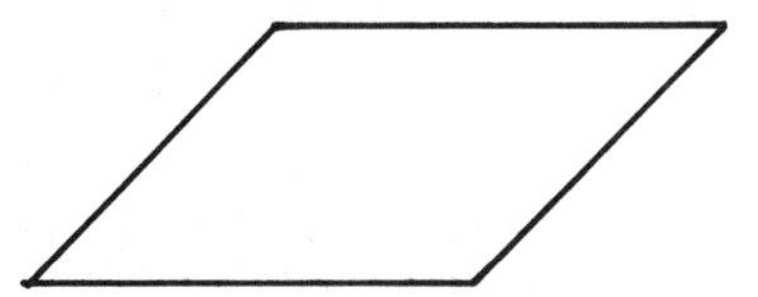

This symbol is used to highlight all activities related to transactions between the memory and peripheral equipment, such as the keyboard, CRT, printer, disk, and so on. The purpose is to allow the flowchart reader to locate such activities quickly. Typically if the Input/Output symbol is absent in a flowchart, one may conclude something is wrong. The usage of the Input/Output symbol is illustrated below:

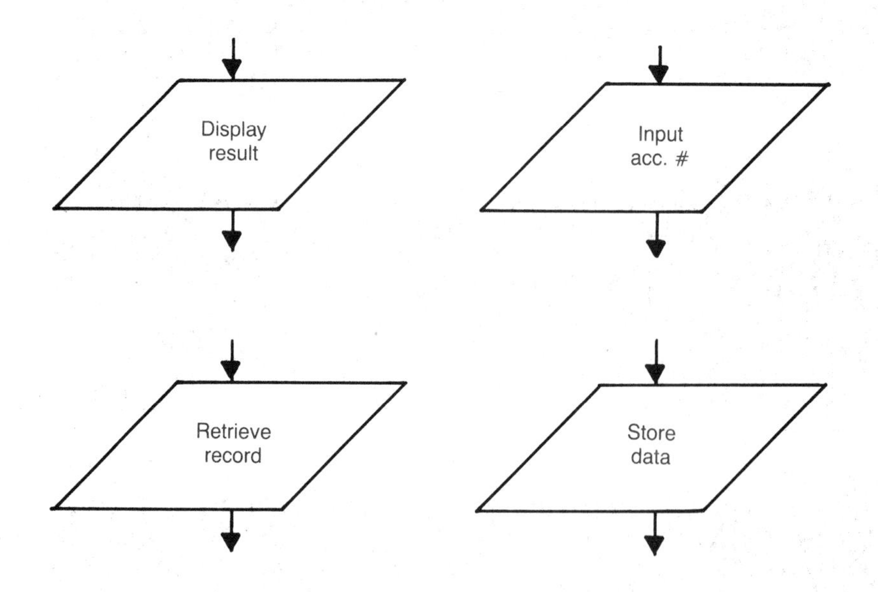

THE DECISION SYMBOL

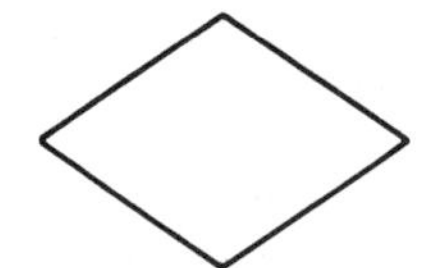

This symbol is used to indicate a controlled branching is to take place. The branching control condition, or the query that must be answered in order to decide the ensuing logic path, is housed in this symbol. Only two arrows may emerge from this symbol, and any diamond vertices may be used for such purposes. Examples:

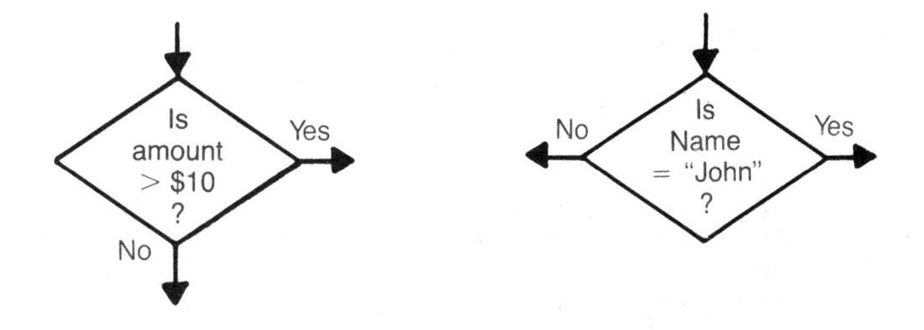

THE MODULE SYMBOLS

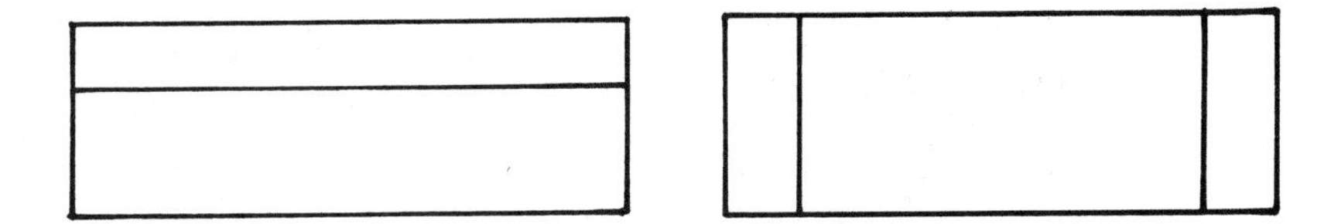

These two symbols are used to indicate that the activities contained in the symbols cannot be implemented by simple language primitives (single program statements) and must be referenced through a separate modular flowchart. The first symbol suggests the modular logic will be implemented as a subroutine (see Chapter 8) while the second symbol simply means the eventual code section will be in the logic flow but is documented separately. Examples are:

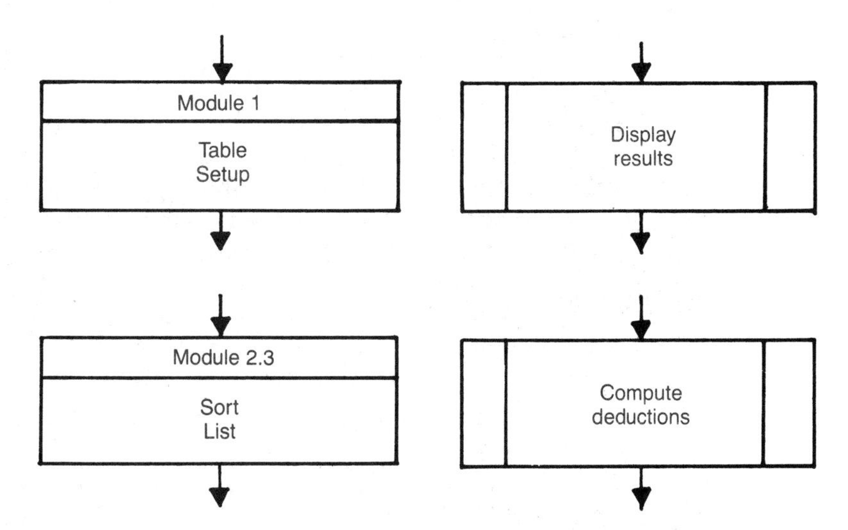

THE PREPARATION SYMBOL

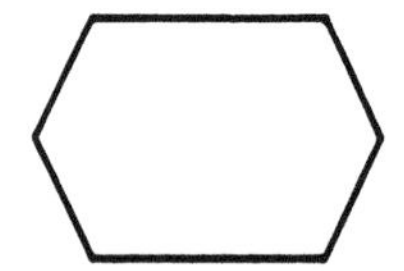

This symbol is used to highlight all activities that involve not a data item but a code, a pointer, or an internal supervisory activity maintained or implemented by the language or system itself. Examples:

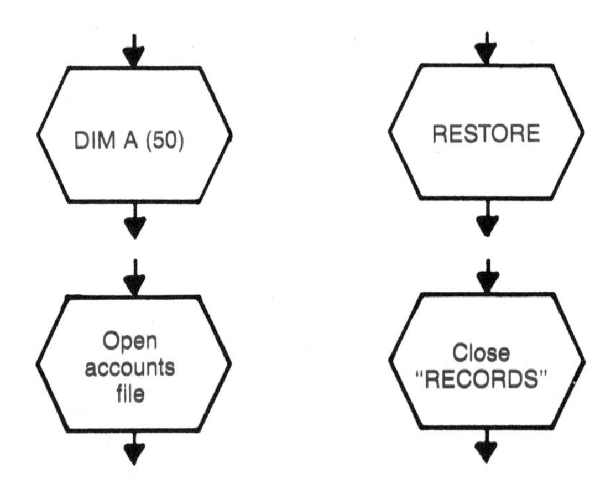

THE TERMINAL SYMBOL

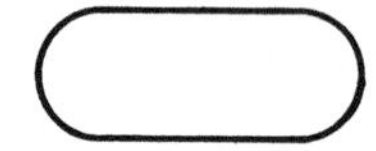

This symbol is used to mark all beginning and ending points of logic modules. The presence of this symbol serves to guide the flowchart reader to various logic modules and indicate the ends of logic flows. The various uses of the terminal symbol are illustrated below.

For master flowcharts:

For inline modules:

For subroutine modules:

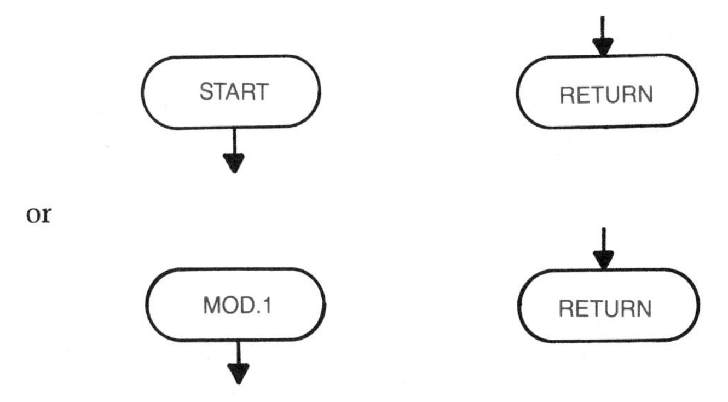

THE CONNECTOR

The connector is used to connect conceptually different logic parts that cannot, or would be difficult to, be physically linked together. The use of the connector usually employs a simple accounting numbering or lettering system to keep track of the linkages. The use of the connector will be illustrated in the Flowcharting Techniques and Conventions section.

ANNOTATIONS

Explanatory notes may be included with the flowchart to clarify the flowchart logic. Such a use is demonstrated by this example:

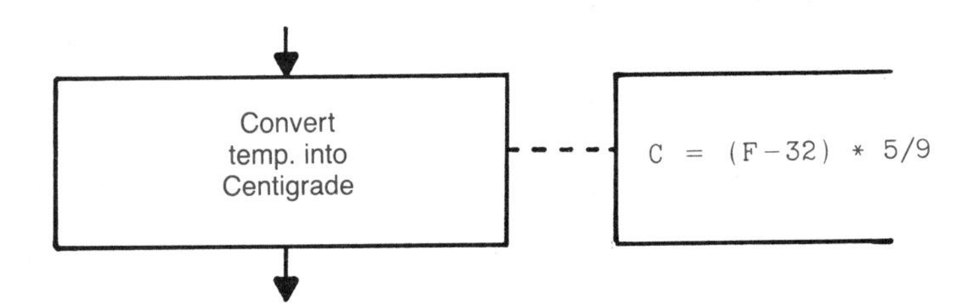

OTHER SYMBOLS

The symbols above represent the standard used by practically all languages. In all languages, however, there are distinct features that are not shared between languages. These special features are often flowcharted with special symbols that are designed to express the language feature in the most efficient way. For instance, the BASIC ON/GOTO statement is often flowcharted as:

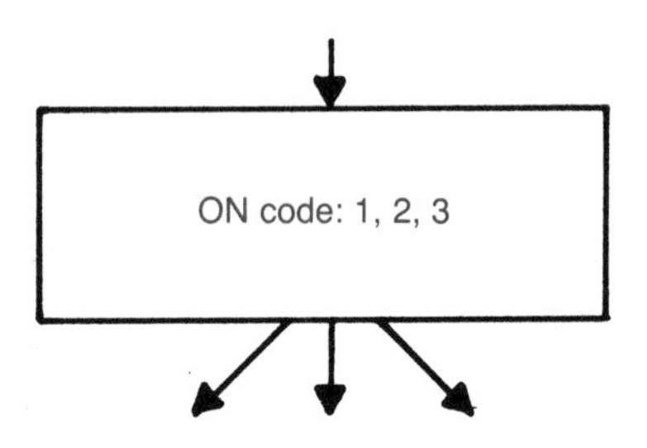

FLOWCHARTING TECHNIQUES AND CONVENTIONS

With the proper use of symbols, the flowchart is drawn with respect to a set of flowcharting conventions and optimized by a few design techniques. These will be discussed in this section.

ARROWS

The flowchart logic always begins at the top of a page, and the symbols (representing logic) are linked together by straight arrows that either flow vertically downward (with exceptions) or horizontally. All symbols must be entered through one inlet (one arrow) and exited through one outlet. The exceptions are the diamond which has one inlet and two outlets, the terminal symbol which has only either an inlet or outlet, and the special symbols. The following contrast some of the correct and incorrect ways of flowcharting:

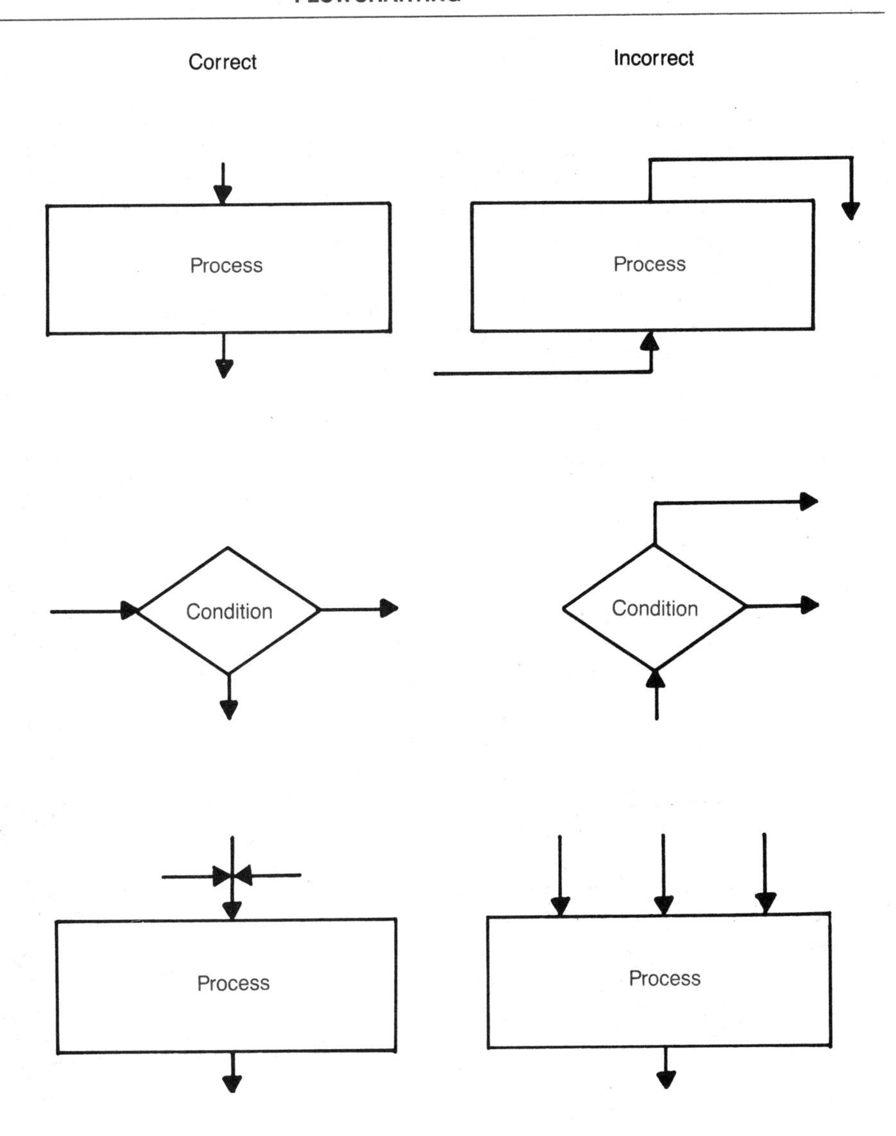

Beginning at the top of a page, the flowchart thus grows downward until the end of the page is reached, then several options may be taken. If the logic is predominantly linear, then the flowchart may be wrapped around and the remainder of the flowchart continues at the top of the same page:

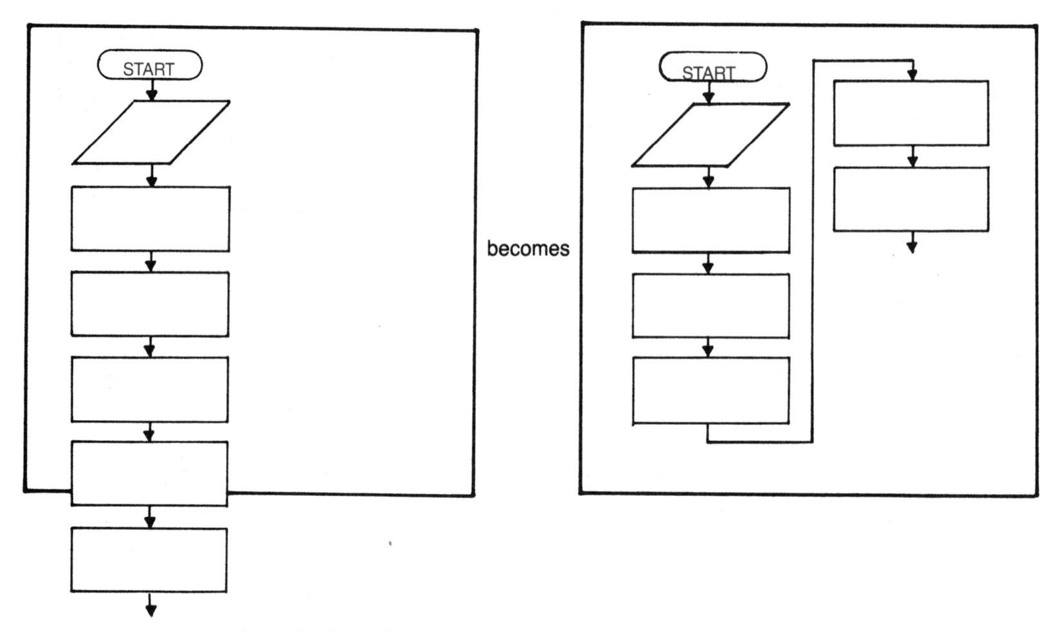

If each flowchart logic column is itself complex and a direct wrap-around may render the flowchart congested or aesthetically unpleasing, then the connector may be used, with the exit and entry points of each column coordinated:

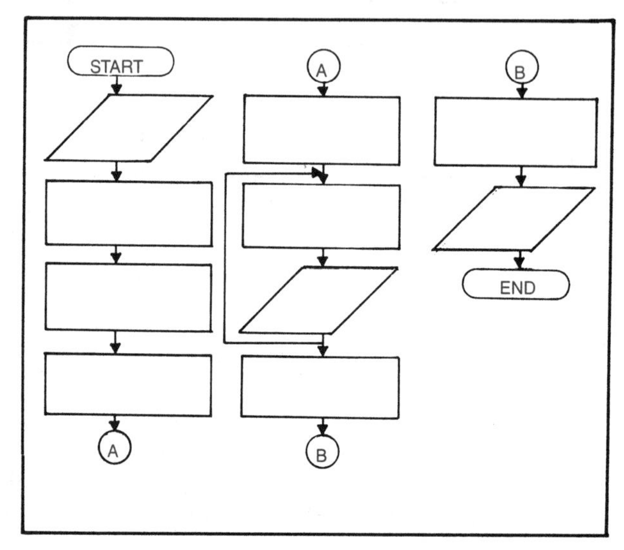

If the flowchart reaches the end of a page and must be continued onto another page, then again the connector may be used.

The design of a flowchart must be visually clear. Arrows must not become luxuriant or cross each other, and "bridging" shall be avoided at all cost. Thus the following flowchart:

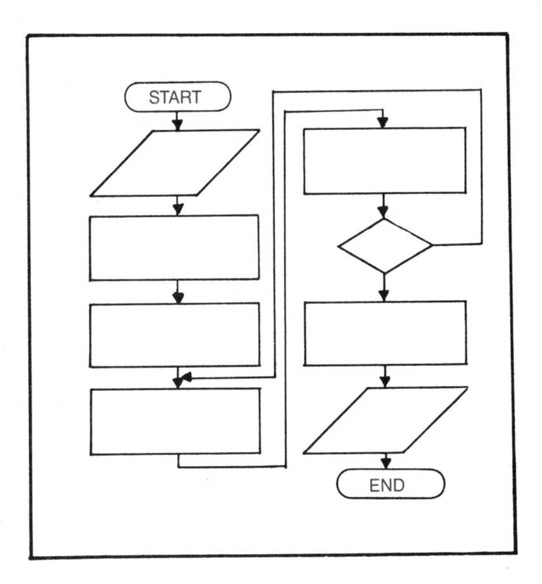

should be designed as:

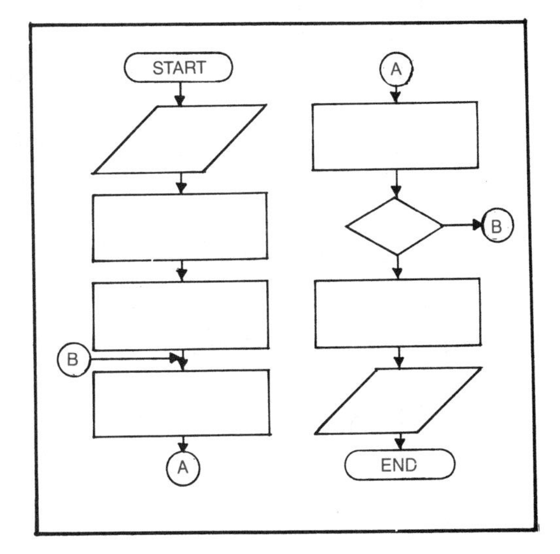

and this flowchart:

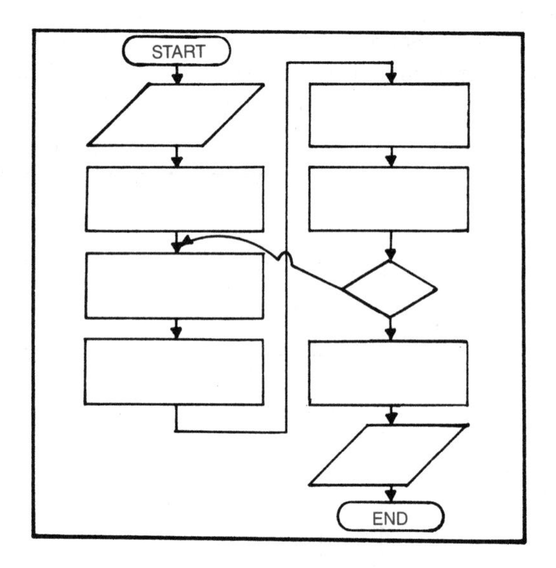

should be designed as:

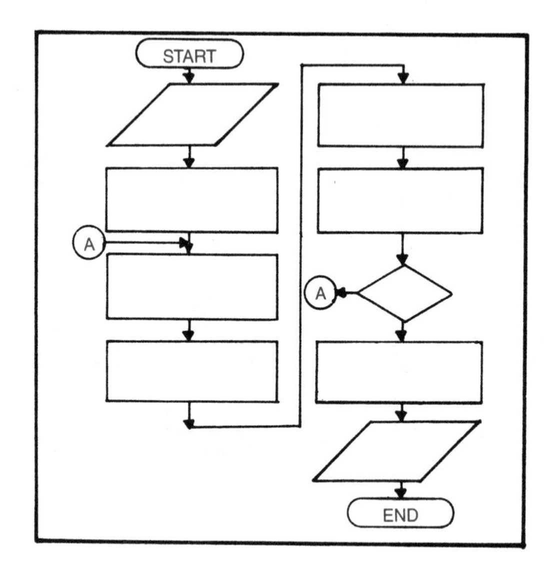

Loop logic also falls into this category. Thus the loop representation:

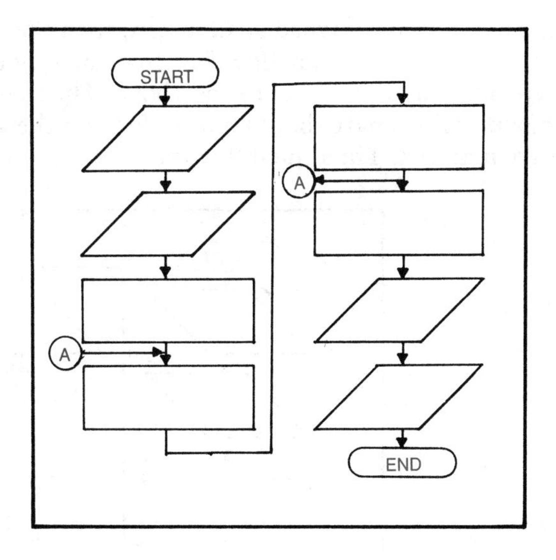

should be redrawn as:

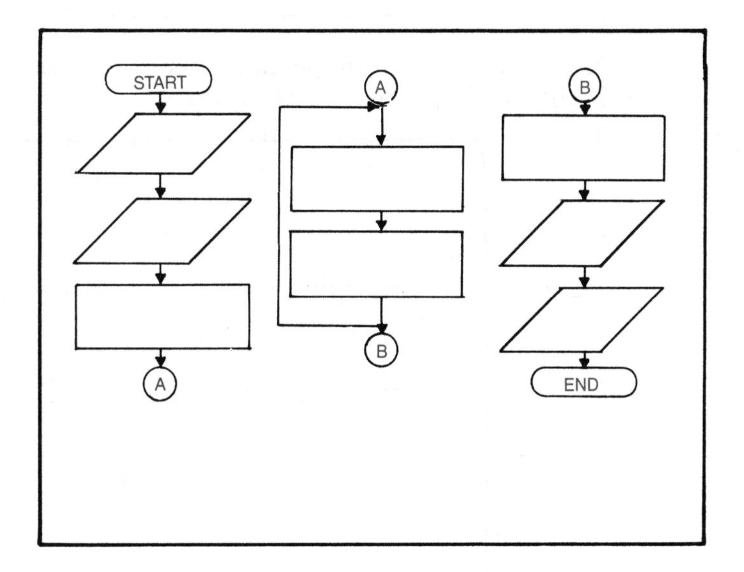

MODULAR FLOWCHARTING

If a program is designed structurally, then the program logic will involve modules. For modular flowcharting, each module must be flowcharted separately and conform to the above. The main logic flowchart and the modular flowchart should not be done on the same sheet of paper just to save material. Thus the following is not recommended:

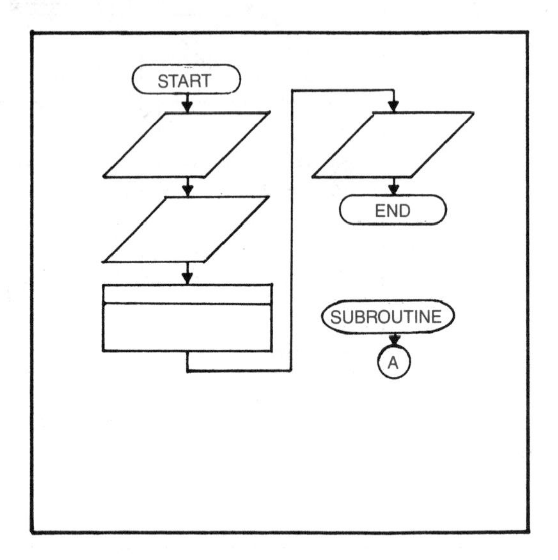

If the module is an inline module, and provided the module is relatively simple, then it may be flowcharted as:

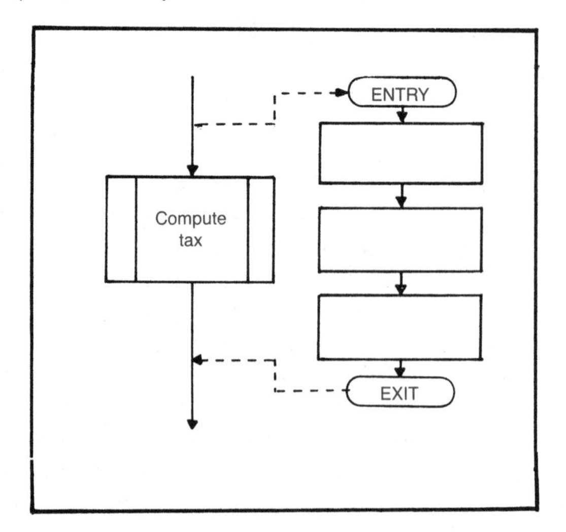

If a program is to involve several modules, then they should be numbered, both in the main logic and the modular flowcharts:

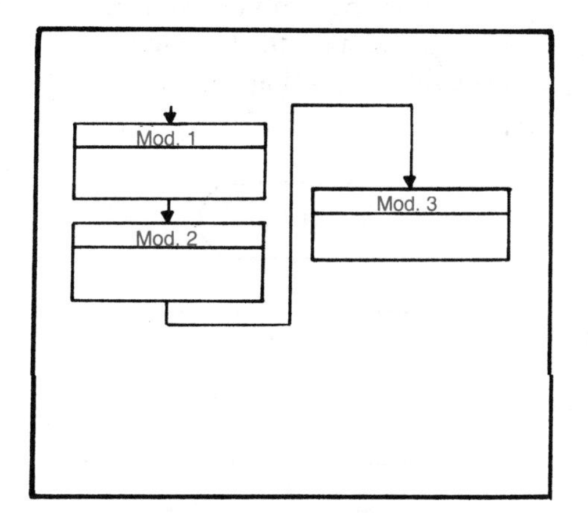

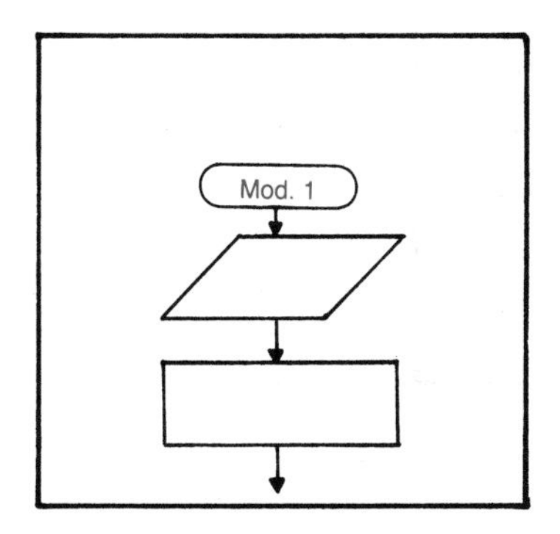

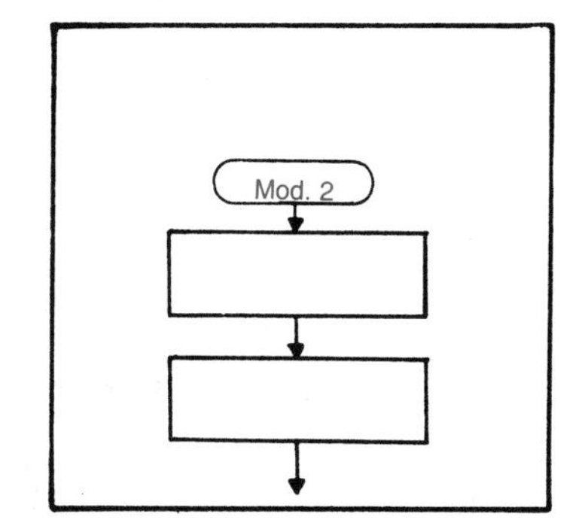

FLOWCHART TRANSCRIPTION

When the flowcharts are thus designed and the logic verified, then they will be transcribed into the language code. The language code is not to be redesigned without regard to the flowcharts. In transcribing the flowchart, each symbol along the main branch of the flowchart will become a language primitive, or statement, except for the START terminal. No off-branch symbol will become a distinct statement. Thus one can always match the number of program statements to the number of symbols along the main flowchart branch. Arrows along the flow of the logic will not become code, while all off-flow arrows will become **GOTO**s. If simple arrows are used to represent loops, then the two ends of the loop arrow will become the **FOR/NEXT** statements. If the off-branch logic is complex and involved, then it will be transcribed into subroutines. (Hopefully, in those situations the problem should have been analysed structurally or the flowchart redrawn to include the use of modules.) The following are some of the flowchart shapes and their corresponding code transcriptions:

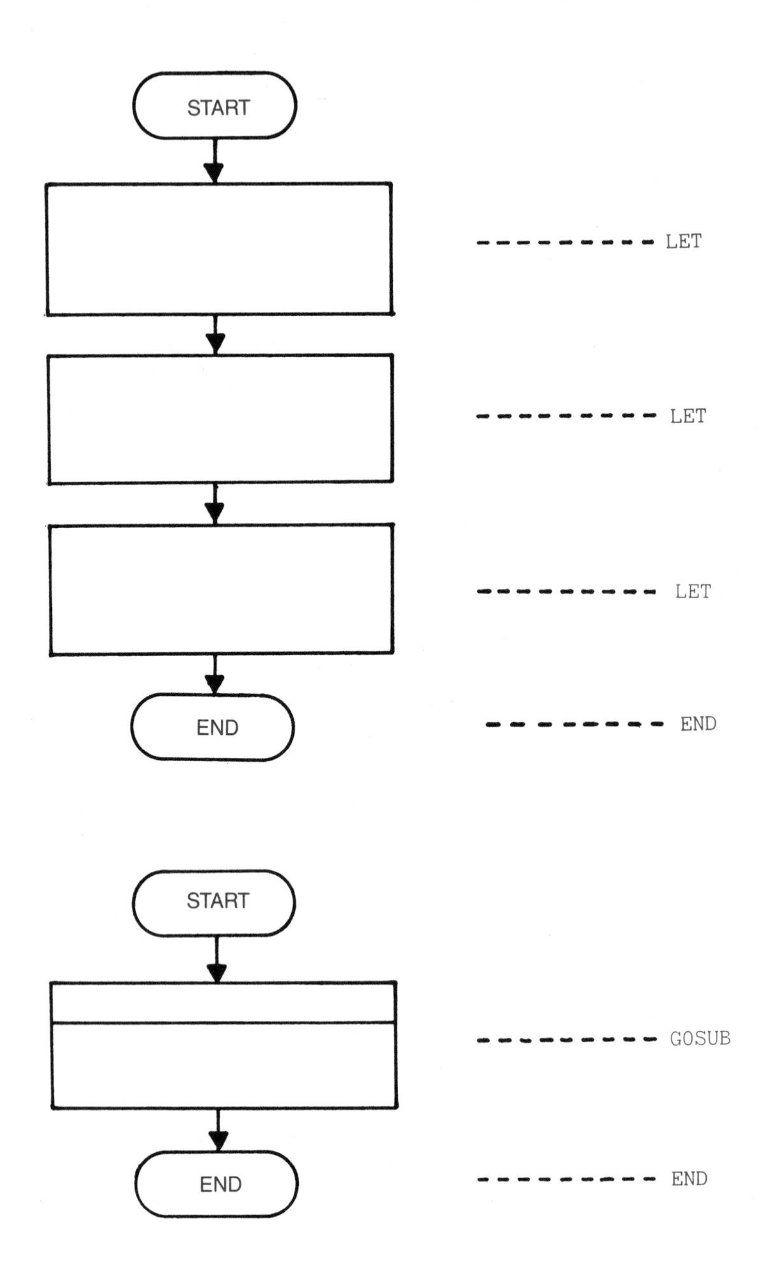

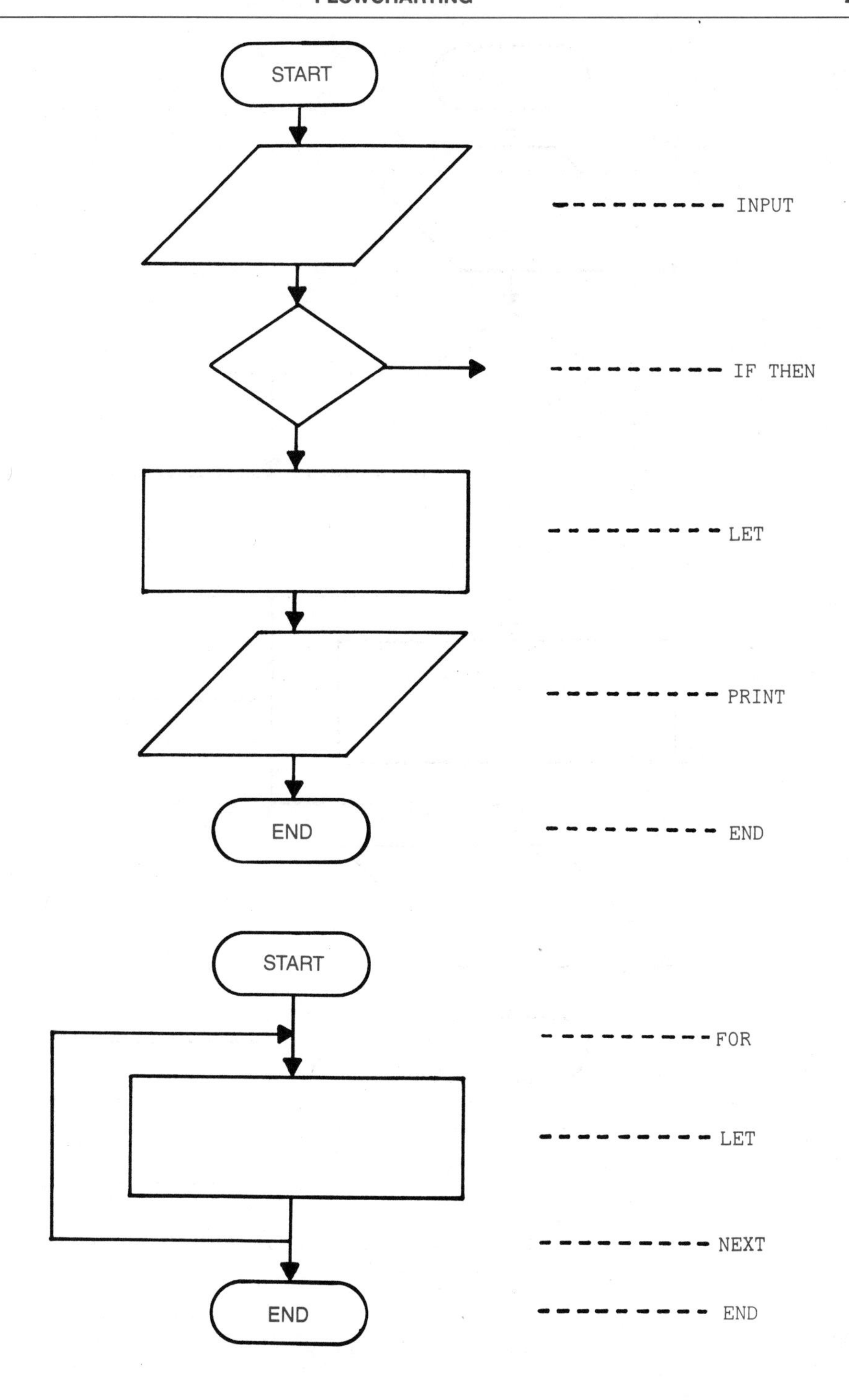
START
INPUT
IF THEN
LET
PRINT
END
END
START
FOR
LET
NEXT
END
END

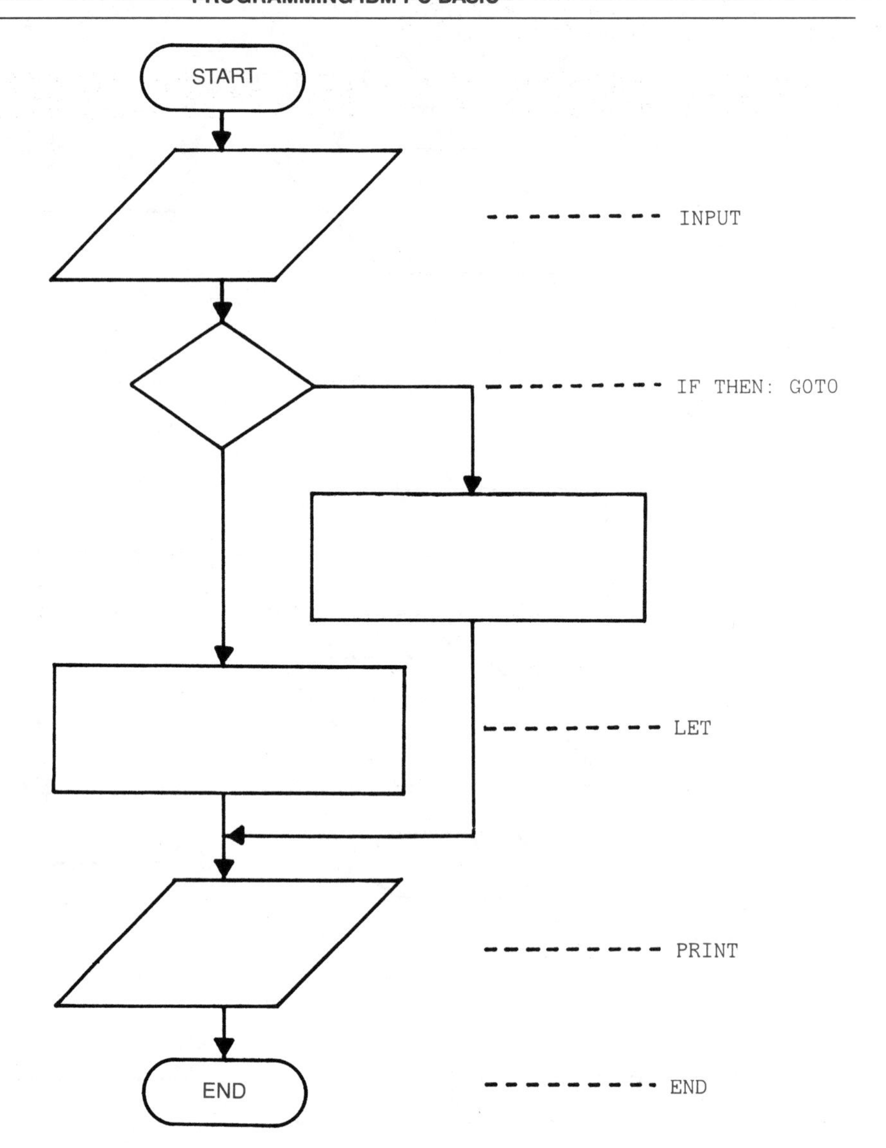
START
INPUT
IF THEN: GOTO
LET
PRINT
END
END

B / SELECTED ANSWERS TO EXERCISES

CHAPTER 2

EXERCISE SET 2.1

C.

4.

```
10 PRINT ,"Exercise 1",, "Date:"
20 PRINT ,"Programmer:"
```

EXERCISE SET 2.2

B.

3.

```
10 CLS
20 PRINT ,"Grades:"
30 PRINT ,"==================================="
40 PRINT
50 PRINT ,"Test 1."
60 PRINT ,"Test 2."
70 PRINT ,"Test 3."
80 PRINT ,"Test 4."
```

```
90 PRINT
100 PRINT ,,,"Total:"
110 END
```

CHAPTER EXERCISES

1.

```
10 PRINT 2.86 + 98.05 + 1.17 + 103.2
20 PRINT ( 2.86 + 98.05 + 1.17 + 103.2 ) / 4
30 END
```

3.

```
10 LPRINT "The total is:"
20 LPRINT 2.86 + 98.05 + 1.17 + 103.2
30 LPRINT "The average is:"
40 LPRINT ( 2.86 + 98.05 + 1.17 + 103.2 ) / 4
50 END
```

CHAPTER 3

EXERCISE SET 3.1

C.

4.

```
10 LET A = 12.6
20 LET B = 7.98
30 LET C = 32
40 LET D = 56.95
50 PRINT A, B, C, D
60 END
```

EXERCISE SET 3.2

B.

4.

```
10 LET A = 10
20 LET S = A * A
30 PRINT A, S
40 END
```

6.

```
10 LET P = 1000
20 LET R = 0.0675
30 LET I = P * R * 5
40 PRINT I
50 END
```

EXERCISE SET 3.3

C.

7.

```
10 CLS
20 LET MM = 1000
30 LET CM = MM * 0.1
40 LET INCH = CM / 2.54
50 PRINT MM; "mm ="; INCH; "inches."
60 END
```

9.

a.

```
10 LET FIRST$ = "JOHN"
20 LET MI$ = "JAMES"
30 LET LAST$ = "SMITH"
40 PRINT FIRST$, MI$, LAST$
50 END
```

EXERCISE SET 3.4

B.

3.

```
10 LET D = 100.64
20 LET D% = D - 1
30 LET C = ( D - D% ) * 100
40 PRINT C
50 END
```

5.

```
10 PI = 3.1416
20 DEG = 1
30 RAD = DEG * PI / 180
40 PRINT DEG; "degree = "; RAD
50 DEG = DEG + 1
60 RAD = DEG * PI / 180
70 PRINT DEG; "degree = "; RAD
80 DEG = DEG + 1
90 RAD = DEG * PI / 180
100 PRINT DEG; "degree = "; RAD
110 DEG = DEG + 1
120 RAD = DEG * PI / 180
130 PRINT DEG; "degree = "; RAD
etc.
```

EXERCISE SET 3.5

B.

4.

a.

```
10 DEF FN H(A,B) = SQR( A*A + B*B )
20 LET HYPO = FNH(3,4)
30 PRINT HYPO
40 END
```

5.

```
10 DEF FN TX(S) = S * .05
20 DEF FN SBT(S,T) = S + T
30 LET S1 = 100.75
40 LET S2 = 24.97
50 LET S3 = 36
60 LET T1 = FNTX(S1)
70 LET T2 = FNTX(S2)
80 LET T3 = FNTX(S3)
90 LET GT = S1 + S2 + S3 + T1 + T2 + T3
100 CLS
110 PRINT S1, T1, FNSBT(S1,T1)
120 PRINT S2, T2, FNSBT(S2,T2)
130 PRINT S3, T3, FNSBT(S3,T3)
140 PRINT
150 PRINT ,,, GT
160 END
```

CHAPTER EXERCISES

1.

```
10 LET CRS1$ = "CS001"
20 LET CDT1 = 3
30 LET CRS2$ = "CS004"
40 LET CDT2 = 2
50 LET CRS3$ = "CS102"
60 LET CDT3 = 3
70 LET CRS4$ = "CS212"
80 LET CDT4 = 3
90 LET CRS5$ = "CS356"
100 LET CDT5 = 4
110 LET CRS6$ = "CS401"
120 LET CDT6 = 3
130 PRINT "Course",, "Credit"
140 PRINT CRS1$,, CDT1
150 PRINT CRS2$,, CDT2
160 PRINT CRS3$,, CDT3
170 PRINT CRS4$,, CDT4
180 PRINT CRS5$,, CDT5
190 PRINT CRS6$,, CDT6
200 END
```

3.

```
10 LET P1$ = "Hammer"
20 LET P2$ = "Sandpaper"
30 LET P3$ = "Ruler"
40 LET P4$ = "Glue"
50 LET P5$ = "Nails"
60 LET S1 = 12.55
70 LET S2 = 3.50
80 LET S3 = 6.78
90 LET S4 = 37.20
100 LET S5 = 5.30
110 LET TTL = S1 + S2 + S3 + S4 + S5
120 LPRINT ,,"Quickie Hardware"
130 LPRINT ,,"123 Industrial Park"
140 LPRINT ,,"(602) 440-6385"
150 LPRINT
160 LPRINT
170 LPRINT "Item",, "Charge"
180 LPRINT
190 LPRINT P1$,, S1
200 LPRINT P2$,, S2
210 LPRINT P3$,, S3
220 LPRINT P4$,, S4
230 LPRINT P5$,, S5
240 LPRINT
250 LPRINT
260 LPRINT "Total",, TTL
270 END
```

CHAPTER 4

EXERCISE SET 4.1

B.

5.

```
10 INPUT B
20 INPUT B
30 PRINT
```

```
40 PRINT "THE DIFFERENCE IS "; ABS( A-B )
50 END
```

7.

```
10 INPUT N1$
20 INPUT N2$
30 INPUT N3$
40 CLS
50 PRINT N1$
60 PRINT N2$
70 PRINT N3$
80 END
```

EXERCISE SET 4.2

B.

3.

```
10 PRINT "Enter 3 integers through 3 input operations
   please."
20 PRINT
30 INPUT I1%
40 INPUT I2%
50 INPUT I3%
60 END
```

EXERCISE SET 4.3

1.

```
10 CLS
20 INPUT "ENTER HOURS WORKED : ", H
30 INPUT "ENTER HOURLY RATE IN PERCENT :", R
40 LET GROSS = H * R * 0.01
50 PRINT
60 PRINT "THE GROSS PAY IS "; GROSS
70 END
```

CHAPTER EXERCISES

B.

3.

```
10 PRINT "Please enter the 5 scores to be averages in 5
   separate keyboard"
20 PRINT "entry operations, each to be ended by pressing t
   <ENTER> key."
30 PRINT
40 INPUT "Score: ", S1
50 INPUT "Score: ", S2
60 INPUT "Score: ", S3
70 INPUT "Score: ", S4
80 INPUT "Score: ", S5
90 LET AVE = ( S1 + S2 + S3 + S4 + S5 ) / 5
100 CLS
110 PRINT "The scores are:"
120 PRINT S1; S2; S3; S4; S5
130 PRINT
140 PRINT "The average is:"; AVE
150 END
```

CHAPTER 5

EXERCISE SET 5.1

C.

5.

b.

```
10 FOR C% = 1 TO 8
20    PRINT C%; ",";
30 NEXT C%
40 PRINT C%
50 END
```

7.

```
10 FOR C% = 1 TO 20
20    LET S% = C% * C%
30    PRINT C%, S%
40 NEXT C%
50 END
```

EXERCISE SET 5.2

B.

5.

```
10 PRINT "ENTER INVENTORY FIGURES:"
20 PRINT
30 LET T = 0
40 FOR C% = 1 TO 10
50    PRINT "ENTER DATA"; C%;
60    INPUT ": ", I
70    LET T = T + I
80 NEXT C%
90 LET A = T / 10
100 PRINT
110 PRINT "TOTAL:"; T, "AVERAGE:"; A
120 END
```

EXERCISE SET 5.3

C.

4.

```
10 CLS
20 PRINT , "A"
30 FOR TIER% = 1 TO 10
40     FOR C% = 16 - TIER% TO 1 STEP -1
50     PRINT " ";
60     NEXT C%
70     PRINT "A"
80     FOR C% = 1 TO TIER%
90             PRINT " ";
```

```
100      NEXT C%
110 PRINT "A"
120 END
```

CHAPTER EXERCISES

1.

```
10 LET CTOTAL = 0
20 LET DTOTAL = 0
30 CLS
40 PRINT "ENTER ALL CREDIT DATA AS POSITIVE NUMBERS,"
50 PRINT "AND DEBIT DATA AS NEGATIVE NUMBERS."
60 PRINT
70 FOR C% = 1 TO 500
80       INPUT "CREDIT: ", CREDIT
90       INPUT "DEBIT: ", DEBIT
100      LET CTOTAL = CTOTAL + CREDIT
110      LET DTOTAL = DTOTAL + DEBIT
120 NEXT C%
130 PRINT
140 PRINT "TOTAL CREDIT: $"; CTOTAL
150 PRINT "TOTAL DEBIT: $"; DTOTAL
160 END
```

3.

```
10 CLS
20 PRINT , "C", "F", "C", "F"
30 PRINT , "======================================"
40 PRINT
50 FOR C = 0 TO 100 STEP 5
60       LET C1 = C
70       LET C2 = C + 110
80       LET F1 = C1 * 9 / 5 + 32
90       LET F2 = C2 * 9 / 5 + 32
100      LET D = C1 * 100
110      LET C1% = D * .01
120      LET D = C2 * 100
130      LET C2% = D * .01
```

```
140       LET D = F1 * 100
150       LET F1% = D * .01
160       LET D = F2 * 100
170       LET F2% = D * .01
180       PRINT ,C1%, F1%, C2%, F2%
190 NEXT C
200 END
```

CHAPTER 6

EXERCISE SET 6.2

1.

a.

```
10 DEF FN NEWDEP(D,R) = D * ( 1 + R * 0.5 ) ^ 2
20 DEF FN IYEAR(D,R) = D * ( 1 + R * 0.5 ) ^ 2 - D
30 LET DEP = 10000
40 LET RATE = 0.08
50 LET ITOTAL = 0
60 LET D = DEP
70 WHILE ITOTAL <= DEP * 2
80       LET I = FN(D,RATE)
90       LET ITOTAL = ITOTAL + I
110      LET D = FNNEWDEP(D,RATE)
120      PRINT ITOTAL
130 WEND
140 END
```

EXERCISE SET 6.4

2.

```
10 LET SALE$ = "Y"
20 WHILE SALE$ = "Y"
30       CLS
40       LET SUBTOTAL = 0
50       LET RESPONSE$ = "Y"
60       WHILE RESPONSE$ = "Y"
70               INPUT "PRODUCT: ", P$
```

```
80                LPRINT P$,
90                INPUT "SALES AMOUNT: ", S
100               LPRINT S
110               LET SUBTOTAL = SUBTOTAL + S
120               INPUT "MORE? Y/N: ", RESPONSE$
130       WEND
140       LET TX = SUBTOTAL * .045
150       LET TOTAL = SUBTOTAL + TX
160       LPRINT
170       LPRINT
180       LPRINT , "SUBTOTAL:", SUBTOTAL
190       LPRINT , "SALES TAX:", TX
200       LPRINT
210       LPRINT , "TOTAL:", TOTAL
220       LPRINT
230       LPRINT "THANK YOU FOR SHOPPING AT RUBEN'S"
240       INPUT "NEXT SALE? Y/N: ", SALE$
250 WEND
260 END
```

CHAPTER EXERCISES

2.

```
10 C% = 10
20 RESP$ = "y"
30 WHILE RESP$ = "y"
40    WHILE C% = 10
50       C% = 0
60       CLS
70       PRINT "Radio telemetry data entry."
80       PRINT "End each entry by pressing <ENTER>."
90       PRINT
100     WEND
110     INPUT "Telemetry data: ", D
120     INPUT "More? (y/n)", RESP$
130     C% = C% + 1
140 WEND
150 END
```

CHAPTER 7

EXERCISE SET 7.1

B.

3.

```
50 IF A < 0 THEN 120
```

C.

5.

```
10 CLS
20 PRINT "Enter project titles and project numbers
   separated by comma:"
30 PRINT "Press <ENTER> to end data entry."
40 PRINT
50 FOR C% = 1 TO 20
60      INPUT "Enter data: ", PROJ$, PN
70      IF PROJ$ = "" THEN END
80 NEXT C%
90 GOTO 10
```

EXERCISE SET 7.2

2.

```
10 CLS
20 LET SUBTOTAL = 0
30 LET RESPONSE$ = "Y"
40 WHILE RESPONSE$ = "Y"
50   INPUT "PRODUCT: ", P$
60   LPRINT P$,
70   INPUT "SALES AMOUNT: ", S
80   LPRINT S
90   LET SUBTOTAL = SUBTOTAL + S
100   INPUT "MORE? Y/N: ", RESPONSE$
110 WEND
120 LET TX = SUBTOTAL * .045
```

```
130 LET TOTAL = SUBTOTAL + TX
140 LPRINT
150 LPRINT
160 LPRINT , "SUBTOTAL:", SUBTOTAL
170 LPRINT , "SALES TAX:", TX
180 LPRINT
190 LPRINT , "TOTAL:", TOTAL
200 LPRINT
210 LPRINT "THANK YOU FOR SHOPPING AT RUBEN'S"
220 INPUT "NEXT SALE? Y/N OR y/n: ", SALE$
230 IF SALE$ = "Y" OR SALE$ = "y" THEN 10
240 END
```

EXERCISE SET 7.3

B.

2.

```
10 INPUT "Enter first number: ", A
20 INPUT "Enter second number: ", B
30 IF A > B THEN LET C = .A - B : PRINT A, B, C
            ELSE LET C = .B - A : PRINT B, A, C
40 END
```

C.

4.

```
10 CLS
20 LET UP = 0
30 LET DOWN = 0
40 INPUT "Enter time: ", T
50 IF T = 0 THEN PRINT "On time:"; UP, "Down time:";
   DOWN : END
60 IF T > 0 THEN LET UP = UP + T ELSE LET DOWN = DOWN + T
70 GOTO 60
```

CHAPTER EXERCISES

A.

2.

Answer:

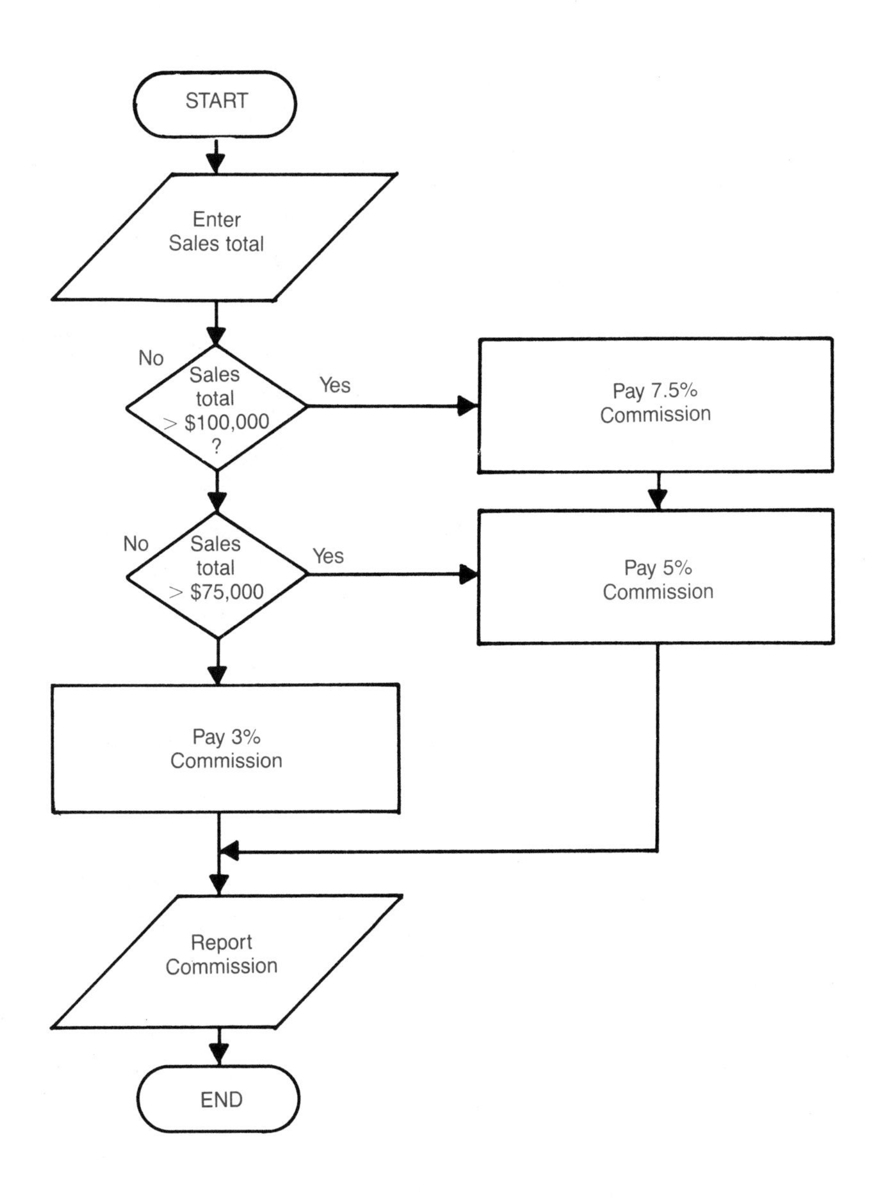

CHAPTER 8

EXERCISE SET 8.2

2.

Answer:

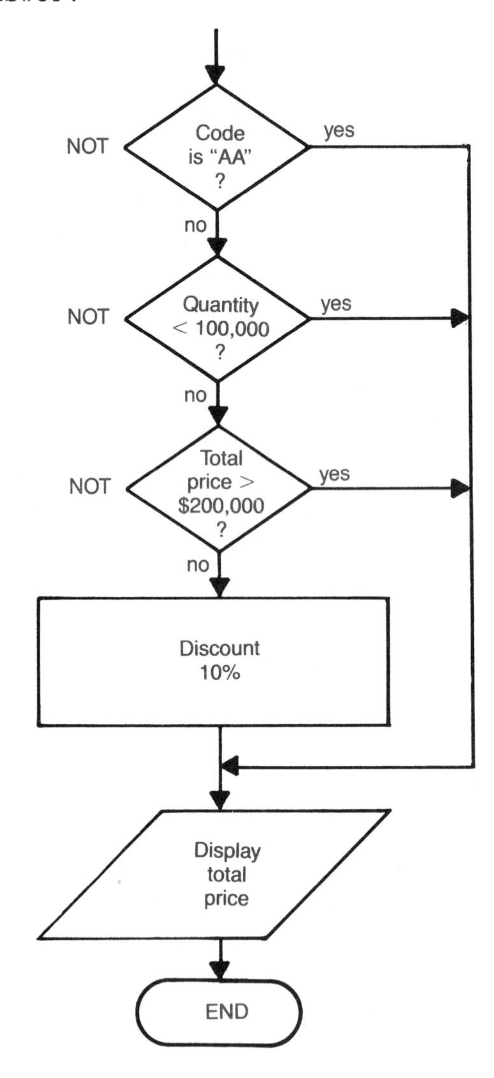

CHAPTER EXERCISES

2.

```
10 WORKERS = 0
20 G0 = 0
30 G10 = 0
40 G20 = 0
50 G30 = 0
60 RESP$ = "Y"
70 WHILE RESP$ = "Y" OR RESP$ = "y"
80 INPUT "Worker hours worked: ", HOUR
90 IF HOUR < 0 THEN 80
100 IF HOUR > 70 THEN G30 = G30 + 1
110 IF HOUR > 60 THEN G20 = G20 + 1
120 IF HOUR > 50 THEN G10 = G10 + 1
130 IF HOUR > 40 THEN G0 = G0 + 1
140 WORKERS = WORKERS + 1
150 INPUT "More data? (y/n)", RESP$
160 WEND
170 PRINT "Overtime more than 30 hours:"; G30
    / WORKERS * 100; " percent."
180 PRINT "Overtime more than 20 hours:"; G20
    / WORKERS * 100; " percent."
190 PRINT "Overtime more than 10 hours:"; G10
    / WORKERS * 100; " percent."
200 PRINT "Overtime up to 10 hours:"; G0
    / WORKERS * 100; " percent."
210 END
```

CHAPTER 9

EXERCISE SET 9.1

C.

5.

```
10 READ A$, B$, C$
20 PRINT A$
30 PRINT B$
```

```
40 PRINT C$
50 END
60 DATA "BANANA", "APPLE", "GRAPE"
```

EXERCISE SET 9.2

B.

3.

```
10 CLS
20 FOR C% = 1 TO 4
30      READ PROPERTY$
40      PRINT PROPERTY$
50      INPUT "Property exists? (y/n): ", MATERIAL$
60 NEXT C%
70 PRINT
80 INPUT "Another material? (y/n): ", RESP$
90 IF RESP$ = "Y" OR RESP$ = "y" THEN RESTORE : GOTO 10
100 END
110 DATA "Electrical Conductance", "Heat Resistance",
    "Vibration Dampening", "Solubility"
```

EXERCISE SET 9.3

A.

1.

```
10 READ A, B, C
20 FOR C% = 1 TO 12
30   READ C
40   LET F = C * A / B + C
50   PRINT F
60 NEXT C%
70 END
80 DATA 9, 5, 32
90 DATA 12.88, 86, 93.4, 5, 100, 23, 77.7, 56.3, 83.6,
   22, 78,3, 56,4
```

CHAPTER 10

EXERCISE SET 10.1

B.

3.

```
10 CLS
20 FOR C% = 1 TO 5
30      INPUT "Enter coefficient: ", COEF( C% )
40 NEXT C%
50 END
```

EXERCISE SET 10.2

B.

3.

```
100 INPUT "Enter row number: ", R%
110 PRINT TITLE$( R% );
120 FOR C% = 1 TO 6
130     PRINT D( R%, C% ),
140 NEXT C%
```

EXERCISE SET 10.3

1.

```
10 FOR C% = 1 TO 50
20    READ STOCK$( C% )
30 NEXT C%
40 FOR C% = 1 TO 50
50    PRINT STOCK$( C% )
60    PRINT
70    FOR D% = 1 TO 12
80       INPUT "Enter stock porfolio data: ", P( D% )
90       IF P( D% ) = 0 THEN 120
100   NEXT D%
110   D% = D% - 1
120   LET P( 0 ) = D%
```

```
130 NEXT C%
140 END
200 DATA
```

EXERCISE SET 10.4

1.

```
10 DIM WORKER$(20), HOURS(20,8)
20 ' SET UP NAME LIST --------------------
30 FOR R% = 1 TO 20
40      READ WORKER$(R%)
50 NEXT R%
60 ' INPUT DATA -------------------------
70 FOR R% = 1 TO 20
80      CLS
90      PRINT WORKER$(R%)
100     PRINT
110     FOR C% = 1 TO 6
120         INPUT "HOURS WORKED: ", HOURS(R%,C%)
130     NEXT C%
140 NEXT R%
150 ' COMPUTE TOTAL AND AVERAGE ---------
160 FOR R% = 1 TO 20
170     LET HOURS(R%,7) = 0
180     FOR C% = 1 TO 6
190         LET HOURS(R%,7) = HOURS(R%,7) + HOURS(R%,C%)
200     NEXT C%
210     LET HOURS(R%,8) = HOURS(R%,7) / 6
220 NEXT R%
230 END
240 DATA
```

CHAPTER EXERCISES

1.

```
10 DIM TITLE$(1000), ARTIST$(1000), INV(1000)
20 CLS
30 INPUT "ENTER INITIAL INVENTORY NUMBER: ", A
40 FOR C% = 1 TO 1000
50      LET INV(C%) = A + C% - 1
60      INPUT "TITLE: ", TITLE$(C%)
70      IF TITLE$(C%) = "" THEN END
80      INPUT "ARTIST: ", ARTIST$(C%)
90      PRINT
100 NEXT C%
```

CHAPTER 11

EXERCISE SET 11.1

1.

```
1020 FOR R% = 1 TO 10000
1030    CLS
1040    PRINT "Entering data for record "; R%
1050    FOR C% = 1 TO 5
1060            PRINT "Data entry "; C%;
1070            INPUT ": ", A(R%,C%)
1080            IF A(R%,C%) = 0 THEN 1110
1090    NEXT C%
1100 NEXT R%
1110 RETURN
```

EXERCISE SET 11.2

A.

2.

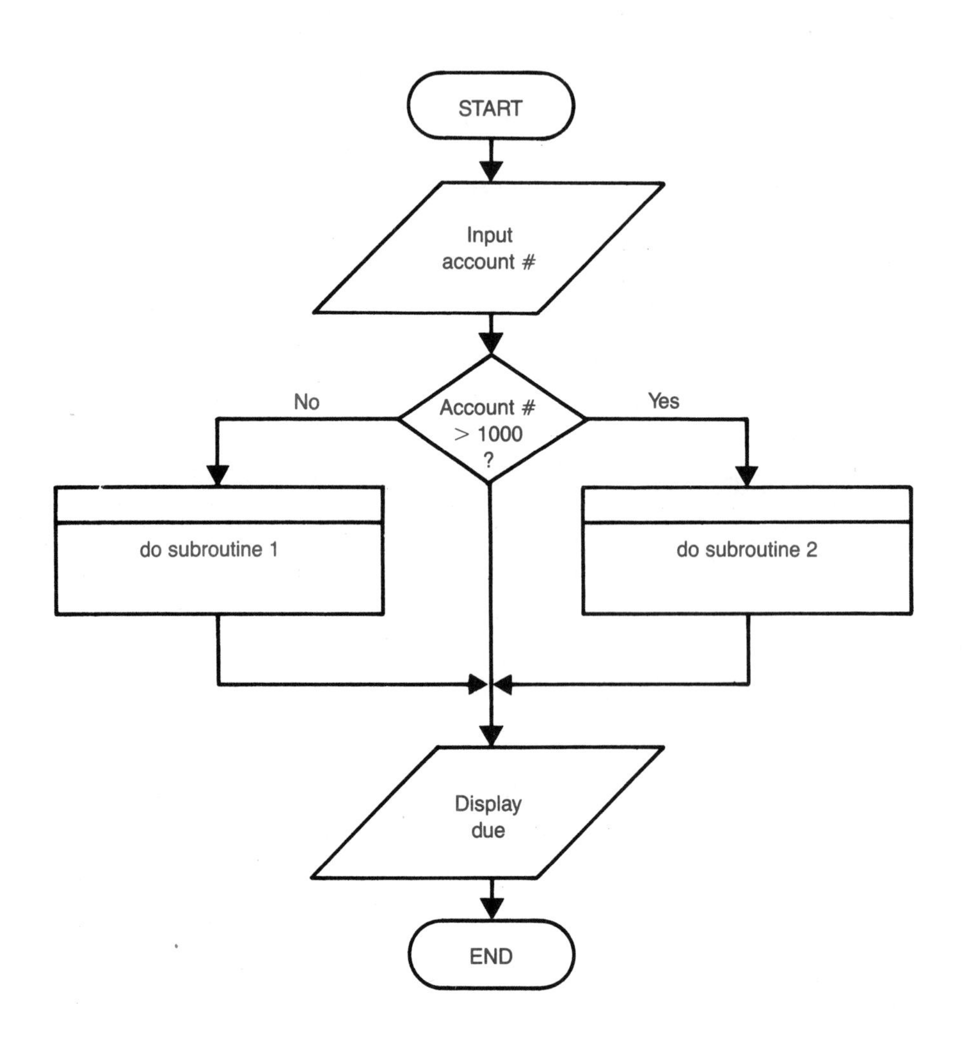

subroutine 1:

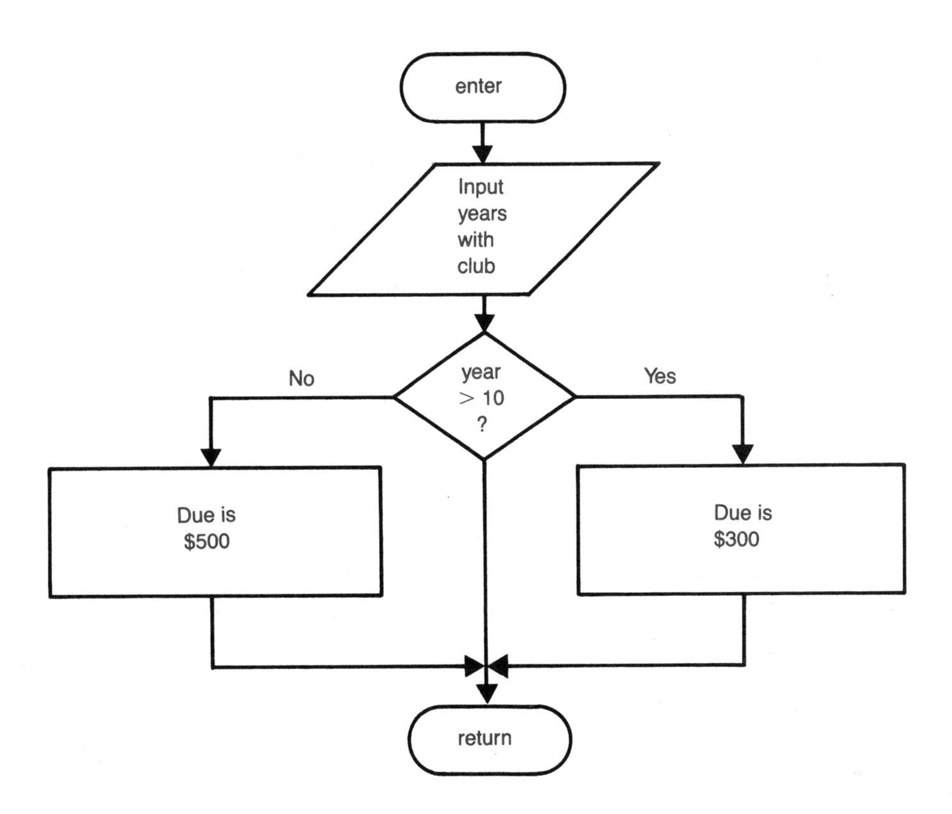

subroutine 2:

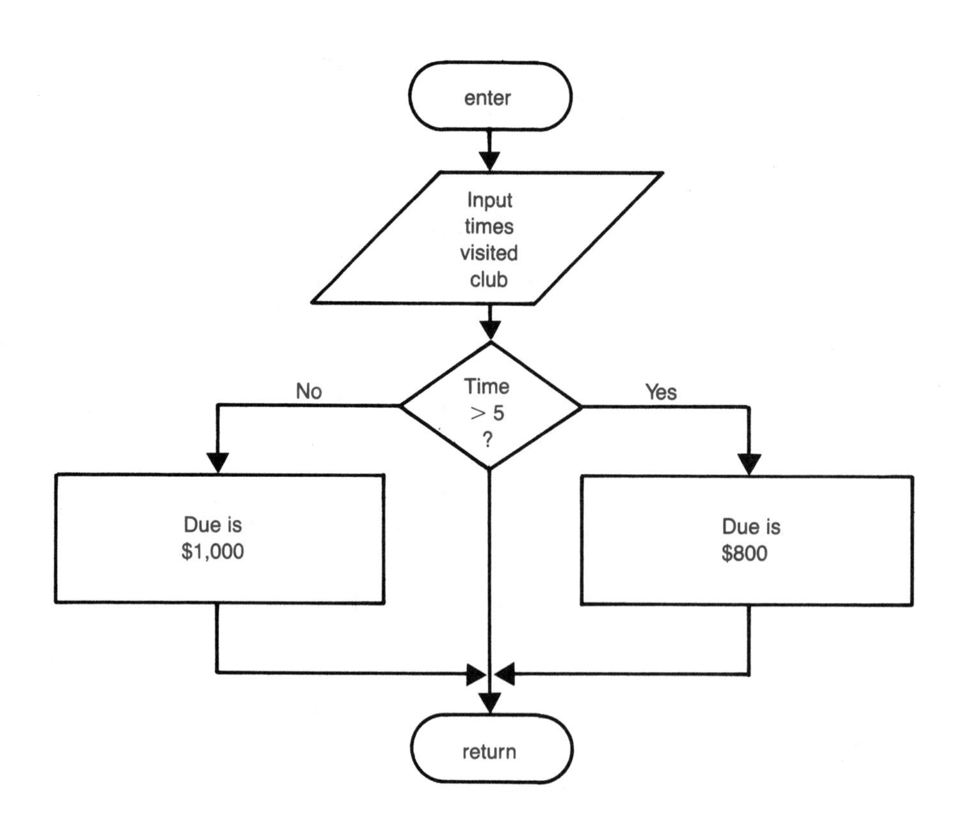

CHAPTER EXERCISES

2.

```
10 DIM PNT$(4), HUE$(7), INV(4,7)
20 GOSUB 1000 : REM ESTABLISH DATA
30 LET SALE$ = "Y"
40 WHILE SALE$ = "Y"
50      GOSUB 2000 : REM MAKE SALES
60      INPUT "NEXT SALE? Y/N: ", SALE$
70 WEND
80 END
1000 ' ESTABLISH INITIAL DATA
1010 CLS
1020 FOR R% = 1 TO 4
1030    READ PNT$(R%)
1040 NEXT R%
1050 FOR C% = 1 TO 7
1060    READ HUE$(C%)
1070 NEXT C%
1080 RETURN
2000 ' SALES
2010 CLS
2020 PRINT "PAINT TYPE:"
2030 FOR R% = 1 TO 4
2040    PRINT R%; " "; PNT$(R%),
2050 NEXT R%
2060 PRINT
2070 PRINT
2080 FOR C% = 1 TO 7
2090    PRINT C%; " "; HUE$(C%)
2100 NEXT C%
2110 PRINT
2120 PRINT
2130 PRINT "ENTER SELECTION ACCORDING TO NUMBERS."
2140 PRINT "e.g. 3, 4 FOR ENAMEL, GREEN"
2150 INPUT R%, C%
2160 IF INV(R%,C%) = 0 THEN PRINT "OUT OF STOCK." : GOTO 2
2170 LET INV(R%,C%) = INV(R%,C%) - 1
2180 RETURN
3000 ' PAINT TYPE
3010 DATA "LATEX", "WATER B.", "ENAMEL", "GLOSS"
3020 DATA "RED", "ORANGE", "YELLOW", "GREEN", "INDIGO",
    "BLUE", "PURPLE"
```

CHAPTER 12

EXERCISE SET 12.1

B.

3.

```
10 SCREEN 1
20 COLOR 14, 2, 2
30 END
```

EXERCISE SET 12.2

B.

3.

```
10 SCREEN 2
20 CLS
30 LET PI = 3.141593
40 CIRCLE( 320, 100 ), 150,, -PI/2, -PI*5/3
50 END
```

EXERCISE SET 12.3

B.

4.

```
10 SCREEN 2
20 CLS
30 KEY OFF
40 DRAW "BM30,1"
50 DRAW "D180"
60 DRAW "R580"
70 FOR C% = 1 TO 5
80     DRAW "BM30," + STR$( C%*30 )
90     DRAW "R10"
100 NEXT C%
110 FOR C% = 1 TO 5
120     DRAW "BM" + STR$( 30 + C%*100 ) + ",170"
```

```
130     DRAW "D10"
140 NEXT C%
150 END
```

EXERCISE SET 12.4

2.

```
10 SCREEN 2
20 CLS
30 KEY OFF
40 LINE (30,1) - (30, 180)
50 LINE - (580, 180)
60 READ X%, Y%
70 DRAW "BM" + STR$( X% ) + "," + STR$( Y% )
80 FOR C% = 1 TO 12
90     READ X%, Y%
100     LINE -(X%, Y%)
110 NEXT C%
120 END
200 ' COORDINATES
210 '------------------
220 DATA 30, 100
230 DATA 110, 100
240 DATA 110, 10
250 DATA 190, 10
260 DATA 190, 130
270 DATA 270, 130
280 DATA 270, 90
290 DATA 350, 90
300 DATA 350, 30
310 DATA 430, 30
320 DATA 430, 110
330 DATA 510, 110
340 DATA 510, 180
```

4.

```
10 SCREEN 2
20 CLS
30 KEY OFF
40 LINE (30,1) - (30, 180)
```

```
50 LINE - (600, 180)
60 READ X%, Y%
70 DRAW "BM" + STR$( X% ) + "," + STR$( Y% )
80 FOR C% = 1 TO 8
90     READ X%, Y%
100     LINE -(X%, Y%)
110 NEXT C%
120 END
200 ' COORDINATES
210 '------------------
220 DATA 30, 100
230 DATA 100, 40
240 DATA 170, 120
250 DATA 240, 1
260 DATA 310, 90
270 DATA 380, 50
280 DATA 450, 100
290 DATA 520, 70
300 DATA 590, 180
```

EXERCISE SET 12.5

1.

```
10 SCREEN 2
20 CLS
30 KEY OFF
40 LINE (30,1) - (30, 180)
50 LINE - (600, 180)
60 READ X%, Y%
70 DRAW "BM" + STR$( X% ) + "," + STR$( Y% )
80 FOR C% = 1 TO 8
90     READ X%, Y%
100     LINE -(X%, Y%)
110 NEXT C%
120 PAINT (150,150)
130 END
200 ' COORDINATES
210 '------------------
220 DATA 30, 100
230 DATA 100, 40
240 DATA 170, 120
250 DATA 240, 1
```

```
260 DATA 310, 90
270 DATA 380, 50
280 DATA 450, 100
290 DATA 520, 70
300 DATA 590, 180
```

CHAPTER EXERCISE

1.

```
10 SCREEN 2
20 CLS
30 KEY OFF
40 FOR Y% = 20 TO 70
50      FOR X% = 160 TO 480
60              PSET ( X%,Y% )
70      NEXT X%
80 NEXT Y%
90 END
```

C / THE ASCII TABLE

ASCII value	*Character*	*ASCII value*	*Character*
000	(null)	022	▬
001	☺	023	↨
002	☻	024	↑
003	♥	025	↓
004	♦	026	→
005	♣	027	←
006	♠	028	(cursor right)
007	(beep)	029	(cursor left)
008	◘	030	(cursor up)
009	(tab)	031	(cursor down)
010	(line feed)	032	(space)
011	(home)	033	!
012	(form feed)	034	"
013	(carriage return)	035	#
014	♫	036	$
015	☼	037	%
016	►	038	&
017	◄	039	'
018	↕	040	(
019	!!	041	)
020	¶	042	*
021	§	043	+

ASCII value	*Character*	*ASCII value*	*Character*	*ASCII value*	*Charac*
044	,	082	R	120	x
045	-	083	S	121	y
046	.	084	T	122	z
047	/	085	U	123	{
048	0	086	V	124	¦
049	1	087	W	125	}
050	2	088	X	126	~
051	3	089	Y	127	⌂
052	4	090	Z	128	Ç
053	5	091	[	129	ü
054	6	092	\	130	é
055	7	093	]	131	â
056	8	094	∧	132	ä
057	9	095	_	133	à
058	:	096	`	134	å
059	;	097	a	135	ç
060	<	098	b	136	ê
061	=	099	c	137	ë
062	>	100	d	138	è
063	?	101	e	139	ï
064	@	102	f	140	î
065	A	103	g	141	ì
066	B	104	h	142	Ä
067	C	105	i	143	Å
068	D	106	j	144	É
069	E	107	k	145	æ
070	F	108	l	146	Æ
071	G	109	m	147	ô
072	H	110	n	148	ö
073	I	111	o	149	ò
074	J	112	p	150	û
075	K	113	q	151	ù
076	L	114	r	152	ÿ
077	M	115	s	153	Ö
078	N	116	t	154	Ü
079	O	117	u	155	¢
080	P	118	v	156	£
081	Q	119	w	157	¥

ASCII value	*Character*	*ASCII value*	*Character*	*ASCII value*	*Character*
158	Pt	191	┐	224	α
159	ƒ	192	└	225	β
160	á	193	┴	226	Γ
161	í	194	┬	227	π
162	ó	195	├	228	Σ
163	ú	196	─	229	σ
164	ñ	197	┼	230	μ
165	Ñ	198	╞	231	τ
166	ª	199	╟	232	Φ
167	º	200	╚	233	θ
168	¿	201	╔	234	Ω
169	⌐	202	╩	235	δ
170	¬	203	╦	236	∞
171	½	204	╠	237	Ø
172	¼	205	═	238	ε
173	¡	206	╬	239	∩
174	«	207	╧	240	≡
175	»	208	╨	241	±
176	░	209	╤	242	≥
177	▒	210	╥	243	≤
178	▓	211	╙	244	⌠
179	│	212	╘	245	⌡
180	┤	213	╒	246	÷
181	╡	214	╓	247	≈
182	╢	215	╫	248	°
183	╖	216	╪	249	•
184	╕	217	┘	250	·
185	╣	218	┌	251	√
186	║	219	█	252	^{n}
187	╗	220	▄	253	^{2}
188	╝	221	▌	254	■
189	╜	222	▐	255	(blank 'FF')
190	╛	223	▀		

D / CRT DESIGN SHEETS

Use the CRT design sheets provided on the following pages to design the desired CRT display, then use the finalized design pattern to generate the program code as example shown below. The column positions are marked at the top of the design sheet, and the row positions on the left. The CRT display zone positions are marked at the bottom.

Make duplicates from the sheets provided if desired.

```
SALE 1 : $ sales amount
SALE 2 : $ sales amount
SALE 3 : $ sales amount
             SUBTOTAL : $ subtotal amount
             SALES TAX : $ tax amount
             TOTAL : $ total amount
```

```
160 PRINT
170 PRINT "SALE 1 : $"; A
180 PRINT "SALE 2 : $"; B
190 PRINT "SALE 3 : $"; C
200 PRINT
210 PRINT , "SUB-TOTAL : $"; SUB.TOTAL
220 PRINT
230 PRINT , "SALES TAX : $"; TAX
240 PRINT
250 PRINT , "TOTAL : $"; TOTAL
```

CRT Column

1 11 21 31 41 51 61 71

CRT Zone

1 2 3 4 5

CRT Row

1 6 11 16 21

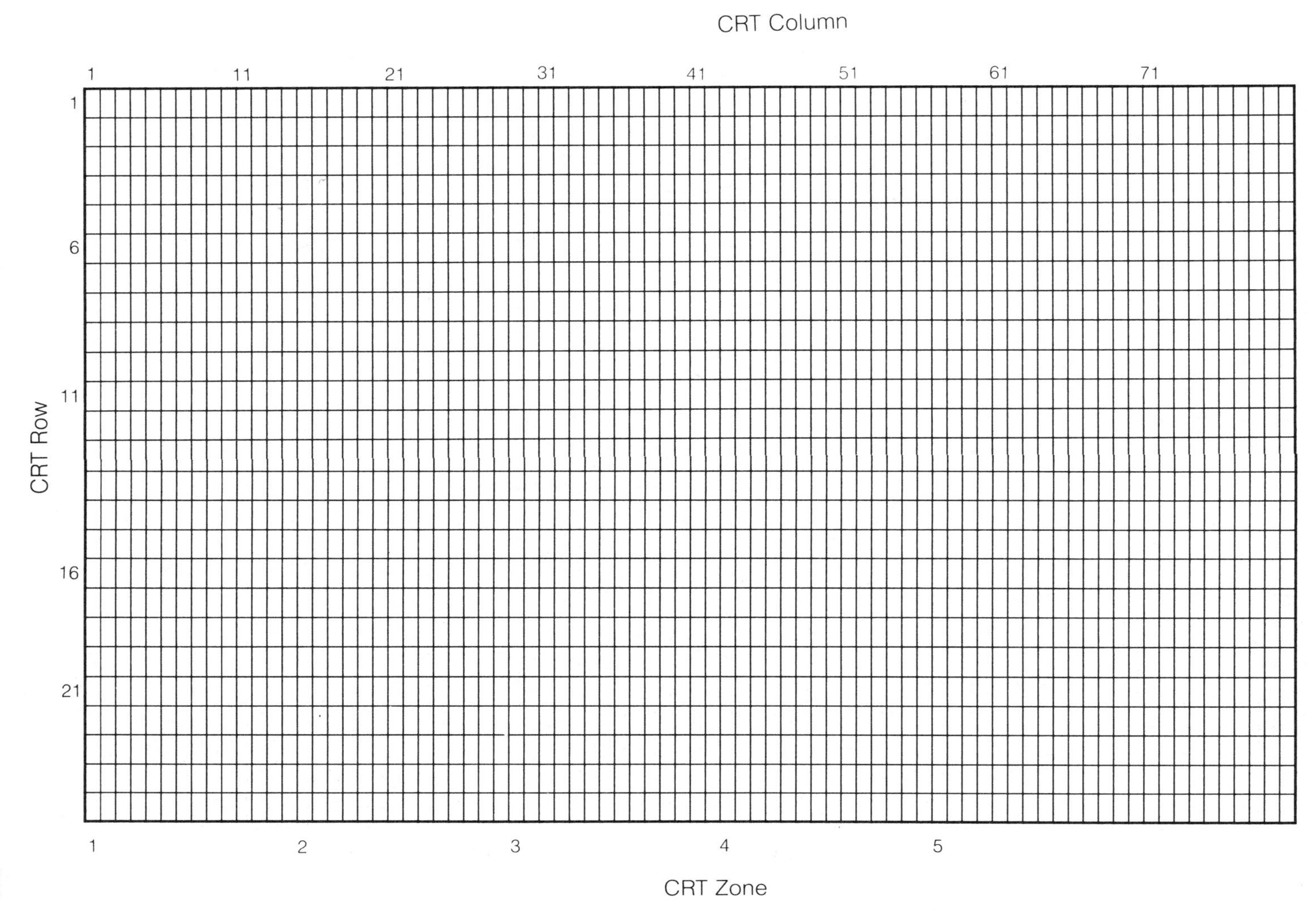
CRT Column
1
11
21
31
41
51
61
71
CRT Row
1
6
11
16
21
1
2
3
4
5
CRT Zone

GLOSSARY

accumulation The summation of a finite series of numbers employing the programming process of looping.

algorithm A general logic scheme that takes an input and produces an output.

alphanumeric data Data made up of symbols and characters that do not possess inherent numeric values.

applications program A computer program designed to solve a user problem.

arithmetic condition The control mechanism, based on the comparison between numeric data, that is used to determine which logical path program execution will take.

arithmetic operators The relational symbols used in the construction of arithmetic conditions.

array An ordered data set.

background A general CRT color attribute; the screen color of the CRT.

BASIC A high-level computer language.

BASICA Advanced BASIC; version of BASIC produced by Microsoft Corporation.

border The outer portion of the CRT screen usually not used for display purposes.

choice A programming structure describing two or more logic paths that can be taken.

compiler A program designed to translate program source code into object code.

compound statement A BASIC program statement that is formed by consolidating several statements into one.

conditional branching The taking of a logical path as dictated by the satisfaction of a condition.
controlled branching See *conditional branching.*
counting A form of accummulation that keeps track of the number of times an event occurs in the execution of a loop.
CRT Cathode ray tube, commonly known as the screen or the monitor.
cursor A symbol that appears on the CRT to indicate where the next display will occur.
cursor control code A symbol used by BASIC to determine the placement of the cursor.
data The quantities or symbols kept in the computer memory to be used in processing.
data assignment The storing of data in the computer memory using the identification system established by a particular computer language.
DATA pointer A counter used internally by BASIC to keep track of the next available data item as set up by the current DATA statement.
default drive The disk drive that the computer is implicitly communicating with; also called the *current drive.*
dependent variable A program variable whose value depends on the assessment of other data.
dimension The number of subscripts required to define an array.
disk drive The device that houses and operates the disk or diskette.
editor A language facility used to input and edit the program source code.
file name An identification code for a program or data file saved on a storage medium.
file-name extension The trailing portion of the file name normally used for file-classification purposes.
filespec The full identification code for a stored file made up of the file name and the extension.
flowcharting The expression of program logic in a pictorial form.
flowcharting symbols Standardized graphics symbols used to represent program logic.
foreground The attributes, such as color, of the displayed images on the CRT.
High-Resolution Graphics mode The detailed rendition of displays made up of a large quantity of dots called pixels.
immediate mode The immediate execution of a BASIC statement.
independent variable A variable whose value is assigned without reference to other variables.

initialization The first-time assignment of a value to a data item.

input The data for a program; the portion of the program governing the obtaining of data from an external source; the process of entering data into the computer.

interactive programming A type of programming in which the computer carries on a dialogue with the user.

interpreter A language translator that translates and executes program instructions one statement at a time.

intrinsic functions General algorithms built into a computer language.

iteration The programming structure of performing an event repeatedly; an occurrence in such a repetitive action or loop.

keyword A word or symbol used by a computer language for specific purposes; usually it is an instruction command.

list A linear organization of data.

literal A data item or constant used directly in a program statement and not separately defined.

logical operators Relational logic symbols used in the construction of controlled branching conditions.

looping The repeated execution of a logic expression; also see *iteration.*

Medium-Resolution Graphics mode A level of display quality that is not the most detailed attainable from an output device.

modular programming A programming technique whereby the program logic is reduced to identifiable components that are handled separately.

module A logic component of a program; also see *modular programming.*

nested loop A set of loops within other loops.

numeric data A data item that has an inherent numeric value.

object code The version of a program that has been converted into machine instructions by a translator.

one-dimensional array An array with one subscript; also see *list.*

parameter A value used in an algorithm.

pixel A dot used to compose output displays.

PRINT zone A predetermined BASIC PRINT position.

program documentation Textual material or prose embedded in program source code that renders the program code more understandable to the user.

program mode The condition under which BASIC executes program statements as a group.

program module See *module.*

program statement A computer program instruction.

program text area The portion of computer memory devoted to the holding of the program source code.
prompt An English phrase or sentence displayed on the CRT that gives direction to the program user.
prompt message See *prompt.*
reserved word Same as *keyword.*
source code Program logic expressed in a high-level language.
spaghetti code A convoluted program construction that is not necessarily incorrect logically but that does not express the overall program logic clearly; usually characterized by many unnecessary **GOTO** statements.
statement See *program statement.*
statement number The number identifying a BASIC source code statement and its relative position in a program.
subroutine A program segment designed to perform a specific function.
subscript An index used to identify a data element within an array.
table A two-dimensional array.
text editor See *editor.*
text mode The output mode under which only textual material and no graphics can be output.
truncation The removal of the decimal portion of a number; rounding of the number may or may not result.
two-dimensional array An array with two subscripts; data organization typified by their arrangement in rows and columns.
unconditional branching The taking of a logical path within a program that does not depend on the satisfaction of a logical condition.
user The person using a completed program to produce results (as opposed to the programmer, the person who designs the program).
user-defined function A general algorithm defined by the programmer.
user program control The taking of logical paths within a program as a result of dictates from the program user.
variable A name defined by the programmer that is used to identify a data item in the computer memory.

INDEX